Teaching Art to Children

CONTENT & VIEWPOINT

3RD EDITION

Blanche Jefferson

Professor of Art Education
University of Pittsburgh

Library of Congress Catalog Card Number: 68-23563

Printed in the United States of America

3rd Edition

To My Husband, William F. Jefferson,
Whose Comments and Suggestions
Were of Inestimable Value
in the Writing of This Book

Preface

In revising this text I have tried to retain an emphasis upon art education as *creative* art and to show how the art teacher works to help children express their ideas. In addition to keeping the core of the original text this revision includes recent developments in art education and creativity at the elementary school level.

Most leading art educators believe an art education based upon creativity as its teaching and working viewpoint does the most to develop the child as an autonomous individual who must make many independent decisions and accept the responsibilities for his own actions in the open society in which he lives. Modern educators teach this point of view in their classes to both prospective and in-service teachers. There is still, however, a widespread discrepancy between what these leaders believe and teach, and what is actually practised with children in many elementary classrooms.

Educators and others concerned with the creative and intellectual development of children have often heard the term *creative expression* associated with modern art education. Much has been said and written about it, and teachers feel that they want to provide creative art experiences for their pupils. Yet many neither understand the concept nor have a grasp of the ways in which they need to operate to put it into effect with the children in their classes. Teachers use the term to describe a range of approaches to teaching art. Its use, however, is a little like the use of the word *democracy*. Most governments say their methods of governing are democratic and that they "free" the individual regardless of how little some may actually do to prepare the individual for a self-directed life. This is often also true of the inconsistency between the use of the term *creative art* and the imaginative, open, individualized practice of teaching art to children that the term implies.

I have visited scores of art classrooms in numerous school systems and have found many excellent situations in which children were learning about art and confidently expressing their own ideas in remarkably well-organized ways. Yet, in many other school systems, I have found a discrepancy between the teacher's assurance that the art was creative and the control and limitation she exerted over the art. In some cases it was a teacher-directed process in whole or in part, resulting in work that was all alike except for some small choice the children could make, such as: "Color it any way you wish" or "Choose any of these three [given] designs to put on the dress." Such small choices cannot be confused with the fundamentally and wholly child-determined aspects of creative expression in children's art.

The discrepancy is shown again in the art teaching aids used by teachers. Even as I revise this book, which for years has presented creative expression as the foundation for art education, new and additional teaching aids of completely opposing kinds are being written, published, and used in classrooms with great numbers of children. Some of these sets of books and other aids are valuable supplements which enrich the teacher's work in ways that would be difficult, if at all possible, for a teacher alone to provide. Others are the very antithesis of this and contradict much of what research and experience have proven to be valuable for children in art. Teachers need some insight into what some of the educationally sound art teaching aids are, and it was partly with this in mind that this text was revised.

The need to clarify and evaluate the different methods of teaching art and to define what creative teaching and working in art involves—what it is and what it is not—was strongly indicated to me in the original writing of this book. Because the ways of creativity are so frequently *not* practised or even fully understood, it seemed vital in this revision to retain this core of explanation and of actual classroom teaching situations which illustrate creative methods and which are presented in the same dialogue form in which they were tape recorded. Pre-service art teachers, too, need explicit descriptions of these creative processes, not only because these teachers represent our hope for excellence in art education of the future, but also because of their role as a deterrent against influences that urge less sound art practices. In their anxiety to help children improve their art practices teachers might revert to methods of teaching that are product-centered rather than the slower evolutionary and developmental ways of child-centered teaching.

The purpose of this book which remains imperative is to present the values of art in education in such a way as to fully impress their importance upon teachers. Art education cannot proceed effectively without clearly defined purposes, for it is then like a ship without a rudder.

An additional reason behind the writing of this text was to make clear the role of the art teacher and to indicate how the teacher puts creative art into practice with children. Teachers may be so aware of the freedom that is a necessary and energizing force in art education that they assume they are to do no teaching. As a result, some teachers reject creative ways of teaching and working in art because, in their limited knowledge of these methods, they see little to support their role as a teacher. As educated and professional men and women they feel responsible for assuming an active leadership role in teaching-learning situations. They feel they cannot accept such a withdrawal status, and they are right.

One of the new sections in this revision deals with curriculum in elementary school art. Although art educators have always been interested in curriculum and have, within local school districts, provided some fine courses of study in art, many feel this kind of planning needs to go further and involve a basic curriculum which extends to greater than local coverage. The interest, research, and content in curriculum are presented. Throughout this revision the close relationship between art and art education has been stressed, because it is, after all, *art* we are teaching children. Some modern art educators have based art education on psychology, others upon anthropology, and still others upon results of statistical studies. All have some relevance, but the practices of art education should remain close to the practices and products of art.

This text has always been rich with examples of the art work of children in the elementary grades. It was felt essential for teachers to have as much exposure to child art as possible in order that they become sensitive to the special qualities and characteristics of children's art. A full appreciation of children's art on its own terms is necessary if the imposition of adult standards upon children, one of the most detrimental factors in art education, is to be avoided.

Choice of illustrations was made on the basis of their value in clarifying the points made in the text. They were also selected to show what is happening in contemporary art classrooms as a result of children's creative art experiences.

This book, then, is directed to pre-service and in-service art teachers as well as to other adults who deal in any way with children and their art.

ACKNOWLEDGMENTS

I wish to express my appreciation to all the children with whom I have had the joy and privilege of working, for the inspiration of their enthusiasm, for their trust, and for the many things I have learned from them which have contributed to this text. I am additionally indebted to those children whose art work appears as illustrations in this book.

Blanche Jefferson

Contents

Teaching Art to Children

1

Methods of Teaching Art

IT SEEMS EVIDENT that the methods of teaching any subject follow closely the nature and character of the subject itself. Education as a process cannot be separated from the subject being taught. Therefore, not all subjects could or should be taught in the same way. They need to change or adapt, taking their lead from the essential nature and purposes of the subject they are implementing. For example, in a mathematics classroom there is relatively little opportunity for originality or the expression of emotions in arriving at a solution. Thus, were the teacher to apply teaching procedures suitable for mathematics to an art lesson, the art work would lose qualities unique to art. Nor can formulas be applied to art or to art products, for their influence tends to standardize both the practice of art and its completed works. Artists seek the opposite of standardization. Their works reflect this fact.

The ways of teaching art, therefore, should be based upon the approaches and ways inherent in art itself. So it is important to continually relate art and art education, for it is art we are teaching children. The core and meaning of art, the ways of the artist, the deep and rich nature of art, the universality and diversity of art, all need to be kept in mind when teaching the subject. Otherwise the classroom experiences children have in the name of art may lack art's uniquely personal, penetrating, and uplifting values.

In their studios, artists work independently. This high degree of independence has been identified with art since time began. Each creates works of a highly personal and individual nature, and this gives us the tremendously varied and interesting world of art. For example, Picasso works alone in his studio following his own ideas and knowledge, and applying his own critical judgment to his work. These same working conditions are a fundamental aspect of high quality art education.

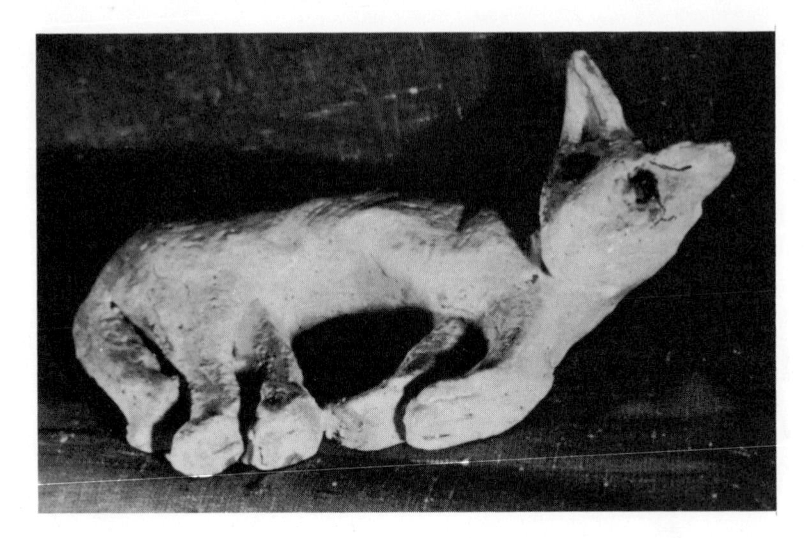

1

A feeling for the subject often motivates the artist. This fifth-grade child expressed the feline quality of repose.

The diverse nature of art requires the teacher to broaden the approaches, to encourage the new and adventurous. Therefore, statements that open up thinking are used, and statements that narrow it down avoided. Teachers need to be extremely cautious about using negatives, for they can destroy the independent essence of art. The minute a teacher says "No," a door is closed; the instant a negative criticism is made, something is cut off.

Of course, study and practice are needed to improve knowledge and skills in art. Adult artists working alone are constantly aware of this need. Children in school need to learn about art and be helped toward general improvement of their own techniques and compositions. Chapter 8 deals with helping children improve their art.

Successfully teaching art to children requires a teacher to be acquainted with art, to realize the breadth of personalized styles in art, to have had some experience with creating original art, and to be able to apply this understanding in teaching the subject. However, knowledge of art alone is not enough. Since it is children we are teaching, a grounding in the special understanding of children is necessary and must become a part of the process of teaching art. It is important to know that art is not taught to children in the same way it is taught to adults. In fact, adult ideas and ways are often dull to children. Failure to adapt teaching methods to the special nature of children and of art accounts for many of the difficulties in art education and robs it of much of its value.

Various methods of teaching art to children are in practice in schools, but not all of them show a relationship to art. Yet, to a great extent, the methods used in teaching it determine how much real value the art experience will have for the children. They have an immediate and marked effect upon the child's painting, drawing, and modeling. They also have a deep and lasting effect upon the attitudes, habits, thinking, and behavior patterns of the child, which are formed during his most impressionable years and carry over into adult life, becoming standards by which the adult functions. Therefore, the art teacher needs to give attention to every method she uses with children. The effects of these methods are so important that not only teachers but everyone who deals with children should understand them.

2

Although children work within a group, each child plans and works out his art in an original way.

Various teaching methods used in art education will first be described in this chapter and then evaluated so that teachers will understand why a certain practice is right for children and why other practices are harmful. It cannot be assumed that the knowledge of right procedures is enough. Other methods of teaching art must also be understood so that a teacher will not use a certain process with children simply because she knows no reason why she should *not* do so.

> Art education, if it is to have a quality of individual but responsible expression and sensible recreation, if it is to encourage creativity and a sensitization of individual understanding of values and their presentation through the forms of art, cannot permit itself to depend fundamentally on foreign, ambiguous, or unrelated interests and knowledge and understanding. Though

the teaching of art may be assisted and guided by the adjunctive information of the social and behaviorial sciences and general educational theory, *the very first source of understanding* for the art teacher, and the most fertile, *lies in art itself* and in the larger body of the humanities.[1] (Italics added.)

IDENTIFICATION OF METHODS

Creative Expression

This is a method of teaching art or a way of working with materials that gives the child:

(a) The opportunity to *choose* his own ideas or subject matter for his art.
(b) The freedom to *express* it (create or make the shape of the forms) and use color in his own way.
(c) The right to *organize* it in his own way.

This complete intellectual freedom of the individual to choose, to express, and to organize is what creative art education means. Wherever the child is given all of these choices, creative expression is the method of teaching and working in art, and it can be readily identified because the content of each child's painting is different from that of every other. According to his own ideas one child might be painting an airplane, another a ball game, another depicting fun at the beach, while his neighbor might be doing an abstract.

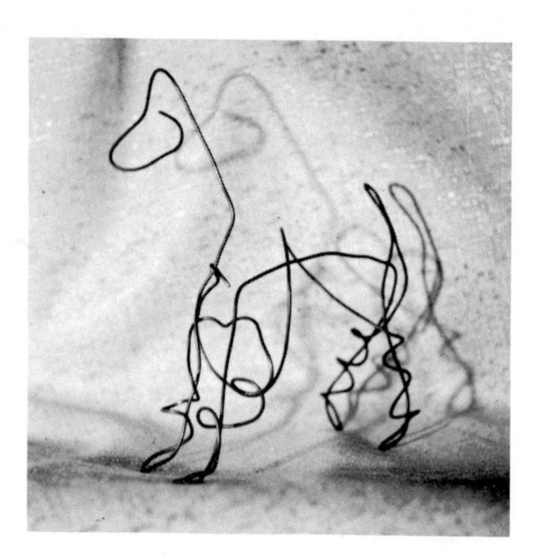

3

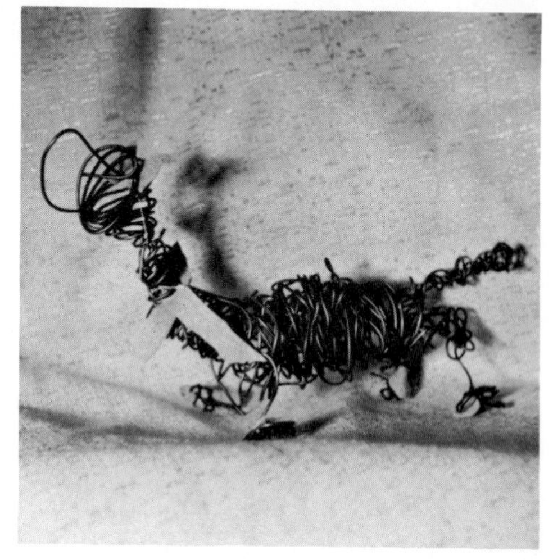

4

These two pieces of wire sculpture were created by different children within the same group. Each child conceived his own idea and interpreted the topic individually.

---

[1] Irving Kaufman, *Art and Education in Contemporary Culture* (New York: Macmillan, © 1966), p. 104. Reprinted by permission of the publisher.

The expression is individual, with each child drawing the shape of the form in the way that seems appropriate to him for that painting. Among those children in the group who might be painting trees, every tree could be different. Then, too, any one child is free to paint a tree, or any form, differently in different compositions and for different purposes.

The putting together of the forms and the placement and arrangement of them is the organization, which in each child's painting is also different. The number of objects, forms, and people that he puts into his compositions is different for each child. Some paintings will be complex, others simple. The forms are put together individually to suit the taste, need, and purpose of each child. The freedom of the child to develop his own combinations of the forms and colors that he includes in his art work is another way to identify the art work as creative expression.

The group of six water color paintings made by first-grade children during one art work period is representative of the range of ideas expressed when children have had a creative art experience (Plates I–VI).* There were 30 children in this class, and every painting was different. Emphasis was placed upon each child working in his own way and choosing his own ideas.

When Linda painted the picture of her house, she said, "This is my house in the night" (Plate I). By looking at the attractive colors she used in painting her house, one gets a warm, happy feeling about it. The house is not expressed in a naturalistic or visual way. It is not the way her house appeared to the eye, but rather the way she felt about it. It is simply the way she wanted to paint it that particular day and hour. Another time she may have painted it quite differently; indeed, she may even have chosen another subject to draw, model, or paint. Surrounding the house with a dark color to show the night helped to emphasize the glow that is seen and felt as one looks at it. The brown outline represents the outside of the house; the interior looks as though she had divided it into rooms, giving an effect of the outside and inside at the same time, as children do sometimes. Children thus frequently express the emotional effect that the object they are painting has upon them, while disregarding the visual aspects.

Donna's picture is unusual and strange in the combination of objects it contains (Plate II). The old valentines she had found at home and brought to school that day must have inspired parts of her painting, creating an extraordinary combination with the Christmas tree. Children get a great deal of pleasure from a familiar toy or possession that has been put away and then found again. The valentines probably reminded her of the fun she had had on Valentine's Day which, in turn, may have called to mind the pleasant experiences associated with other holidays, and so objects associated with these experiences and her feelings about them inspired her painting. Donna was remembering, selecting, and organizing her experiences and feelings. This is an outpouring process that helps the child focus upon his own ideas and reactions. Through such permissive creative art experiences, the child grows and matures as he receives encouragement and praise for his achievements.

---

* Roman numeral plate designations refer to reproductions in color insert.

Mary Sara has painted herself with a new red and black plaid dress which she wore to school that day for the first time (Plate III). She was proud of her dress and aware of it, and tried to call attention to it in indirect ways by smoothing it as she sat down and brushing it occasionally with her hand. The way she has placed herself in the middle of the paper, as well as the pose and expression in the picture, has communicated something of the pride she felt in having such a pretty dress. The orange part is Mary Sara, and the red and black parts on each side are her dress. The dress is on her and goes down around her, so both the girl and dress can be seen at the same time, which is Mary Sara's own way of showing herself wearing her dress. If children are not interfered with or directed during their art experience, they evolve their own ways of expression that are meaningful to them and interesting to those who look at and study their art. Mary Sara's new dress was an important and exciting thing to her that day, so she chose it for her art experience.

Jackie's rich painting of various stripes is bold in the way it fills his entire page (Plate IV). He has experimented with lines of various widths, using rich and beautiful combinations of colors. In some cases he has kept each color separated with distinct and sharp lines between; in other instances he has let the colors run together and flow into each other, creating soft, almost dreamy spots.

Susan's two vigorous trees are large, full of rich, green leaves, and red fruit, and are well supported by strong trunks (Plate V). They are fastened securely to the ground but go up and touch the sky. Most first-grade children draw trees in this manner, with a trunk and a round ball of leaves at the top.

This commonly used tree form is a generalization of a tree: a trunk with a clump of leaves at the top. In some cases a child is not aware of the structure of a tree; in others he wants only to generalize without giving it too much importance or an undue amount of his attention. He wants a tree form that can be both expressed and recognized quickly and easily.

Another picture in this group is an abstract (Plate VI). Connie has created a sensitive, varied, and well-organized painting. Through her intense concentration upon her ideas and feelings as she worked, Connie has achieved an aesthetic quality that comes from the variety and organization of sensitively expressed colors and forms. The ladder form on the right is not only different from every other form but has rich and interesting variations within itself. The composition is unified by the rich, green form on the right as it continues around the other forms. The red line also around the forms is varied as it moves from inside to outside the gray line, from wide to thin lines, and from bright to dim shades of red. Although these structural elements are important, the aesthetic experience in looking at the painting comes even more from Connie's concentration upon and expression of her feelings as she worked.

This small sampling from one group of children gives some insight into the products resulting from creative expression. Also revealed is the personal nature of the subject matter that motivated each. Calling attention to the qualities of paintings such as Connie's helps children become aware of aesthetics in art. Although there are times for teaching, it is while working that the child is independent of teacher control or from influence or pressure of other children or adults. There is opportunity to choose, to express, and to organize with no interferences. The child has the power of self-determination. He has no obligation to anything except his own standards of quality.

These standards are not *your* standards; they are not the standards of another "average" or "more fluent" child in the group; nor are they voted upon by the class. They are *each child's own individual* standards, and they must be recognized and respected as such.

Within this small group of six paintings there is not only a range of ideas, but there are also marked differences in the ways the paintings are organized and expressed. When the subject and feeling of each painting is studied in relation to its origin, a striking harmony is evident.

There are many kinds of ranges existing within the art work of any group of children. There is variety among the children themselves which is reflected in their art. This diversity should be expected, for creative expression is built upon and refined through the individuality of each child.

Assigned Topics to Interpret

Sometimes the teacher or the children decide upon a topic that all of the children in the group use as the subject matter for their art. Such a topic might be "Snow," "A Game I Play," or "Halloween." Every child in the group builds his art work from ideas he finds within this chosen topic. Each is free to express and organize it in his own way, without teacher control. Specifying topics for interpretation as a method of teaching art is identified by the opportunities each child has to develop the selected topic in his own way.

The group of four crayon and chalk drawings, done on blue paper, illustrates the use of specific topics as a method of teaching art (5).† Because of a recent snowstorm, the children in this first-grade group along with their friends had been having a variety of experiences in the snow: sled riding, sliding, snowballing, making snowmen, seeing cars skid, falling, shoveling snow, and a number of other activities, both pleasant and unpleasant, including being cold. With this background, "Snow" was the topic selected for individual expression in the art class. After an exciting verbal exchange of ideas including the recalling of both sensory and emotional feelings about the snow, each child was encouraged to choose any interpretation of the subject in which he was most interested.

The feeling of cold wintry winds is shown in the way Joseph bent the trees and drew the child's hair blowing to suggest the power of the wind. He said, "The wind blows the snow, and trees, and everything. It makes the snow blow in big piles in places. The wind makes me cold." More than just a picture of "things" is shown here. Joseph's art also expresses sensory and emotional feelings about winter. It is obvious from looking at the picture that he was impressed by the effect of the wind and by his feeling for winter, more, perhaps, than he was by the visual representation of the objects. He

---

† Parenthetical Arabic numbers refer to black-and-white illustrations.

5

Four examples of first-grade children's work from the topic "Snow" are representative of the variety that can result from the teacher's emphasis upon individualized expression. Each piece of art reflects the child's interest and feeling about winter.

shaped the objects to show *feeling* in addition to ideas. The bush in the background, not affected by the wind, is graceful, creating a contrast with the motion of the trees. Probably this is aesthetically the most beautiful spot in the composition. Children have complex experiences and reactions. Joseph felt the cold, the wind, and the beauty. His art reflects them all.

Marian was one of several in the first-grade group who included herself in her art. In the pre-work discussion, she talked about the warm clothing she wore when she went outdoors to play in the snow, emphasizing the need for snow boots, warm gloves, and cap: her anticipation of the cold. Her art shows herself drawn large with details of her clothing, suggesting her close relationship to a cold winter experience. The tree is shaped and bent to take advantage of the space left after the figure was drawn. Children sometimes shape objects to fit a space; they seem to have a certain feeling for design and space division. Children learn about art when a teacher points out these and other art qualities.

Wayne's charming and debonair snowman rests quite solidly on the snow. The unusual shape of the two rolls of snow underneath the body suggests feet, adding to the somewhat human character. Wayne, too, has shaped the tree forms to fit the space. The branches on one side of the evergreen are smaller than the others because of the limited space. Children seldom draw objects partly cut off by the edge of the paper, as adults do. They seem to want to draw the entire form, changing it when necessary to fit the space.

Joanne's large tree dominating her art gives it beauty and a feeling of strength and protection. The shelter of the house and the hole in the tree for a squirrel's nest give a sense of warmth against the cold. She included herself "going home after playing in the snow," she said.

A study of these four pieces of art will show that, although snow is falling in every picture, none is falling in front of the objects and people. Children seldom show snow or rain falling *on* the people. They simply show the snow falling, realizing that those who see their art will understand what is happening. It makes their art clearer; the objects are easier to identify. This is *art*; it need not be naturalistic.

Learn to look thoroughly at children's art. Try to see as much as you can of what the child has done, for there is often a great deal accomplished and expressed. Learn to see deeply into it. Express your appreciation of it to the children. Comment upon the art achievements of each child, avoiding personal evaluations such as indicating what you like and dislike.

Other examples of child art that reveal ideas and experiences are shown throughout this text. Some of them, such as Plates XXXVIII and XXXIX, show very different interpretations of one idea *not* assigned to the group, in this case, but chosen by the children themselves. Plates XVII and XVIII and Illustrations 38 and 39 on page 118 also reveal the individuality possible within one topic.

Creative expression and *topics to interpret* both give opportunities for choice on the part of each child, but creative expression is more open in opportunities than the other. At no time should a child be required to conform to a topic when he has ideas of his own which he would prefer to express.

There are other practices used in the name of art education that deserve critical consideration by teachers because of their restrictive effects upon intellectual freedom and thus upon art expression. Adults need to be aware of them and to consider their departure from the nature of art and creative ways of working in art education. The following discussion considers some of the more common of these practices.

Copy Activities

Activities in art which consist of reproducing the likeness of a model or an imitation of a form are copy experiences. The child undertakes the duplication of a picture, a shape, or a design as nearly as he can. A copy activity can be done by one child or by a group of children reproducing a picture or shape, and can be recognized by the sameness of intention on the part of every individual within the group. The resulting products are as nearly identical as the children can make them.

Dictated Methods

Following a prescribed course set by the teacher and controlled by her in a step-by-step procedure is referred to as a dictated method of teaching art. The teacher, standing before the group, cuts, draws, or shapes one part or fragment of the whole drawing or composition, and all the children in the group cut, draw, or shape the same part or fragment as nearly as they can in the same way. Deviations from the teacher's drawing are frequently corrected by her on the spot. The whole class follows the direction of the teacher and goes forward in the lesson in the same way and at the same time. This method of teaching not only controls the ideas that each child must use, but also the size and shape of these ideas as they are put into form. In addition, the teacher controls the placement of each form on the page. This means that the teacher controls the organization. Since this method of teaching is a step-by-step process, the teacher also controls the speed at which the children work. This control is one of the identifying characteristics of dictated methods; identical art products is another.

Patterns

As the name implies, patterns are shapes drawn or cut by another person and passed on to the children to duplicate. Most frequently the children duplicate these patterns by drawing around the outside lines. Tracing is another form of pattern work. There is sometimes a step-by-step teaching process involved in this method, too. This is usually the case when the object to be made is composed of more than one part. For instance, if the project is the making of a boat from colored paper, the teacher might give each child a piece of red paper just about the right size for the hull of the boat, a piece of white in approximately the right proportions for the sail, and a strip of black for the mast. She would then provide each with a cut-out red shape of the hull to place upon his own piece of red paper, and the child would be instructed to draw around it and cut it out. After all pieces were completed in this manner, they would finally be assembled.

Prepared Outlines

In this case the drawing is already done on the paper and given to the child, and he simply colors inside the lines that someone else drew. A teacher who uses prepared outlines in art class usually reproduces enough for all of the children from one master copy. Pilgrims or turkeys during Thanksgiving are familiar examples. Color books and many workbooks contain prepared outlines and will be discussed in Chapter 10.

EVALUATION OF METHODS

As must certainly be evident from the description of methods of teaching art, there are two that stand out because they give to each child many opportunities for using his own ideas. These methods are creative expression and assigned topics. Both are liberal, modern methods of teaching art, and sometimes the distinguishing line between them is thin. The other four—copy activities, dictated methods, patterns, and prepared outlines—give the child little opportunity to use his imagination or to depend upon himself in any way. There is a place for assigned subjects in a program based upon creative expression. Just how and when assigned topics can be used will be discussed in a later chapter.

In either case, whether creative expression or topics to interpret, the child must be able to identify himself with the idea, have personal feelings about it, react to it, and be free to determine the form of his own art.

Creative Expression

From the selection of ideas through the process of creating the art the child needs to be free, to be on his own to use his ideas and to let them flow through his emotions by way of his hands into his painting, or modeling, or other art activity. This action is an art experience. Freedom, permissiveness, and a warm, appreciative, emotional climate are elements necessary to art education. Therefore, those methods that give to the child opportunities for making his own decisions are the most beneficial.

Art is a personal matter and depends upon the individualizing of ideas and emotions by each child. There is, in fact, really nothing to make art from except the application of ideas and emotions to materials; but it must be the child's own ideas and emotions, not the teacher's. This great distinction between the child's way as the right way for himself, and the teacher's way as the right way for the child, constitutes the broad difference between creative methods and other less desirable practices in art education.

Art, to be creative, must be original with each child. It must be concerned with the imagination. Art brings into being something new through the exercise of the imagination. Art work involves labor and ingenuity, an unfolding of the child's ideas, as well as the experience of and the expression of feelings ignited by his inspiration to make this "something" that has not existed before and is not likely ever to be repeated. The deep educative benefits that can be derived from creative art experiences need to be kept in mind as other processes of teaching art are discussed. The satisfaction that comes to children from solving their own problems through art expressions that are individual can be shared by a teacher who understands *why* such activities are beneficial and *how* other methods fall short in these values. The term *creative expression* is popularly used to describe a wide variety of ways of teaching art regardless of how broad or how limited the children's opportunities for making choices may be. An evaluation of *all* methods of teaching art will help establish a more specific idea of what it is and what it is not.

Assigned Topics to Interpret

Only broad topics provide leeway for individual interpretation. A topic needs to have many facets opening up various possibilities. It should be the kind that can be exploded in all directions to provide the excitement of personal choice and the opening of a greater range of ideas. Although a child's attention is directed toward one general subject, he may still organize and express any aspect of the topic he has selected.

At the same time, the topic must be one about which every child has an abundant source of ideas and feelings. The topic needs to be child- and not subject-centered. For example, "Fun in the Snow" is a common experience in some parts of the world, but would not be a choice in others. It is used as an example here merely to show suggested ways through which any topic might be approached. It opens more choices than "Putting on My Skates" does. It can be developed from many points: building a snow fort, sledding, rolling in the snow, jumping in deep snow, sliding on slippery sidewalks. A child can include many people or few in his art and put them in various kinds of positions. He can select many interesting objects to enrich his art and organize the forms to suit his purposes.

The topic can also influence the emotion the child will try to express. "Fun in the Snow" indicates humorous or enjoyable activity. If the child or his family were involved in a skidding mishap, such a frightening event may be uppermost in his mind in art class. As the topic "Fun in the Snow" is discussed and developed he will usually suppress his own more urgent emotion and comply. A broader topic, "What Happens in the Snow," is more inclusive. It would include this child's experience and maybe that of others. It would still, however, not include the child who may want to draw about his puppy or about playing with his train, or any of a multitude of ideas that may be especially important to some of the children that day. Since the subject matter for art needs to be highly personal to the artist and individual to everyone working in art regardless of age, assigned topics, broad as they may be, are often lacking in this close personal quality.

Unfortunately, in some cases the subject of an assigned topic is limited in scope, such as "My Mother Combing My Hair" or "Walking to My Desk in School." They are experiences common to every child in the group. There is no question about the background each has from which to work, but there is little opportunity for originality. What possibility is there for the imagination? How can the child learn to be inventive within such a limited subject?

The narrow scope of the topic strongly suggests only one or two persons and a very limited organization of these persons. There is little or no suggestion of emotion. It is such a commonplace occurrence that it fails to stimulate much excitement on the part of the children. It is difficult to imagine a child choosing such a topic from among the many exciting, new, and fascinating events in the daily lives of children.

Topics to interpret can broaden a child's scope of expression and may open up a new area of interest to him. Some art activities are so broad and general in nature and provide such rich opportunities for choices, that it is difficult and meaningless to categorize them as either creative expression or assigned topics. The making of a puppet may be one example, provided that each child has broad choices of types of puppets, materials to use, and ways of constructing, forming, and assembling the puppet; an example of individuality in making puppets is shown in Illustrations 67 and 68 on page 193. If the choice of the type of puppet or the topic for the puppet is open, it provides for the creative element of free choice. Examples might be: a sailor puppet, a butterfly, a flower, a group of dancing oysters, a tree, a mule, a space man, or an abstract puppet.

If the child may use any method of assembling or organizing the parts of his puppet, this also provides for many creative possibilities. For example, he may assemble it from wire and boxes, stuff paper into a cloth form, or make it of wood and foil assembled by springs and other materials; he may construct it out of papier-mâché and fabric, or any number of materials and their combinations put together ingeniously, depending on the child's imagination.

When the child determines the shape and color of the object with no limitation imposed upon him, he is expressing it as he wishes. Such freedom of choice not only develops the child's individuality but also creates more interesting and varied puppets.

Keep the opportunities for choices open; keep widening and extending them. As this is done, the climate is set for creativity.

Other Methods

Experiences with art materials previously identified as copy, dictated methods, patterns, and prepared outlines have little or no art value for a child. They give the child little opportunity for choice, nor do they provide him with any expression for his imagination or emotions. Copying is simply a mechanical process, with the success of the work depending upon each child's ability to make his work resemble the original. The products are all alike. Any differences among them depend more upon the child's lack of ability to reproduce exactly someone else's ideas, expression, and organization than upon his own ability to have and to express ideas. There is no place for the inclusion of his personal relationship to his art, his thoughts, feelings, or ideas about it. Avoid giving children anything to copy. If a child working alone occasionally copies something for the purpose of learning more about it, to develop a particular skill, or to sharpen his sensitivity to it, it becomes a needed learning situation and probably should not be interfered with unless copy work becomes a way of working he relies upon.

The dictated method of teaching art, as the name implies, is a lock-step process of having each child follow in a step-by-step manner the directions of the teacher. She has worked out in detail the idea ahead of time, and the class participates in mass-producing her idea. Such an activity can take place in any art medium, such as clay. Dictated methods are teacher-centered. The teacher thought of the idea, she decided upon the shapes of the forms, and she put it together in organized form. She, or whoever originally developed the idea, is the only one who profits by the thought-provoking challenge of creating. When the teacher directs the children in making the same object that has already been developed, she is not providing them with either art activities or sound educational experiences. They do develop habits of following directions, of doing exactly what everyone else does at the same time and in the same way, and of doing exactly what the leader directs, but these things hold little value in preparing children for individual thinking and activity. Children, under this practice, learn to rely upon the leader (the teacher) and feel secure only when doing so.

Some people may think that copy experiences and directed activities provide a child with a vocabulary of forms that he can draw upon later for his creative art work. Such people lack confidence in children and fail to realize that each child *can* and *wants* to do original art work, and seem not to be concerned with the kinds of art and educational qualities inherent in original art work. By such controlled ways of teaching art they continually discourage and prevent the child from using any of his ideas. He loses confidence in his ideas and in himself. Then, when faced with the necessity of actually creating from his own ideas, he finds he has trouble. He does not know what to draw, and when he does draw, the work is often stiff and limited in its organization and complexity. Directed methods do little or nothing to prepare a child for later creative activities.

When all children are held to the same speed, as they are in directed or teacher-controlled procedures, the faster, more capable, more enterprising children learn to form an indifference to work by learning to do one small part of a job and then stopping for a while to wait for others. They learn that working up to their capacity is neither wanted nor appreciated and often meets with disapproval. They find ways of evading this challenge of working to capacity. They learn that conforming to the speed of slower workers brings rewards. The slower workers, on the other hand, learn evasive ways of avoiding the frustrations caused by not being able to keep pace with some others.

Children's individuality can be damaged by such conformity, because many are prevented by their teacher from learning the satisfaction and exhilaration of plunging ahead and following the depth and speed determined by their *own* abilities.

The art work done by John in Illustrations 6–11 demonstrates the case against teaching methods that result in conformity. During the first three grades John attended a school in which dictated methods of teaching art were used. Illustrations 6–9 show his work done under direction. One rainy day the first-grade teacher, in trying to relate the art to life situations, directed the children in making a drawing of an umbrella such as the one in Illustration 6. Under her step-by-step direction, everyone drew the big curve for the top, then the smaller curves below, and then the handle. The child's feelings about rain and his personal experiences with rain and umbrellas were completely omitted. Children like to stamp in puddles or see reflections in them. They have different reactions to rain experiences, such as getting caught in the rain, falling in the mud, or playing in the water that runs along the curb. These activities and the children's reactions to them make interesting pictures for children to make and for others to see.

In the first grade during Halloween John's group drew pumpkins by the step-by-step dictated way of teaching, as in John's drawing in Illustration 7. The smiling expression and other features varied in size, but otherwise they were almost identical. When they were displayed, one quick look was enough to see them all. None required any special notice, for there was nothing different about any.

In the second grade the composition of three cherries and the word *Washington* (8) was decided upon as the art lesson by the teacher in recognition of Washington's birthday. In view of the many exciting events and adventures in this great man's life, this group of cherries is trite. Few, if any, children would have chosen it for their art. If they had been free to decide, their art would have reflected their own feeling for his many adventures and contributions.

These illustrations are examples of John's work done at a school in which dictated methods of teaching art were used.

If you have difficulty trying to determine the subject of Illustration 9, you are not alone. Few people who see it know what it is. Difficult to recognize though it is, the teacher has placed a star on it indicating that it was among those that turned out best. It is the head of a girl wearing a green scarf in recognition of St. Patrick's Day. It looks grotesque because John was only following directions without any other purpose in mind while developing this project. He was not interested in the subject. What active third-grade boy would think of such an idea for his art? It is an adult's choice, and a dull one.

The star on this piece of John's art shows that the teacher's motive was to have the children imitate her own model as nearly as possible, under her direction. Those who, in her judgment, accomplished this purpose were rewarded by the star; the recognition of receiving a star was withheld from the others, regardless of the sincerity of their efforts. Such discriminatory practices have no place in art. They discourage those who fail to receive teacher approval and cause these children to lose interest in art. It is difficult for a child to understand why he did not receive recognition. Children become confused by such practices, trying to gain the satisfaction of receiving the star rather than of doing a satisfying job. The premium is placed upon following directions, mass-producing the teacher's idea, complete acceptance of the ideas and expressions of the leader, preparing plastic young minds for totalitarian practices. No wonder children are confused and bored by such "art" activities. They are in opposition to life in our culture, to the interests and choices of children, to a respect for individual differences, and to art itself.

After John's third year in this school his family moved to another town, and he was enrolled in a school in which creative expression was the method of teaching and working in art. For a while John was disturbed in art class. He seemed not to have any ideas. He was ill at ease and lacked self-confidence. During the first part of the art work period, following a lively teacher-pupil motivational discussion of the topic, the other children went right to work, but John just sat and looked around. He seemed to have difficulty deciding for himself what to do and how to do it. When he finally decided upon an idea and got started, he drew one object and quit. One object on a page had been his background of art experiences for three years, and he had a difficult adjustment to make.

When John's teacher noticed he was adjusting faster in other subjects and still having trouble in art, she discussed it with his parents. Fortunately his mother had saved his art work, of which Illustrations 6–9 are examples. This revealed to his teacher a deeper problem for John than just adjustment to a new school. The teacher realized that building John's confidence in himself and in his own art ideas was the first task, and encouraging him toward more complex relationships in the work he did was another. Determining the cause of his trouble and taking steps to correct it did not immediately solve it nor greatly upgrade the quality of his art, for much damage had been done in these three formative years. It only gave a clue to ways of dealing with it. Correction was a rather slow process.

Illustration 10 shows how John tried to draw a group of seated men. Because for the first three years his own ideas of how to draw were continually interfered with by the teacher's imposing her ideas upon him, he was confused about how to draw people. He was not prepared for creative art, and his drawing of these people seems grotesque. He did make some independent accomplishments, which the teacher pointed out to him and encouraged. He shaped the people to fit the chairs and formed the figures into a group facing the center. He was working on his own and organizing his ideas, which was a step forward for John.

10

11

John's art in the fourth grade, at a new school, was based upon creative expression. These examples of his work show the influence of previous experiences as well.

More and more he discovered the excitement of using his own ideas as he wished. He became intrigued with designs and put them on everything, even all over a train as Illustration 11 shows. John became interested in art and was just as full of good ideas and just as eager to express them as were his other fourth-grade classmates.

Filling in prepared outline drawings is another questionable activity.

> The activity of coloring pictures drawn by someone else is such a commonplace one that children and adults have come to accept it. It is not only the variety of kinds of coloring-in experiences that are determined for children but also the prevalence of them that should receive the critical attention of thoughtful adults who look beyond the immediate occupation of the child to the long-range effects of this activity and to its transference to other areas of his thinking, deciding, and behaving.[2]

Some people believe there is value in the use of prepared outline drawings because they impress upon children the "right" idea of the styles peculiar to the subjects being colored, for example, how Pilgrims were dressed or how an Indian looked. There is value in this knowledge which can be gained without having children fill in the prepared outlines of a form with color. Art for children should be centered more in the *child's* ideas, imagination, and emotions.

Another reason sometimes given for the use of prepared outlines is that they teach motor control. The child learns to stay within the lines when he colors—but he would be much more interested in coloring inside the lines of a form that he made than in one already drawn according to an adult's idea. The child takes more pride in what *he* does. Therefore, it seems logical that he would take more pride in coloring within the lines of his own picture *if staying inside the lines is what he feels would express his ideas best.* There are times when the effect is more satisfying if he does not stay within the lines. He will learn this and other skills better in relationship to his own work than by applying an isolated operation to a prepared outline. Examples of the effects of coloring in prepared outline drawings upon the creative art of two children are shown in Illustrations 75 and 76 on page 202.

There are other activities for children related to this one and found both in school and out of the classroom that deprive them of interesting and valuable art and educational experiences. There is an abundance of materials such as ready-made molds to fill in with prepared mixes; three-dimensional forms of various objects to paint; airplanes and cars, ships and animals, billfolds and belts cut out and ready to assemble: all a child is required to do is follow directions and not digress. To alter the directions would cause trouble, and the object would not then fit the preconceived plan for it.

Teachers have a grave responsibility in choosing the methods of teaching art because children trust their teacher's judgments. This trust and confidence causes children to become impressed with the teacher's choices and decisions and to feel that they are "right." The art experiences chosen for children should be those that do the most for them educationally.

---

[2] Blanche Jefferson, "The Color Book Craze" (pamphlet), Association for Childhood Education International, Washington, D.C., p. 1.

SUGGESTED ACTIVITIES

1. *Visit a class in any elementary school while the art class is in progress. Be there for the beginning of the lesson. Try to determine for yourself what method of teaching art was used, and discuss it with your classmates.*

2. *For class discussion, have two or three sets of art work made by children in the elementary grades. If possible, these sets should represent different grade levels and different school districts. Each set should contain all of the art work made by the group during the art work period. Hang each set together and discuss them to try to see:*

    (a) What method of teaching art was used, and what clues the children's art gave that led to this decision.

    (b) What, if you were the teacher, you might say to the children during the next art class to help them toward more freedom in creating.

    (c) What achievement you could find in his art to mention to each child.

2

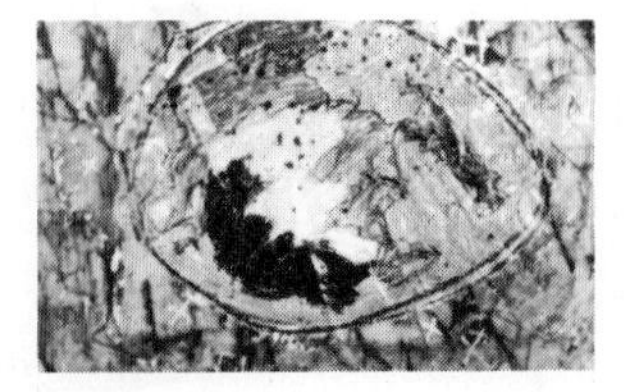

Values of Art Education

ART HAS universal appeal for children. They feel attracted to it, take pleasure in doing it, enter into art eagerly, and derive many satisfactions and benefits from it.

Because of its popularity with children some adults tend to think that art lacks the depth of intellectual involvement and challenges present in some other school subjects. Some believe that because it is so generally liked by children that it must be easy. Many adults consider art "fun" and try to motivate children with this unnecessary lure. They believe that its diversionary use is the major or perhaps only value in art.

These attitudes have frequently resulted, unfortunately, in placing art in a minor educational position, regarding it as a peripheral area of the curriculum, or viewing it as recreation. Unaware of its educative values, some people are hostile toward the use of precious school time for art. Others, lacking convictions of their own, are also swayed in this direction by the present emphasis upon other subjects.

The values of art are too numerous and too deep to be thought of as only providing a pleasant change in the curriculum, although even this has its educational values. Learning is enhanced as children enjoy the satisfactions that come with the highly personalized creative art expression. When learning takes place with a feeling of enjoyment and gratification, it is often better remembered and more frequently applied. We need to look beyond the happy atmosphere of the art class to understand what there is about art to give such deep satisfactions; the educational advantages of creative expression need to be examined.

Anyone teaching art or studying child art should be convinced of its values and also be able to convince those less familiar with modern art education of its worth. To do this the teacher needs to be familiar with the open positive processes of creativity as a way of originating art forms, as a way of expressing ideas, as a way of solving problems, as a way of dealing with others, and, in fact, as a way of life. Habits and attitudes are formed from the creative working process which will help a child understand himself and his classmates better, and help him adjust to life around and within him. Art experiences will give him confidence and personal opportunities, help him learn how to make art judgments, and improve his own art work.

When the values of creative art education are clearly understood, the place of art in the curriculum is strengthened; the quality of the art experience the children have is improved, and the general public attitude toward art is upgraded.

For its deepest educative benefits, the art experience for children in school needs to be closely related to, and in many ways much the same as, the art experience for the artist in his studio. For it is *art* we are teaching children, and art can only develop from an art process in which the child in his art class and the artist in his studio have the same type of intellectual freedom to do self-determined art, with opportunities to learn as they work, an appreciative audience, and the right to set as their own standards the results of their best efforts with that particular subject at that time and under those circumstances.

In recent times there has been an awakened concern for the development and encouragement of art in the United States. Two presidents, John F. Kennedy and Lyndon B. Johnson, have given leadership in this direction. New legislation for the arts and new art galleries and collections are bringing art into focus. Emphasis upon preserving and appreciating the beauty of our country is making us aware of the application of art. It seems essential that Americans, for whom these things are intended, be able to participate, to share, and to respond to them. It follows that such education be a vital part of every child's daily school experiences, and that adequate time be provided for them to build art judgments and to create art work of quality.

There are a great many reasons why it is important to teach art to children and why it should be taught as creative expression; some of these reasons will be explored in this chapter. Among the major divisions of this chapter there is some overlapping among the values themselves, for the nature of art and the benefits of an education in art are all interrelated.

> Nothing so bolsters our self-confidence and reconciles us with ourselves as the continuous ability to create; to see things grow and develop under our hand, day in, day out. The decline of handicrafts in modern times is perhaps one of the causes for the rise of frustration and the increased susceptibility of the individual to mass movements.[1]

> In creative problem-solving the solution offers tremendous satisfactions, not only because a problem has been solved and a job completed, but because the product has aesthetic qualities and the creator has given of himself to the project—something of himself has emerged in a form which he recognizes (and which others recognize) as his own unique contribution to the solution.[2]

---

[1] Eric Hoffer, *The True Believer* (New York: Harper & Row, 1951), p. 38.

[2] Page 14 from *Setting Conditions for Creative Teaching*, by James A. Smith. © Copyright 1966 by Allyn and Bacon, Inc., Boston. Reprinted by permission of the publisher.

AESTHETIC AWARENESS

A major purpose in art education, quite possibly its primary purpose, is to deepen and quicken pleasure in seeing: to make people more discriminating in their judgments of art, so that they can enjoy it more and be able to improve their own art work, their response to nature, and to their environment.

Awareness of the qualities of art can be guided and developed through art education, provided the art education is based upon creative expression. Because each art product is different, each needs to be approached individually, bringing a constant need to be alert for qualities in the art work that give it meaning and distinction. This awareness of art qualities carries over into an awareness of other visual forms including clothing, furniture arrangements, and city planning.

Through their constant exposure to modern-day media and culture, children easily become sensitized to the different art forms of their day. Through the study of the various types of art resulting from the imaginative, original processes of creative expression, and from the emphasis given to the qualitative parts of each, children learn to like and to expect many different kinds of art.

There is no method of teaching art that provides the rich opportunities for the child to make as many aesthetic judgments as does creative expression. Personal judgments and personal choices are the very essence of art. Beauty, pleasing proportions, and harmonious relationships between the forms and the colors are basic to the structure of art. Since we are teaching art to children, it is imperative that they learn about these art qualities too, and know how to make art judgments. These learnings can take place in daily art classes by pointing them out in the children's own art work and that of others.

The expression of his ideas and feelings in organized form makes the creating of art a personal experience for each child. Because of this, judgments of art, also, can only be made on a personal basis; there is an interaction between the personal expression of the artist and the personal reaction the observer gets from looking at the art work. This high degree of diversity makes every approach to art an opportunity to refine taste and to raise the level of each child's art judgment. For example, in a fifth-grade painting, expressing her fear of the big waves at the seashore, Jane has shown a high, dark, ominous wave and a dark, threatening sky (12). The trees and her hair blown by the wind reflect the natural forces involved in the danger. Jane's expression is clear and dramatic. The observer sees this, feeling the power and threat of the sea, and reacts to it according to his own feeling and experience.

Expression is an individual matter. Another child's painting about the sea might be called "Fun at the Beach." His purposes would be different from Jane's; so, of course, his expression of it would be different, too. Although the same subject of the seashore was chosen individually, the interpretations would not be the same. It is necessary for a teacher to project herself into the art activity of the child before she can determine what his

Good

12

By concentrating upon the expression of an emotion associated with an exciting experience, a child can create an aesthetic art product, as Jane has done in this example.

purposes are and, thus, encourage or help him. In fact, this is necessary if we are to make meaningful contact with any work of art. The viewer is not only cognizant of his own feelings about the art but also studies it to see the intent of the artist. The choices the child makes as he works are determined by his purposes and intentions. Even though he may not always be able to verbalize about them, they guide him. The child concentrates upon his ideas, constantly searching for shapes and colors to state them. As these selections are motivated by his deep purposes, the resulting art work is harmonious with his intent.

Harmony in art means that forms and colors are related to the purposes of the art, and that the forms and colors within the art are related to each other. Each provides something that adds to the effect of the other. But it also means something in addition to structure: a feeling for the subject or a reaction to it expressed in the art. When colors, shapes, and emotions are harmonious or related, each supplies a quality that adds unity among them, giving the whole a feeling of "oneness," which we respond to as aesthetic quality.

The observer is aware of the aesthetic qualities in Jane's painting. The emotion of fear is further expressed by the fact that Jane is alone on the beach, and there is no one to help her. The feeling for the subject (a sudden dangerous wave) is shown in the girl's narrow escape, her abandonment of the sand pail, and her reaching toward help. The dark sea and sky encompass the light sand, giving unity to the composition. Every form and item in it add to the feeling created by Jane as she concentrated upon her work. The resulting painting is truly a work of art. It has aesthetic quality, and it is necessary for the teacher to make the children aware of it. If some people feel that they do not like the painting, they are probably reacting to the danger and fear. Certainly, we react strongly to these things, and we respond in this way to Jane's painting because she has been so earnest in expressing this feeling.

Children and adults can learn to understand art better and to accept a greater variety of art works if they are helped to realize that the artist and his art are successful when the emotion he expresses (whatever it is) is felt by the viewer. In this case Jane was motivated by a strong purpose. She concentrated on it as she worked, and was successful in expressing it. These factors bring about an aesthetic work of art. Persons looking at it need to study the art work to sensitize themselves to the child's intent and then see how she has related the forms and colors to her purposes and to each other.

Making aesthetic judgments indicates that the finished art product is viewed in terms of its artistic qualities. Practice in making aesthetic judgments comes most abundantly in creative art expression in which each piece of art work is different, each having qualities peculiar to it that must be judged independently of every other piece of work. Practice in making aesthetic judgments, richly provided in creative art education, builds within children a responsiveness to quality in art.

Personal likes and dislikes alone, without being founded upon art knowledge, are inadequate as bases for quality judgments of the art. Whether a person likes or dislikes a work of art is such an individual matter, dependent upon knowledge and background, that it gives no substantial basis for the guidance of children's aesthetic judgments. Teachers need to guard against expressing opinions that are backed by nothing more than this.

There are sounder reasons for making art judgments than one's likes and dislikes. "We like what we know" is a frequently used statement. If we have seen only naturalistic scenes or likenesses of objects and people, we will understand them best and like them best. Abstract art would be disliked and meaningless because we have no experience with it and consequently do not know it.

The child's ability to make art judgments grows under the guidance of an art teacher who knows how to make such judgments herself and knows how to guide children in understanding how such *art* quality is achieved and why it is recognized as art quality. This is an excellent way to provide knowledge and information that lead to better art judgments. This ability leads, also, to better art expression, deeper appreciation of art, and more qualitative selection of art products.

Art education without emphasis upon aesthetic quality lacks the very core and meaning of art. Art educators need to reflect upon and stress the values of *art* in art education. The creation and contemplation of beauty and expression in art is still the base upon which art has operated everywhere in the world from our first records of man to the present.

One of the most important things that a teacher or parent can help children to retain as they mature is their awareness of experiences through the use of their senses and emotions. The creative person keeps his openness to experience and in this respect he is childlike. The child does not feel that a new experience will be a risk to him. He perceives the world without feeling he has to make judgments about it. During early childhood he collects much raw material without deciding "what" or "how" he will use it. How much information is collected and what is done with it will determine his creative potential not only as a child but as an adult.[3]

THE TOTALITY OF THE EXPERIENCE

The totality of the experience in art is one of the reasons for art's appeal to children and is also one of its unique and important values. The totality of the art experience implies a complete enterprise each time an art project is undertaken. The child starts with an idea and some raw materials, a ball of clay or paper and paste, for example, and with only his own resources makes and completes an art product. From the inception of the ideas through the creative process to the finished piece of art it is one unfragmented whole.

Not only is art a complete experience, but it is also an involved problem-solving situation. It is a sum of many different and related tasks, undertakings, and responsibilities, reactions, judgments, decisions, and adjustments. It imposes many different demands upon a child, requiring him to deal with them simultaneously. No wonder children like art, for it completely challenges and absorbs them.

Although there are various kinds of undertakings to be dealt with, they are mutally dependent and intrinsically related. The whole task is one of harmonizing them and bringing each part and the whole project under control.

The totality of the art experience involves the child's need to conceive of an original idea; to shape each form to suit his mental image and feeling dominant at that moment; to put the parts together into a whole unified structure.

While engaged in bringing this complex project about, the child takes advantage of skills he has already mastered to some degree and at the same time deals with the awkwardness of underdeveloped ones, bringing right along with it the need for further emotional adjustments. He feels and responds to his own competences while he feels and reacts to his disappointments and inabilities. This vacillating and continual emotional adjustment is present not only in his awareness of his lack of manual dexterity but also in his awareness of the effect this has upon his art. This give and take of adjustment is in itself excellent education.

There is frequently a wide gap between the mental image a child has as he first begins his art and resulting visual images he sees in his art product. However, a growing child is, from experience, well acquainted with his inadequacies. He keeps trying and learning, building skills and power in many ways. He is not easily discouraged by his *own* confrontation with disappointments and inadequacies in art. It is only when adults reenforce his feelings

---

[3] Earl W. Linderman and Donald W. Heberholz, *Developing Artistic and Perceptual Awareness* (Dubuque, Ia.: William C. Brown Co., 1964), p. 11.

of incompetence that he is overwhelmed by them and discouraged. Every child needs to build his own balance of adjustments which is, of course, a necessary part of every art experience. He may make changes in his art to accommodate his feelings and judgments about the relative successes of the comparisons he himself makes of it as he works. Changes take place in his art as they take place in his ideas and feelings.

As he does all of this, he must deal with the lessening opportunities and growing difficulties he faces with his art as it progresses. Every time he adds a form to his art, he has less space to work with, and the leftover spaces are irregular in size and shape, increasing the difficulty in using them. Every form added complicates the problem even further by requiring whatever forms he does add to be related to the already existing ones and to the space he has to put them in.

As he works, he expends himself. Every idea he expresses narrows his choices and energy. His attention span gives way to its limitations. The child has many things going for him in art; but he also has many problems.

Most art work requires color to which children respond vigorously. Yet the choice, use, and application of color have problems all their own which are added to the already complex situation multiplying the involvement of the total art undertaking.

Throughout the entire complex of the art experience, each child is faced with the exciting bombardment of new and changing ideas and moods that come to him as he works. He selects, rejects, reacts, and revises to suit himself and to accommodate the other aspects of the on-going process.

There is also the constant awareness of his own responsibility for what he does, his use of materials, and the effectiveness of his art product. The art materials he is using at the time also bring their own limitations and delights to be used as advantageously as possible. The present general atmosphere of censure in our daily lives tends to make people avoid responsibilities, but in art, there is no escape from the acceptance of responsibility for one's individual actions. The evidence is there for all to see. This, too, has solid educational value.

From the beginning of each art working experience, somewhere in the back of each child's mind is also some consideration of how others will react to his work. Although each is free to choose his own ideas, to organize and express them in his own way, there also exists the wish to display the completed art and have others respond to it. The importance a child attaches to the reactions of others also affects the judgments he makes as he works. He rejects or tempers his ideas to accommodate them. The truer he remains to his own ideas and expressions, the more personal and original his art will be. Teachers and parents can help by avoiding negative value judgments or strong positive ones and creating a permissive appreciative climate.

Artists of all ages, including children in school, are protective about their art work because there are so many of their own personal qualities and hard work in it. From the beginning to the end of the art experience children are reluctant to tolerate another person's different ideas that interfere with their own.

Through the ages, art is and has been created in its wholeness and remains an individual performance. Few things of this nature remain. Few things consume us so completely or give such deep satisfaction. Art experiences embody both the creative and performance aspects of art, and intertwine them as almost no other undertaking does.

> Much of the ache and the brooding unhappiness in modern man is the result of his difficulty in using himself fully. He performs compartmentalized tasks in a compartmentalized world. He is reined in—physically, socially, and spiritually. Only rarely does he have a sense of fulfilling himself through total contact with a total challenge. He finds it difficult to make real connection even with those who are near him. But there are vast urges of conscience, natural response, and goodness inside him demanding air and release. And he has his own potential, the regions of which are far broader than he can ever guess at—a potential that keeps nagging him to be fully used.[4]

> One need not minimize, however, the arduousness of a task requiring intense concentration and effort; it is as hard as learning to read and write concurrently. The additional complexities of aesthetic composition, of appreciating and interpreting the beauty in what one sees and does, would be too much to expect, certainly too much to require of pupils at this stage. At best, the teacher can call attention to distinctive qualities and be enthusiastic about specific instances when they do appear in a student's work. Here, too, the sense of the whole, the feeling for unique and expressive character are gradually acquired.[5]

> It is implied, I think, that the act of a man creating is the act of a whole man, that it is this rather than the product that makes it good and worthy.[6]

One of the powerful values of art in education comes from this totality of experience. The wholeness of it is unlike anything else the child encounters in the curriculum of the elementary school. There are times in the teaching-learning situation in art, however, when one of the facets of art may need to be dealt with separately to improve it. This is a learning situation that relates to art, but the work done is not a work of art. Art results only from the sum of all the parts—the totality of the experience.

The general nature of the art experience and the common bond in all art experiences, child or adult, are pointed out to clarify the close relationship between art and art education, and *not* to imply that adult standards, tastes, ideas, or purposes are to be imposed upon children, or that these personal factors in art are ever to be imposed upon any person by another.

INDIVIDUALITY

Individual differences among children have long been recognized and teachers of every subject urged to provide for them. Art education has gone further and done more in this direction than any other field in the elementary school

---

[4] Norman Cousins, "What Matters About Schweitzer," *Saturday Review*, September 25, 1965, p. 32.

[5] Miriam Lindstrom, *Children's Art* (Berkeley, Calif.: University of California Press, 1957), p. 75.

[6] Jerome S. Bruner, *On Knowing* (Cambridge: The Belknap Press of Harvard University Press, 1962), p. 19.

curriculum. No art lesson need be reconstructed to provide for individual differences; consideration for individual differences is inherent in every aspect of creative art education. Art is based upon the individuality of the person doing the art. In fact, every child is required and expected to work differently from every other. Therefore, if each child is *not* working in a personal and original way, it is *not art.* Individual expression and development through art are accomplished within the context of group teaching as each child is encouraged to rely upon, to use, and to extend his powers, skills, interests, knowledge, and background. This demand upon the individual makes him search for and build upon his own unique resources instead of being led along by the group or doing something because everyone else is doing it. Since we live in groups and depend upon each other in many ways, we need to learn how and when to take strong individual stands. People need to learn that not all actions are group actions, that individuals make groups, and ultimately, even within the group, that it is the individual who must decide for himself.

Individual action can become lost unless provision is made for it. In the work that so many people do, they are unable to see the effect of their ideas and personal contributions on the finished product, for it is often a piecemeal operation which denies them a feeling of association and pride in a contribution that is peculiarly theirs. People support causes as a group. They participate less actively in sports, drama, and other activities, becoming more passive as spectators. With this trend, it is imperative that all persons working with children insure their daily participation in creative expression through art, for it provides richly for and develops the individuality of each child. Every individual by nature feels an urge to reach out toward something that will distinguish him. Art can satisfy this need in constructive refining ways. There are several ways through which individuality is strengthened by art.

Personally Meaningful Opportunities

Creative expression gives to every child the *opportunity to choose the ideas or subject matter for his art that are most meaningful to him.* Each child in the group has the privilege of choosing what is the most interesting to him at that moment. Children's ideas and interests constantly change; different days bring different interests and moods. What seemed urgent to a child yesterday may be dull to him today. What excited him and inspired him in the morning may be replaced by a newer interest in the afternoon. In creative expression the emphasis is on the child's choice, which lets him take advantage of his immediate interest.

Whatever subject he chooses, the teacher encourages each child to think about his feeling for the subject and try through colors and shapes to express it. The subject for the art itself is less important than the expression of either a personal emotional involvement with the subject or an expression of the feeling for the character of it. For example, the graceful qualities of the cat, its soft flexible body or its quiet stealthy movements, expressed in art work reflects the response made to the character of the cat,

13

Joe felt an indefinable fear of going home alone at night. Expressing this fear, he gave it form and organization.

as in Illustration 1. Personal emotional involvement is expressed when the child shows excitement or happiness in a playground picture or an amusing clay animal, for example, or the drawing of the face of a distressed child as in Illustration 89 on page 222.

During one art work period there would probably be as many different ideas being expressed as there are children in the room. One child might be drawing a picture of himself and his friends playing baseball after school, another might be involved in expressing his experience in coming home after dark, while another does an abstract or nonobjective drawing.

Of the many ideas that come into a child's mind, one is selected mainly because at that moment he feels some close emotional identification with it. This is true of adult artists as well. An idea with strong personal meaning can be expressed with clear feeling. Expression of personal reaction must be the constant that runs through art work; otherwise it becomes a sterile academic exercise. This gives it human content and lifts it above a mere visual plane, because the child (or artist) has invested into it something of his own life and given it life and feeling of its own to which people who look at it can respond.

Each child is not only permitted but also encouraged to select an idea that is uniquely his own. In forming the shapes of objects according to his own ideas of how they should appear, he develops a style of expression that is just as much his own as his handwriting or his physical appearance are.

The organization of his work is developed according to his own ideas, too. The art work of some children is identified by its complex nature, that of others by its simplicity. It is considered important in education that each child continue to develop in his own distinctive way.

Individual Challenge

Art education gives to each child the *maximum opportunity to develop his own ideas to the best of his ability.* This opportunity provides well for individual differences. Children within a group vary greatly in their abilities to solve problems. Each will be able to solve a problem as far or deeply as his ability will permit. Some children, more gifted than others, may see and express much more than others. It is unlikely, then, that any two children in a group will develop their ideas to exactly the same extent. Some will stop with only a few ideas expressed in a simple way, while others will see deeper meanings and relationships and be able to express them in a much more complex manner.

Ability, meaning mental ability, is not the only factor influencing the depth to which a child might go in depicting his ideas. Inspiration or motivation is a very important element. The child's interests inspire him. The teacher has a very real responsibility in recognizing this and in helping each child develop his ideas to the fullest. (Her role in motivation will be discussed in a later chapter.) An uninspired child is not apt to have the incentive or drive to carry an idea to any great extent. This lack of incentive can block his expression and cause him to stop short of what he might have been able to do. When the topic is not of his own choice or when he is forced to work when he does not want to, the result will show this lack of incentive.

> Nothing has been said of ability, or abilities. What shall we say of energy, of combinatorial zest, of intelligence, of alertness, of perseverance? I shall say nothing about them. They are obviously important, but, from a deeper point of view, they are also trivial.[7]

Recognition of Each Child

Another related reason for using creative art work is that *teachers* use such processes with children because they *have confidence in each student as an individual who can and wants to create.* Confidence gives support to children's abilities to create in art; creative art expression fosters confidence. So confidence is both an ally and a product of creative expression. The child must have confidence in the teacher and know that she will accept his every serious attempt regardless of how it may appear or how different it is from the others. This is one place where the child need not be afraid to be different. His different ideas are encouraged and accepted. Sure that the teacher will not reject his original work, he feels free to create. The teacher sets the

[7] Bruner, *op. cit.*, p. 29.

stage for this through her faith in children, by verbally saying so and revealing it in other ways.

The teacher, then, has the real responsibility in establishing the rapport necessary for such confidence. By feeling and knowing that every child is creative she can communicate this feeling to children by building their confidence in themselves and so increasing their chances for improvement in art.

Every child is creative. You have only to watch a child at play to see him constantly finding new ways, and changing, inventing, and turning to new things. You have only to listen to a child to hear him tell fascinating tales built upon reality and upon his imagination. Children are so rich in imaginative powers that they frequently cannot tell where the factual stops and the fanciful begins—nor do they care. They make it their story, the way they want it. All this is creativity and is the basis for art. Every child has all this; it is the responsibility of the teacher to cherish and encourage it.

If an adult feels that a child cannot create, he simply does not know children. He makes this decision from his lack of knowledge of children and his own lack of experience with and observation of them. If an adult feels that a child cannot create, he simply is not accepting the child's work. Many adults do this. Because adults are unfamiliar with the characteristics of children's art, they expect the child to draw or paint as they would. This is impossible. A child is not an adult and therefore does not act as an adult in many ways, including the doing of his art work. This is a very old truth that adults, at times, disregard.

> All children are creative—of this I am convinced. My recent work with children has made me more and more aware that it is impossible to predict where creative talent can be found. It is everywhere: among the slow-learning, the brilliant, the average, the privileged and the culturally deprived.[8]

When children are permitted to use their own ideas and are inspired to do their best work, they become excited by the art experience. Helen Parkhurst shows this in discussing art with children. The children say:

> "You have a nice feeling when you make things with your hands."
> "You have a good feeling because you know it is your own."
> "This feeling is all over."
> "You feel a little excited and nervous."
> "When I start [the art work] I am very curious to see how it will come out. When I do it I get all excited. My hands get very excited and keep going. They get a lot of energy from your head."[9]

Individuality of Working Speeds

Art gives every child the *opportunity to work at his own speed.* The rate of speed of working and the promptness with which people go about beginning a task are highly individual matters. Some children work fast, seeming

---

[8] Smith, *op. cit.*, p. 14.

[9] Helen Parkhurst, *Creating with One's Hands*, a recording (New London, Conn.: Alpark Records, distributed by Arthur C. Croft Publications).

14

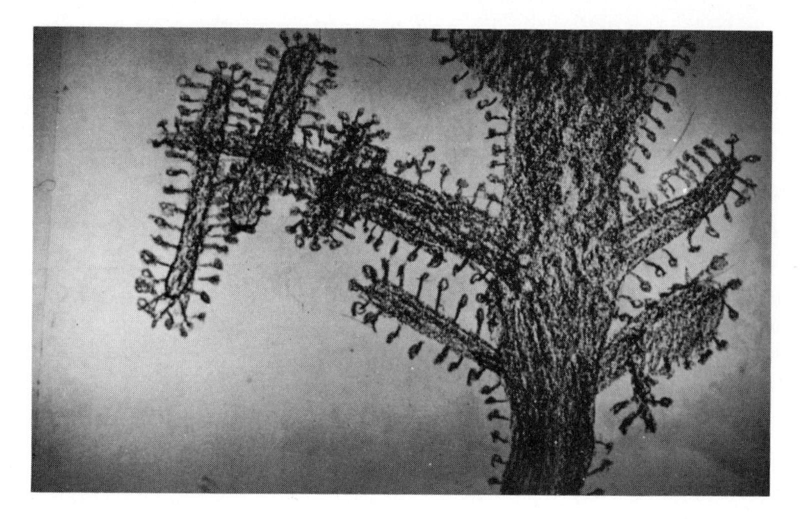

15

The time and apparent effort a child puts into his art are poor bases for grading or evaluating the child's work. One child may paint a tree quickly, while another works slowly and includes details. Both paintings have quality.

to be anxious to get every thought and idea into form as quickly as possible. Some work fast but slow down occasionally and then begin again. Some work slowly and deliberately from the start until they complete their work.

This variety in rate of speed is determined by many factors that are individual to each child. Some children move slowly in dressing themselves, eating, and walking, and in every other aspect of their behaivor. Art work is another aspect of a child's behavior, and he may be expected to function in this as he does in everything else. The same pattern applies to the child who is excitable and jumps into everything; this child gets an idea quickly and pursues it immediately. It does not mean that one speed of working is better than another. It simply means that each child's own speed of working is best for him. Interfering with or trying to control the various speeds of work within one group during an art work period confuses children.

Control of working speed might also interfere with ideas. One child, working quickly, might be expressing only the large shapes at first, returning to complete them when he has exhausted his fast flow of ideas or inspiration. Another, working slowly, might have only a little completed, while others are much farther along. Slowing the first child could cause him to lose some of the ideas that come so fast. Insisting upon speed from the second child could discourage his ability to work at all.

Children approach their work or start to make the first form at different speeds, too. Just looking at a blank sheet of paper or a chunk of clay causes some people to hesitate in starting; others are anxious to get something started and go on from there. This is not only a child's problem; artists of every age work this way. Some artists apply a flat color over their canvas just to get over the hurdle of beginning. There are no other educational experiences except the creative ones in which the child begins as wholly from nothing. Only his experiences and his thoughts guide him; there is no form to follow, no logical step-by-step pattern; each child is on his own. This very feeling at the beginning causes children to work at different speeds.

Then, too, some children have more trouble with motor control than others. Manipulation of materials is a problem. This causes different rates of speed within a group.

Differences in working speeds are normal and to be expected within a group of children. A few will do two paintings during an art work period while one might say, "I didn't have time to finish mine." Because a daily program of varied school activities must be administered by the teacher, sometimes children are unable to complete their art work in a given amount of time. When this happens, additional time should be provided, either during the next art class or in the child's free time.

Child-determined Task

The child enjoys the privilege and responsibility of *setting the task for himself*, individualizing education for him in a very important way. It is not always easy to decide what to do and to determine the amount of time and efforts to spend on a job. It takes thought and planning to determine what task is important enough to undertake. To decide what ideas to omit and what to include in his art work takes judgment on the part of the child doing the work, and is a measure of their value to him. It is a privilege to make these decisions and to set the task for himself. A confident student will want to do it. Not to want to set the task for himself is evidence of too much dependence upon the teacher.

Setting the task for oneself implies responsiblity for the outcome of the job. Children like responsibility. It makes them feel grown up. Children will enjoy this responsibility unless it becomes burdensome or unpleasant by standards that are set too high by too much being expected, or by too much pushing. When this occurs, the child tries to avoid such responsibilities. This escape from obligation deprives him of the opportunity to develop judgments and assume obligations, which are qualities of character just as important in childhood as in adulthood.

Setting the task and working it through to completion should be a pleasant experience for every child. If a teacher is negative in her criticism of the way a child works or of what he does, it is discouraging to him, and accepting the responsibility for its outcome then becomes unpleasant.

Learning to set the task for himself helps the child learn his capacity for achieving certain goals. He knows, by trying, whether or not one job might be too difficult for him, or whether only a difficult and complicated task challenges him. This knowledge helps him estimate other tasks in relation to what he has learned about himself. He also discovers how long he can remain interested in any one job. Some children, by the nature of their personalities or their abilities, cannot work through a long undertaking, whereas others prefer it.

Emotionally Personal Expression

Creative expression *helps each student to face his own thoughts and feelings.* We do not always face what our own feelings really are. We rationalize. We try to hide our real feelings, especially those that we suspect may meet with disapproval or ridicule. We try to hide our disappointments and fears. Children do this, too. They care so deeply about what their parents, teachers, and friends think of them that they try to conform to what they think they are expected to do or feel. If they sense disapproval in, for example, being afraid in the dark, they might say that they are not afraid and make some other excuse for their fears. It is not always easy to face true feelings. Children need help to do it. The teacher needs to help the child focus upon what his real feelings are and to help him identify them.

In one instance when the children in a group were talking about ideas and activities that they might use in their paintings, one child whose name was Joe said: "I ran all the way home from Jimmie's house last night. I was afraid to come home after it got dark. All the way home I thought there was something behind me in the night—something big. I couldn't tell what it was, but I felt it was going to get me." Before Joe had quite finished this statement, many of his classmates laughed and some of them said: "Ah, I'm not afraid at night." "What are you scared of?" "You shouldn't be scared when you are big enough to be in third grade." Joe said: "I wasn't just afraid of the dark. I was afraid I might be late getting home. My mother would be mad."

He changed his story from the first statement of what he really felt and was afraid of to what he thought would be a more acceptable reason for his fear. He chose the second reason because he sensed approval of it. This is a common experience and one that children share and talk about—something that they are not ashamed of, or have not been made to feel ashamed of.

The teacher, being sensitive to Joe's need to face his real feelings, said: "It's all right to be afraid. Sometimes we are all afraid, but not all afraid of the same things. I have things I'm afraid of. Your parents have fears, too. All adults have them, only we call them 'worries.' Most of the things we adults worry about never happen. Joe is afraid of something outside in the dark. We are all afraid at times. Maybe some of the rest of you are, too. Maybe your fears are different from Joe's." From this experience and emotion, Joe created his drawing (13).

Such a brief discussion helps children to bring their feelings into focus, to realize that their feelings are shared by others, and that there is no reason to be ashamed of them. Learning to face his fears and his other feelings helps a child focus more keenly and understandingly upon his emotions. His art work profits as a result.

16

When children experience strong emotion along with an idea, this becomes communicated in their art, as in this composition of a person going swimming.

Another example of an intimate expression of emotion is shown in Michael's drawing of a boy crying (89, page 222). Every child has strong feelings of sorrow or joy at times. Michael's intense feeling of sorrow at the loss of his beloved pet dog is clearly and sensitively expressed in this small drawing done at a friend's home on a torn piece of notebook paper.

Development of Self-evaluation

The child *learns how to evaluate* his work as it progresses as well as to evaluate the finished art product. A child begins his art work in high hopes that it will be successful and that he will be proud of it. He is excited and inspired to begin to put his ideas into form. But it is not always as easy as it may seem for a child to put his ideas into organized form. He is not always able to shape the form in just the way he imagined it should be. Then, sometimes, his anticipation gives the idea such an emotional glow that seeing it expressed in form is disappointing: "It doesn't always come out as right as I want it to," said one child in discussing her painting.

The child decides to what extent he has been successful in every shape or form he creates. He evaluates it. In doing so he measures its worth and the degree of its excellence. He determines to what extent he is satisfied with it. Every form or part he adds to his composition affects the total undertaking and causes him to reappraise his previous work. Evaluation is a continual process, becoming more involved as the composition grows. The decisions the child makes as a result of this evaluation guide him in deciding what to do next, what changes to make, what needs to be added, and how he can improve his work. It also tells him when his work is completed. Other persons may feel that perhaps he has omitted parts which, to them, are important, or that he could do more with the idea than he has done. These persons are looking at the child's work through their eyes, putting their values upon his work. It is difficult at times for other people not to do the evaluating for the child.

An adult may think a child cannot evaluate; he can. Naturally, the child cannot evaluate a piece of art work as an adult would, any more than he is able to do many other things on an adult level. When he is six, he will evaluate his work as a child. When he is sixteen, he will look at it as an adolescent. Only when he becomes an adult will he be able to see and evaluate his art work as an adult. Teachers need to keep this obvious fact in mind when dealing with children and their art. Unless some teacher-guided evaluation takes place, children may not develop in their art expression beyond the childish stage. They may lack the further knowledge required for more advanced art expression and judgment. It is important that children learn from their experiences, but this learning in *art* must take place in a pleasant positive manner and in accord with their achievement level at the time. It should not interfere with a child's right to make his own evaluations, but should enhance it.

Each child has his own values or measurements of quality that he applies to his work, and they are affected by what he has learned about art. Self-evaluation means constant improvement for each child, permitting each to develop at his own speed. This provides, in some measure, additional opportunities for the gifted child, whose greater mental ability makes it possible for him to do more and to see more deeply into causes of success or failure. He can discern more speedily what needs to be done. It provides just as well for the slow learners who will evaluate their work according to their own less involved purposes and simpler intentions. It provides for every child to learn how to recognize and measure his own achievements and appreciate them. Each child learns to judge his less successful attempts or areas of a composition and to correct them or to discover the reasons for the failure. He does this for himself and by doing so learns to depend upon himself.

When creative activities are provided in art education, each child develops an ability to evaluate that carries over to other situations in which he is called upon to make decisions and determine action.

Just as the child learns to evaluate his work as it progresses, he also learns to evaluate the finished product. When he feels satisfied that he has expressed what he had in mind and how he felt about it, he looks at the work, appraising the results. He may feel satisfied with the task, as a whole, but feel dissatisfied with some part of it. He needs to learn to see and to estimate the whole work and not continue to look at only the less important spot that may not have turned out as well as he hoped.

When the child sees his art work exhibited, he evaluates it again. He privately studies its strengths and weaknesses. He also studies it in relation to his classmates' work. Studying his work in this manner is a learning situation for the child, and he should not be deprived of it either by having all of the evaluating done for him or by having his own or some other children's work omitted from the showing. Each child needs to see every other child's work. Nor should the art work be hung in any order of preference, such as hanging the "best" first. When the teacher does this, it deprives the child of the opportunity to make his own comparisons and decisions. To study the art work from the viewpoint of the teacher's preferential hanging would only confuse him and may discourage him as well. An important role of the teacher is to discuss the children's accomplishments with them. This discussion helps them learn. (Just how the teacher does this will be discussed in Chapters 5 and 6.)

Satisfying a Need for Power

Children often feel powerless in an adult world. To some extent, the power to control and to determine their own art compensates for this feeling of helplessness.

Many abilities are developed through art education, bringing with them reenforced feelings of power and confidence, but the very way that a child makes decisions in art gives him a sense of command. In this situation and for a while, he alone is the authority making decisions to create or to destroy, to include or delete, actually controlling and determining a whole undertaking.

EXPRESSIVENESS

Expressiveness is the ability to depict thoughts, feelings, and moods through the language of art. One of the three basic elements in creative art expression (Chapter 1, page 4) is *the freedom to express:* create or make the shape of the forms and determine the colors. Expressiveness, the power to state clearly and with feeling exactly what is in the mind, is an important asset to any person. It improves daily communication with others, and gives a feeling of confidence and power. Although expressiveness is important in any area of communication, it is especially so in art, because art is personal, individual, and truly an international language. To a great extent it is the expression of feeling in art that viewers respond to which creates an immediate bond among peoples.

Freedom to express implies the right that each child has to determine how objects will be shaped or formed to serve the needs of his art for that time. Many elements determine the shape the child will create and the colors he will use: the extent to which he feels confident in his right to express, which is a reflection of the teacher's confidence in him; the materials which help determine the shape and color; his own changing abilities; the warm appreciation he feels which inspires his art expression; the mood he is in; and the feeling he has for the subject he has chosen.

17

Barabara's (second grade) "newspaper cat" reflects the freedom to choose and use materials in new ways.

As the teacher teaches about art indirectly through presentations of new materials and ways artists have used them, as she discusses art with children, she is building knowledge which helps children become more eloquent in their expressiveness in art; as was previously discussed, this expressiveness is closely tied to individuality. Expressiveness becomes unique so that each person's art work bears the stamp of his own individuality. To facilitate expressiveness, it is necessary to build each child's confidence and to discourage rivalry which acts to deter it.

Building Self-confidence

Modern creative art education *builds the child's self-confidence through acceptance*. Many of the other outcomes of creativity depend upon the confidence that the child feels as he works. Self-confidence is an important asset in the success of those who possess it. Most of us have been in situations in which we have failed to make a contribution because we feared it might be met with criticism or not be accepted. Even though we felt the contribution might be worth considering, we failed, not because we did not have an idea, but because we did not have the self-confidence with which to express it. Certainly we make mistakes—we all do—but the fear of such a possibility should not overcome our desire and need to make our contribution. Self-confidence does not mean boldness, or a boasting or swaggering pretense; it is rather simply a feeling of assurance in one's own judgment, ability, and power.

The attitude of teachers and parents toward his work and their acceptance of it is valuable in building a child's confidence. Encouragement and praise are the tools to help the child grow and express his ideas, but too strong and exaggerated praise may be damaging. There is pressure in praise—pressure to go on or to try something else. Too much pressure can be felt as a burden to the child. He may begin to feel that he cannot live up to such extreme expectations. He may also sense the disproportion in the praise and feel aversion to its falseness.

The child needs help in seeing and recognizing his achievements. This task requires an adult who knows how to make such choices and how to help the child improve.

The building of self-confidence in a child is an important educational value, for threats and fear are a part of most children's daily relationships with adults. Acceptance and warm pleasant response to children do much to restore intimidated children and to help them regain or further develop their expressiveness in art.

Rivalry as Hindrance

Freedom to express ideas implies freedom from pressures to conform or to discourage. Rivalry or competition has deterring effects upon the free flow of ideas into the expressed language of art. Since the art work of each child is accepted and respected for its own quality, no comparisons are possible or desirable. Comparisons imply a common basis for judgments. Creative art implies the opposite. In art a premium is put upon differences, individuality, and personal expression. Imposed competition and intellectual freedom are incompatible.

Each person feels within himself an urge to excel in some way, which is natural and should be encouraged. Comparisons made by the teacher or by another person of the work of one child with that of another defeat the purposes of art. Comparison depends upon a quality in one work against which another can be measured. Comparing art work makes each child feel apprehensive. The feeling of confidence is gone, and confidence is a strong asset to success in art. The embarrassment of an unfavorable comparison can damage further desire to create. A child may think after such an experience that he "can't do that" or that he "won't try that way again."

Competition is rivalry for the purpose of gaining some advantage over another person. When this atmosphere prevails, the child is aware of what the others are doing and how they are doing it. He must keep in mind that he will be measured against their ideas and ways, which confuses him. The quality of his art work lessens because concentration is lost. His art work ceases to be purely his idea and becomes mixed up with the impression that the work of others is making upon him. Individual personal involvement is lost. The resultant art product is less dynamic, less aesthetic, and has less artistic quality. Only that which comes from the strong personal inspiration of its creator is art. Competition destroys art as it destroys the child's self-confidence. The processes of teaching creative expression free the child from competition. (In Chapter 13 fuller consideration will be given to competitions.)

Communication and Expression

Some art educators stress art as expression; others feel that it is communication. A few take definite stands one way or another. Art is both. An idea must be expressed before it can be communicated, and communication is open once it has been expressed. The relative importance of one or the other may change and vary with the art and the artist, but expression and communication go together.

Art for children in the elementary grades emphasizes the expression of ideas, for children, like all artists, are more interested in their own art than in the art of others. Expressing their ideas in art is important to each child. However, this alone is not enough. They also want others to see their work, to look at it, and to respond to it. They want it to mean something to someone else, too, as was indicated earlier in this chapter.

The role of art as a communication medium has expanded, in fact exploded, in the last two decades. To a very great extent communication in our time is achieved through pictures. We are fast becoming or already have become television- rather than book-oriented. By way of motion pictures in both theatres and television, it is likely that, generally speaking, people watch more stories than they read, and they watch and hear news more frequently and with greater coverage than they read.

Television is used to entertain and to implement education in schools and homes. The most popular magazines are largely picture books devoting more space to pictures than to text. Pictures are extensively used in textbooks.

Communication through pictures is a totally different kind of experience than communication through the written or spoken word. The basic difference between them comes from the slower sequential presentation of verbal materials on the one hand and the faster all-at-onceness of pictorial materials on the other. The building of concepts through textual materials consists of a build-up of ideas, one following the other, while pictures are abrupt, presenting their total materials all at once. All of the rich content is there together and shown in relationship. The settings, costumes, moods, feelings, locations, action, theme, and counter-themes are assimilated in this multifaceted total presentation.

Much direct and indirect learning results from the hours of picture-watching most people do. Learning is broadened and deepened through this activity. This is not to imply that this learning is or is not all desirable, ennobling, or beneficial. Nevertheless, it happens. The effects upon the mind, emotions, and sensitivities of this frequent mental fare need desperately to be considered and studied.

The impact of communication through pictures upon our way of life, our thinking and responding, and our decision-making is tremendous. Through the impact of quantities of pictures we have whole new bases for comprehending and deciding with only a limited knowledge of the art of pictures and picture-making to draw upon for guidance.

People in general have not yet learned how to look at pictures much beyond the narrative presented through them; nor have they learned to recognize the dominant objects in them. There is a need to see deeper into the total presentation within the frame of the picture or within the motion picture to comprehend its fullest meaning: to see *how* the picture is constructed and expressed to communicate the message and absorb us in its purposes. Education and experience in creating and dealing with pictures and other forms of art amplify the ability to respond more advantageously to our present mass consumption of pictures.

We are all well aware of the hours spent in front of television screens and how intent people of all ages become as they watch their favorite programs. Those who watch or look at pictures would be helped to respond more intelligently to the area of communication at hand when they are made more deeply aware of what is presented visually and learn to recognize art elements that affect their reactions to pictures. Minds, feelings, and actions are led and conditioned through the communicative role that pictures play. A certain amount of wisdom about the medium is needed to "read between the lines" and gain deeper insight into what is seen.

Dominance and subordination in a picture affect our response to it; so do many other structural aspects of art, such as light and dark, size, color, contrast. The one who determines the picture—the artist, photographer, or producer—can stimulate both intellectual and emotional response by the selection and organization of these elements within the picture. When viewers also have this knowledge, they can use it to help themselves become more critically evaluative on the one hand, or respond more appreciatively on the other.

Art is a particular quality within the realm of visual products. It seems evident, then, that teachers need to point out the relationships between visual forms in art and any other visual forms, television included, and to call attention to the application of conceptual learnings about art structure and art appreciation.

Since communication through pictures has become such a vital tool in our time, it is important to strengthen the education of children in art which is the very area that will help most in consuming, interpreting, and evaluating the tremendous quantities of pictures that they look at every day. Thus art education is given another role and gives another value to education.

Through the ages in every culture, continent, and age wherever people are or have been, pictures have been used to record and to inform. Found in caves in France were pictures believed to have been created 30,000 or 40,000 years before recorded history. Pictures cut through language and time barriers. People who cannot make themselves verbally understood by other nations can often grasp meanings through pictures.

INVENTIVENESS AND RESOURCEFULNESS

Education that leads to creativity, resourcefulness, originality, and inventiveness must be provided for each child daily if we are to maintain the *adaptive* qualities needed by each person who must meet the demands of a fast-changing world of art, of commercial products, transportation, communications, and employment. From an early age people need to learn how to apply their natural reservoir of imagination to a multitude of new materials, new situations, and new work patterns. They need to learn how to transfer skills and apply knowledges they have to evolving or revolutionary changes. They need resourcefulness to help them adjust, adapt, and transfer to new tasks and changing demands. They need to be resourceful to maintain employment and some form of creative expression which gives purpose to life.

18

Resourcefulness is developed when children are inspired to create art from a shape or form they see or find. This piece of scrap wood suggested a fish to a child who used other materials to complete his form.

Opportunities to learn how to be creative with raw materials help children develop inventiveness, so necessary if we are to maintain our place among the nations of the world as a country of opportunity, and to keep and to extend our high standard of living for ourselves and for other peoples. Inventiveness, a direct outgrowth of creative art, is essential for a high standard of living. What every free open society must have is ample opportunity for people to learn to invent and to try new ideas; and the people must have courage to invest their efforts and confidence to rely upon their individual powers, abilities, and judgments. People who do this are richly rewarded. In art class when a child is faced with raw materials and must rely totally upon himself to bring into existence some object never before created in just this same way, inventiveness is nurtured.

The use of "found" objects in art helps to develop inventiveness and resourcefulness. The fish in Illustration 18, made by a nine-year-old child, was inspired by a piece of scrap wood that suggested a fish shape to him. Adult sculptors use found objects in much the same way.

Along the same line are drawings made from a found visual cue on the paper. Illustrations 61–65 in Chapter 9 show how each of five children created a different art composition from the same given line (60). Not all drawing or sculpture should be centered around found objects, but it does give variety to the approach to creative art and builds inventiveness and resourcefulness which are aspects of creativity important to art and to many other activities.

Responsibilities

Learning how to be inventive and resourceful brings with it acceptance of responsibilities for the choices children must make in creative art expression. Since the child is faced with the necessity of making his own choices in art, the responsibility for the outcome of those choices can only be placed upon the child. Accepting the responsibility for our choices and actions is a desirable character trait. The more obligation the child feels toward making these choices, the greater the responsibility he is accepting. He matures as he accepts responsibility.

It does not necessarily follow that because it is better for the child to make his own choices that he *wants* to make his own choices. It is easier to have someone else do our thinking and make our choices; it takes initiative and energy to do our own. The child likes to depend upon others, but since he cannot always remain a child, he must learn to depend upon himself. Art work helps him toward this end. Once a child has learned the feeling of personal satisfaction that comes with self-reliance, he will not want to give it up.

Others, however, never seem to have learned to accept the responsibility for their own actions and choices. They try to evade "blame," but are eager to accept "praise." They do not want to face the unsuccessful attempts or the less perfect areas of their work. Perhaps this is because too much emphasis has been put upon the finished art product. The child should feel free to experiment. If his work turns out badly, he has learned what not to do and that his idea does not work in that way. He has made this decision himself. The teacher accepts this for what the child intended it to be (an experiment) and for what he has found the outcome to be.

FREEDOM

Freedom is not only basic to self-government but basic to both art and art education. Intellectual freedom is not to be interpreted as a self-indulgent lack of restraint, for this behavior brings chaotic working conditions. Actions of one person that result in interferences in the rights of others, or cause interruptions in their concentration, are not to be misconstrued as freedom. Each person's freedom to make his own decisions and to enjoy a classroom atmosphere conducive to learning must be preserved. Self-discipline is essential to a productive person. The teacher helps children toward this responsibility by maintaining teaching-learning conditions in which each child feels confident of his right to intellectual freedom.

A child needs to learn to be his own master: to discipline himself without the need for outside authority. To work in original ways in art requires this self-mastery, for the child charts a lonely course in art as he parts company with the ideas that others are pursuing and seeks, explores, and discovers new ideas and ways. The more clearly original the idea, the more marked the division from the others: the more alone the child feels. This departure into the uncharted can be frightening or bring feelings of uneasiness. A child needs to be strengthened by reassurance, which, in turn, builds his courage for other adventures into the world of art.

Open opportunities for freedom of intellectual choices is a major right of the child in art, but there is another: his right to have and to keep his own art work. His art work is a record of his ideas and feelings as well as tangible proof of educational progress, and again he needs the freedom of determination to keep his own work. It is *not* the teacher's property to keep or dispose of. It is his.

To protect the free open nature of art expression itself and to educate those who are eager and confident to make their own choices, this free creative approach must begin and continue to grow when a child first picks up a pencil or crayon. Children need continually to experience intellectual freedom, for it is inherent both in life and in art. Art experiences support and strengthen intellectual freedom and are in turn dependent upon it.

> We teach the meaning of freedom when we teach the young to explore the world of imagination and art. We give the private instruction which can enable young men and women to hold out against the torrent. We help to restore the intellectual vitality, the self-confidence, the moral dignity of the contemporary individual by the imaginative reconstruction of human experience. In doing so, we can show that human life is greater, more noble, more wide-ranging in its possibilities than the particular embodiment it now takes in the politics and disorder of our present moment.[10]

> The Iron Curtain has become an iron wall, with all forms of modern art outlawed and with fear the password—fear of diversity, of personal expression, of exploration, of analysis, of invention, of experimentation, of anything, in fact, that might lead to official displeasure.[11]

Preparation for American Culture

There is no method of teaching art that prepares the child for life in our culture so well as does the creative. The ways in which creative expres-

---

[10] From "Moral Values and the Experience of Art," in *Art and the Intellect* by Harold Taylor, p. 62, copyright © 1960 by The Museum of Modern Art, New York, and reprinted with permission.

[11] Katharine Kuh, "An American Critic Reports on Art in the Soviet Union," *Saturday Review*, August 24, 1963, p. 18.

sion best develops the individual have already been discussed. Whatever prepares the child to be a better person also better prepares him for life as a citizen.

There are few areas in education that provide such a wide range of individual choices as art does. The tangible results of these choices can be looked at, handled, and evaluated. This tangible evidence of his choices helps the child to see the value of depending upon himself and of making good choices. The constant evaluation associated with art education helps the child improve the quality of his choices. The better the art choice, the better the art product. The better the civic choices, the better the government.

Our American system of private enterprise needs persons who have ideas, who can think creatively, and who can not only present new ideas but improve existing ones. The risks inherent in this system extend to art, as well. Children enjoy uncertainty in their art endeavors. As a child originates his own art, he never quite knows what will happen next or how it will all come out. He is investing his art materials in the worthiness of his ideas, and taking chances on his abilities. Then, too, every art experience is an adventure into the future: nothing quite like this has ever been done before by him or by anyone else. He is out there alone and on his own. The uncertainty that is involved in this investment of self and materials fascinates him, generating energy to keep him going as it does in other exciting investments of one's resources.

Improved transportation gives us the opportunity to mix with people from all over the world, to become involved in the affairs of other people. We are learning to work with, to understand, and to appreciate them, to feel less hostile toward strange ideas and ways. Creative art experiences with all the variety of processes and products help prepare a child for the variety of people and ways he will find everywhere. He will learn also that others respond as he does to praise and encouragement and that they share his hopes, fears, and ambitions.

Ideally, our American democracy has a deep regard for the intrinsic value of every human being. We believe in the rights and privileges of every individual. This quality is developed when children learn to expect their classmates to work differently from them and to appreciate their individually different work.

Safeguard Against Obsolescence

> If we indoctrinate the young person in an elaborate set of fixed beliefs, we are ensuring his early obsolescence. The alternative is to develop skills, attitudes, habits of mind and the kind of knowledge and understanding that will be the instruments of continuous change and growth on the part of the young person.[12]

Our society is experiencing obsolescence of machinery, skills, and jobs at a fast rate. Certain things and ways of doing things are continually becoming outmoded. This means that those who can produce only by learned and patterned methods become nonfunctional, too. They fall into disuse

[12] John Gardner, *Self-Renewal* (New York: Harper & Row, 1964), p. 21.

along with their jobs. They find themselves without the personal resources necessary to make the changes progress demands. They have not learned flexible, imaginative ways of thinking, of working, and of approaching a piece of work.

To maintain the flexibility of mind and the agility of adaptation so important in meeting and dealing with the rapid changes in our lives, it is necessary to build these processes into behavior patterns. A part of every educational program at every level needs to be activities that require a student to think independently and originally from a stimulus of materials, to meet new things and situations courageously, and to approach them with an appetite for adventure. Flexibility of personality, outlook, and working methods can be developed through creative thinking that takes a topic in diverse directions and lets it develop differently with the demand of each varying personality involved in it.

However, some stability must occur. Jobs need to be completed, but a mental door is kept open through which new ideas may merge into the evolving work. As materials and ideas are organized, direction is stabilized. The personal interpretation that comes from each child gives it meaning.

The emphasis upon depth education and specialization in our present society can bring with it a certain resistance to change because of the vested interests in it. Total commitment and involvement are a part of our way of life, but it does not follow that rigidity needs to set in because of it. The processes of art, of free and open ways of working, the constant search for new and better ways, continual evaluations of the emerging products, and the attitude of appreciation for achievements, all counteract the stultifying effects on progress of vested interests. This is true in the elementary school classroom as well as in adult life.

As children face raw materials in art with only their own resources and drive to rely upon, they are learning the very working processes so vital to our day. As they see and study the range of their peers' completed art, they are making the same kind of adjustment needed to respond to the vast resources of material products in life out of school.

Social Unification

Freedom in art, which brings with it an appreciation of differences, helps to realize a better relationship among people, because it encourages each person to accept the fact that the right to choose is not only his but also everyone's. Involvement in the creative process helps him accept the multifaceted approach to art and to life. It helps condition him to differences in people, in what they do, and in what results from their actions and choices. It helps him realize that people can work together and yet not conform. Art work gives each child many chances to study, to understand, and to appreciate the work of his classmates. People are important, what they do is important, and how we get along with them is important.

The way each child works is different. The teacher accepts the varied work of each child by setting up an atmosphere in the classroom, so that each feels free to try any idea in art in any way. These and other processes, procedures, or methods used in modern art education should be accompanied by an appreciative attitude toward every piece of art work produced. This is necessary if individual expression is to survive. Children, like all people, want to receive favorable attention. When they fail to receive it, they may abandon their own ideas and be influenced by the work of those children who receive the favorable attention. This not only destroys creativity, but it sets up a feeling of personal inadequacy that destroys self-confidence. It also sets up feelings of envy and jealousy, which can lead some children actually to dislike other children. Such feelings of hostility can be avoided if the individually different work of each is appreciated for its uniqueness—if the differences can be enjoyed.

A part of teaching creative art expression is to see something of beauty or value in every child's work. Every child is important; the way he feels about himself is important, the way he feels about others is important, and the art work that he has decided to do is also important or he would not be doing it. Since it is important to him, it should be important to his teacher and to his parents.

Any favorable comment made about his art work is in effect an acceptance of the child's own personality—of himself. Any unfavorable comment, or the absence of a favorable comment when others receive it, appears to be a rejection of the child. The teacher should, of course, make comments to every child about his work, and these comments should be positive and helpful in the effect that they have upon the child. Rather than "correcting" children's art expressions, the teacher should try to understand and enjoy the interesting and unusual forms that children create. In this respect, an adult approaches the teaching of art differently from that of factual subjects.

Appreciation comes through respect. Tolerating differences is inadequate; it indicates that the differences are distasteful and that we put up with them. Acceptance is little better. Appreciation is a deeper, more positive, and more outgoing quality. It can be developed. When it is developed in the classroom, it carries into community life. Creative art education provides almost unlimited opportunities for children to learn how to get along with and to appreciate others. Herbert Read speaks of the importance of creative activity in relation to war and feelings of hostility:

> For when the individual has been deprived of his creative functions, he is ready to take part in collective destruction. And then, if he can't have the real thing, which is war, he will indulge in fantasies of cruelty and mass murder, mass produced for one and all.[13]

As the child matures, he wants to know how he can improve the less successful areas of his composition. Pointing out and discussing these areas of his art should be privately done between the teacher and the child when the teacher is sure that such comments are sought by the child. It is embarrassing to have the personality of the child identified with poor work. It might be done in some general way if the teacher feels certain that no child would associate the art work with the creator. Such disassociation is difficult in

[13] Herbert Read, "Education Through Art—A Revolutionary Policy," *Art Education*, National Art Education Association, Washington, D.C., VIII, No. 8 (1955), 5.

group teaching. In the elementary school it is best to concentrate upon the achievements of each child.

Balancing of Classroom Activities

Children need varied daily activities to *give a balance to classroom activities.* Creative art has many values that no other subject contributes to education; so, of course, have the skill and precision subjects. In the elementary schools it is essential to teach skills of many kinds, for they are the tools of education. Without them we could neither communicate nor protect ourselves against being cheated. The word "house" means a building in which people live or work. Words in reading must mean the same to all readers, or we could not share ideas with each other. In spelling the child must not only have all the correct letters but also have them arranged in the correct sequence. In arithmetic he learns that two and two are four, and that he had better not be very creative about it! Art is not rigid. Put two and two together, and the result is always four. Put black and white together, and the result is countless shades of grey that must be chosen to fit various situations in which colors must relate to each other, to the subject, and to the emotion to be expressed.

The methods of teaching the skill and precision subjects and those used in creative art differ greatly, and conflict sometimes arises because this difference is not understood. These teaching methods and working procedures differ, because the values they contribute to education differ.

Children are adjusted to having their individuality provided for when they come to school, so most children feel immediately at home in art. The child comes from a home in which he is usually the only one of his age and the only one with his particular needs and interests. He is unique and is accustomed to having his uniqueness recognized and provided for. In school he finds about 30 other children of the same age with approximately the same needs, about the same size, and trying to play the same games and study the same lessons. The child is apt to get lost in the sameness. Children find their own ways of gaining recognition for their individuality. Some of these means are acceptable, others are not. Creative art experiences are excellent ways of providing for the unique personality of each child.

Art adds another dimension to the intellect by giving each child another way to approach problem-solving.

> Curiosity about things which can be known through the mind suggests a like wonder about things which one comes to "know" through other than purely intellectual effort. Do not the schools have responsibility for helping to nurture sensitivity to the sweep of a line, the intricacies of rhythm, or the subtleties of melody? If one heeds the laments of teachers in other than narrowly defined academic fields, there is a real danger that the curriculum may be purified to exclude non-cerebral fields, or worse yet, that courses of study may be redefined to provide more intellectually respectable information about rather than direct experience in the fine arts.[14]

---

[14] Robert J. Schaefer, "Anti-intellectualism in the Pursuit of the Intellectual," *Teachers College Record*, Teachers College, Columbia University, LXV, No. 2 (1963), 9.

The goals of art education may be summarized in one sentence. Art education seeks to develop sensitive, creative, and artistically literate individuals who may grow aesthetically, emotionally, and intellectually through active expression or reflective appreciation in the arts.[15]

SUGGESTED ACTIVITIES

1. *Plan a motivation for a group of children that will help them develop deeper awareness of nature or their environment.*
2. *Plan the kind of an art awareness notebook that a child might keep and use. Think of possible titles for it. What would children put into it? How could these notebooks be displayed? When? How often?*
3. *Discuss art with some children. Try to determine how well they are learning how to make aesthetic judgments.*

---

[15] Kaufman, *op. cit.*, p. 33.

3

Responsibilities of the Teacher in Art

THE TEACHER PLAYS an active and important role in art education, and her responsibilities vary according to the changing situations within the art class. It is important for a teacher, or anyone involved with children and their art, to know what she is expected to do, what leadership she must assume, and what leadership and responsibilities she must inspire in each child. In short, as an art educator, the teacher needs to know specifically what to do and what not to do. During every minute of the art class the teacher is needed by the children. It is not a time when the teacher can put the children to work on an art problem, provide them with materials, and withdraw to correct work from a previous session or to put some work on the chalkboard.

Since teachers may not show children how to draw, direct progress of the art class, or provide the children with examples to copy, it may seem to some that there is little the teacher *can* do. There is, however, much that the teacher *can* and *should* do, for much of the responsibility for the success of the art experience depends on the teacher. She has a job to do at every step of the way.

Although the teacher's responsibilities change as the art lesson progresses, there are some constants in all aspects of her work with children. Among them are her warm acceptance and respect for each child, for his divergent ideas and his art products. Creative art cannot survive without this attitude and working relationship.

Throughout the whole art experience the teacher's role is that of an inspired educator stimulating children to clarify and translate their ideas, feelings, and reactions into organized aesthetic art forms. At times during the pre-work discussion or later with individuals as they work, the teacher adds richness to the children's ideas and suggestions, and depth to their feelings and emotions related to the art. In this way she enlivens, encourages, opens new vistas, extends concepts, and sharpens focus upon the emotional expression so vital to their art.

The various tasks of the teacher during the art class are clear and specific but not rigid. Every teacher needs to understand them and then to implement them according to her own personality and the needs of the children. A study of these roles will be approached through general topics with subdivisions. Although each will be considered separately, they overlap and blend.

The responsibilities of the teacher during the art class are clear and specific. They include:

(a) Planning.
(b) Motivation.
(c) Guidance.
(d) Evaluation.
(e) Exhibition.

PLANNING

Although every art experience needs to be a creative one, as defined in Chapter 1, it does not imply that the teacher makes no preparation for art. It is imperative that every art experience be planned and contain educational advantages for every child. Art can become a rich educational experience if the teacher makes it one. To do this, the teacher plans beforehand:

(a) *What* art materials will be used and *what* art content needs to be taught.
(b) *Why* this art experience is being undertaken (the educational advantages it has).
(c) *How* to present and conduct it.

Lesson planning is as simple as that but *is* all of that and seldom just any one phase of it. Chapter 9, "Curriculum in Art," will deal with the content of art education in the elementary school.

The art materials need to be readied, by the teacher or by someone under her supervision, before the art work period begins. This important aspect of a well-planned lesson helps to make the art experience an organized one. It seems self-evident that a teacher would be very sure she could do the lesson herself before attempting to teach it to children. If, for example, a teacher is planning mosaics for the group, she must have tried and executed mosaics with the same materials the children will be using, not only to provide examples to show the group, but also to gain some mastery and skill as well as to see into the problems that arise with this particular medium.

Another essential part of the teacher's continuing preparation is to see and study current exhibitions of differing types of art, and to feel and sense the ever-changing and highly individual nature of it. Although the teacher will have her own preferences among the shows and the pieces, these are her own responses. Because she recognizes her right to her own preferences, the sensitive teacher will provide this same allowance for each of her students, giving equal acceptance to those ideas and preferences which are different from her own.

MOTIVATION

When a person is prompted to do something, he is motivated to do it by having some incentive for the action he undertakes. A motive is an inner urge that causes the person to act in one way or another. An art activity, to be a truly creative one, should come from the child. Within a group the art work will be as different as the children are different because the method of creative motivation has a different effect upon each, inspiring each to his own ideas and ways of working.

At times a child will not need to be motivated in art by another person. The child frequently paints or draws simply because he wants to. Children at home will, without urging, get their paints or clay and create. This happens in school, too. Sometimes a child will want to paint or draw in an activity period or when he first comes into school before classes begin. This is a matter of individual self-motivation. People working alone can work in this way whenever they choose and for as long as they choose, but groups of children in school cannot.

Because we have group teaching, a program of education must be administered that will provide learning opportunities for every child in every subject. Therefore, art activities are scheduled for a specific hour and a specific length of time every day. Although each child wants to create, this set time may not be the moment when he is most inspired. If the children have been deeply involved in the lesson just preceding the art class or if a new process in arithmetic is still occupying their minds, other interests may be crowded out. Art is only one of many interesting areas of education that demand the child's attention. It seems highly unlikely that there could ever be one selected time when every child would feel his most intense urge to create. Therefore, the teacher, from her education and experience with children, selects the time she feels would be best for the art class.

There are five aspects of the pre-work discussion referred to as motivation: incentive, recall, emotional association, association of ideas to materials, and broadening of knowledge.

Incentive

It takes little to excite interest in art, for practically all children enjoy it and look forward to the art class. Yet some mental adjustment occurs when children leave another interesting area of the curriculum to begin art work. The teacher takes an active part in helping children make the transition from another focus into the special mental and emotional attitudes needed for art.

Creative thinking precedes creative working, so a climate needs to be set for the intellectual readiness for art that is conducive to imaginative and original thinking. Just seeing the art materials prepared for use or helping to distribute them aids in this readiness. However, this is not enough. A teacher who enjoys imaginative thinking herself can easily transfer her own incentive for art to the children. A brisk reassuring verbal classroom interchange sets a promising groundwork for creative art work.

Every artist of every age needs to be inspired before he creates. It is not easy to create. There is perhaps no other area of learning in which the child begins so wholly from nothing as he does in creative work. In art he has a blank paper or chunk of clay and maybe a few tools, and that is all. He must get his own idea, and when he runs into difficulty he must work out his problems. Since creating is a demanding task, as described on pages 25–27 in Chapter 2, the child needs to be strongly motivated to begin and to carry it through. To take the lead in helping the child become inspired by his own ideas is the teacher's responsibility.

The teacher needs to learn how to induce action, to rouse the child enough to work hard in his own best manner. She should continue the motivation until she senses that every child is excited to begin. With questions directed toward their interests she stirs up the feelings of every child until each is eager to go to work with whatever materials he has.

It is plain from this explanation of incentive that it is closely allied to the child's emotions. Emotion causes motion. The more intense the emotion, the more intense the expression; the stronger the emotion, the stronger the will to produce the ideas associated with it. Through the emotions, art comes from deep within us; the clearer the focus upon the emotion, the

19

Before the work session begins there is usually a time for creative thinking. When the teacher feels the children are thinking imaginatively and are motivated, she closes the discussion, and the children begin to work with materials.

freer the product will be from confusion. There will be a definite purpose and a strong inspiration that will keep the child's mind centered on his one idea.

To accomplish this strength of motivation the teacher cannot function in a matter-of-fact, dull, dispirited, or lifeless manner. To arouse children successfully, to excite them, to make them *want* to create and to make them *eager* to do so, the teacher must be lively and alert. Discussion, to be motivating, should be encouraging and enlivening. The teacher takes her cues in the discussion from the children. She receives their suggestions with enthusiasm, and she responds warmly and approvingly to each contribution, no matter how brief her responses. Some teachers can do it with only a quick gesture that indicates and communicates admiration. Every child needs to feel this radiation of the teacher's respect, regard, confidence, approval, and pleasure in his ideas. Such a position taken by the teacher inspires children and makes them *want* to create.

Dramatize a little. Children love it. They catch the spirit quickly and soon feel the glory and the excitement. They are ready to create because they have been motivated.

Teachers can learn to motivate in the specific way that creative activities require. Become the inspirer, and be enthusiastic enough to make every child become fired with drive to put his thoughts and feelings into organized form. See what wonders it will do for your own enthusiasm for art as well.

Recall

Since ideas for art come largely from the past experiences of the artist, it is important for the teacher to help children recall as much as they can of their knowledge and experience to help them bring a rich amount of ideas into their conscious thinking.

Everything that has happened to a person can be remembered with the right stimulation. The mind is like a deep well of resources from which many kinds of related and imaginative experiences and emotions can be drawn, brought into new associations, organized, and a new art form developed.

To do this the teacher asks a general question such as "Who has an interesting idea for his art today?" and follows it with some variations of the question: "Who has a *different* idea?"—stressing the word *different* or any of its synonyms to help children go deeper into their resources.

To bring richness into their ideas, the teacher then helps the children focus upon ideas related to their central idea such as "Where were the children playing?"—calling attention to the environment and forms from it that could be included in their art. It is not necessary for every child to answer these questions, for each projects them into his own silent responses. The teacher also injects ideas into the discussion, adding further depth and breadth.

> When the teacher gives praise for originality, ingenuity and "different" ideas, she gives the child status for his creativity, and he stands a better chance of rising above the status need.[1]

[1] Smith, *op. cit.*, p. 36.

Emotional Association

The expression of feeling or emotion associated with the idea an artist or child has chosen affects the expressive and communicative qualities of the art. It is most frequently the emotional tie between the art and the viewer that gives art its appeal.

Blended with the questions and discussion suggested for recall of experiences can be others that call attention to the feeling recalled or imagined.

Association of Ideas to Materials

Children need help in translating and pinning down their free flowing mental imagery into forms that are possible to achieve with the art materials at hand and yet reflect their experiences and reactions. The teacher's questions can again help: "What colors could show fear?" for example, or "How would you shape the trees to show the feeling of wind?" Again one or two of these questions during the pre-work discussion serve as reminders and are not intended as an exhaustive analysis.

Illustration 2 on page 3 is an example of how the bulky massive nature of clay lends itself to large generalized forms rather than the thin line quality that is possible with wire as shown in Illustration 3. The fish sculpture (18) on page 42 is another example of how the quality of the material helped the child associate his thinking with it. Materials do not always suggest ideas; sometimes it is the other way around. However, materials do help to determine the way the idea can be expressed.

Broadening of Knowledge

Each art experience in art education needs to include some measure of concept development about art, such as that in color and design. It can be a part of the pre-work discussion; it can come after the art work is completed; or it can occur on an individual basis with children as the work progresses. (The content of an elementary school art curriculum is discussed in Chapter 9.)

Amount of Motivation

The cooperative motivational discussion between teacher and children continues until a high point of anticipation is reached, *not* until the topic is exhausted. If the discussion is carried too far, the children will tire of it because they feel that they have worked it out pretty well verbally—then there is no need to work it out in art. It takes only a little practice for a teacher to learn how to judge the high point of anticipation. Be alert to the indication of eagerness on the part of the group, feel satisfied that the children are ready, and then know that the motivation is over and the children ready for their most important role—to create independently.

It is difficult to say just what amount of time is required for a motivational discussion. In a 45-minute art period, for example, it is difficult to determine just how much of this time is needed for the focus of attention upon creativity and the stimulation of sufficient emotional drive to begin and to carry through a complex task.

If the art project is a long-range one, the time required for this pre-work discussion will likely be much longer than a problem lasting for just one day. A long-range project requires a combination of introduction, motivation, explanation, and development of the idea with the children. The teacher needs to build a cooperative discussion with the children and continue it until each child has an overall view of the whole job. Each child should understand the whole problem and have a mental picture of it in his own mind before he begins any part of it. With children in the upper elementary grades it may take at least one entire class period to accomplish this type of motivation. Then additional separate stimulations will be needed for each phase in the process. The motivation for each phase can be brief and to the point as required.

Some art experiences that are quickly done still require a motivation that may consume as much time as the actual work if an explanation of some procedures is included, as in finger painting. Since finger painting and clay work are considered "messy" media, some procedures for cleaning up of the work areas and the children themselves need to precede the actual motivation. This additional explanation requires time, but time so spent pays in orderly organization of work. Time so spent also aids the motivation because the children are already considering what ideas they might choose.

Effects of Motivation

Some educators feel that actual first-hand experience is the best kind of motivation for creative art work. It is true that first-hand experience gives the child a good background from which to create, but it is sometimes not enough in itself to start him painting or modeling. Lawrence McVittey made an experimental study with fifth-grade children on various methods in art motivation, to determine the effectiveness of each. As methods of motivation he used:

(a) Verbal stimuli.
(b) Emphasis on hearing.
(c) Reading.
(d) Visual stimuli.
(e) Active participation in an event.
(f) Informal unplanned activity, extrinsic stimuli which cause the child to be moved or accelerated toward expressing himself spontaneously.

McVittey concluded:

> The motivations which included the "Personal Factor" of student-teacher participation resulted in the greatest degree of creative growth. . . . Motivations which do not include student-teacher participations should be carefully considered before they are used. Mere participation by the student alone does not guarantee learning.[2]

[2] Lawrence McVittey, *An Experimental Study on Various Methods in Art Motivation at the Fifth Grade Level* (Doctoral dissertation, Pennsylvania State University, 1954), pp. 91–92.

The effect of lively discussion-type motivation between teacher and children is shown in the accompanying samples of two children's art work (Plates X–XIII). The first example in each case was drawn with little or no verbal exchange before the drawing began. The second was a result of stimulating discussion between teacher and children.

The first two drawings were made by Donald, a second grader. The lesson was an assigned topic. Since Thanksgiving was near and since the class had been studying about the Pilgrims and Indians, the teacher selected this subject as an appropriate one. The introduction to and motivation of the art work period consisted of the teacher's saying: "We have been studying about the Pilgrims and the first Thanksgiving. Draw whatever you want to about the first Thanksgiving."

The first drawing Donald made resulted from his serious attempt to comply with the teacher's assignment (Plate X). He drew whatever ideas came to him in association with the subject. He drew two Pilgrims and, from their appearance, it is evident that he has achieved an understanding of their character. The Pilgrims are plainly dressed, wearing the straight hats we so frequently see in other pictures of them. Color is noticeably lacking in the picture. Donald knew that the Pilgrims cooked outdoors over a fire, so he has drawn a piece of food on a spit held by two forked sticks.

A few days later the teacher repeated the topic of the first Thanksgiving with her second-grade art class. Instead of merely assigning the topic, she engaged in a lively discussion of *many* things that the children had learned about the Pilgrims and their celebration of the first Thanksgiving. They recalled many facts they already knew that served to remind the children of the many interesting things from which they could choose or could include in their compositions.

Not only were facts recalled, but emotions were discussed. The children, through the questions of the teacher, tried to imagine themselves as among the Pilgrims. They tried to project in their imaginations the ways that the Pilgrims might have felt under the various new and sometimes frightening situations in which they found themselves. The exchange of ideas continued until many aspects of the first Thanksgiving were discussed. During this time the children were reviewing what they knew and were thinking about it from a different viewpoint—as a subject for their art.

Donald's second drawing (Plate XI) is much more interesting than his first. The Pilgrims are seated at the table. Donald has shown people on both sides of the table. He has included a log cabin with a roof colored to suggest a primitive one made of leaves, sods, and branches, as some of the Pilgrims' early homes may have had. Donald has drawn three trees without leaves to indicate that he knew it was late fall and the leaves were gone. As in the first picture, Donald shows food being cooked outdoors over an open fire.

Donald probably knew all these things when he drew the first picture, but these facts were not predominant. He needed to be reminded *again* of what he had learned and to think about what he would select for his drawing and how he would arrange his picture. It is the responsibility of the teacher to help children to recall and to excite, stimulate, and encourage them to think and to draw. Motivation is a powerful force in art that gives to children the responsibilities of selection and organization. Children can reach new heights of achievement with teachers who inspire them, and the results are as gratifying to the teacher as to the children.

Another example of the power of an intensive motivation is shown in the work of Debby, a kindergarten child, five years and one month of age. Her two drawings are the result of the assigned topic of Christmas. The first drawing was made without a discussion-type motivation (Plate XII). The second is the result of a dramatic, warm, and exciting motivation (Plate XIII).

Before the first drawing was begun, the teacher gave each child a large sheet of grey paper and crayons, saying: "Since Christmas is coming, I thought you might like to draw something about Christmas. Go right ahead and draw and color anything you like about Christmas."

Debby drew simple shapes on her paper and colored each with a bright color. She worked the entire time on the forms shown in the first example of her work. When her work was finished she said: "These are the shiny balls you hang on your Christmas tree." This certainly is an idea associated with Christmas, and Debby remembered the loops for hanging some of the balls.

Several days later the teacher decided to use the same topic of Christmas for the art lesson but with much more emphasis upon her role as the guide in a stimulating discussion before the actual art work began. The children talked about the many things they think about when Christmas is mentioned. In many instances the teacher asked questions that caused deeper thinking about some of the people and objects named and discussed by the children. She inquired about details of appearance and relationship of ideas that might encourage the children to group or to associate some of the people and objects when they put them into their pictures. Never at any time did the teacher tell them what to draw or even suggest how they should draw it; this would have been directed teaching.

Children of any age learn through their own efforts to express themselves in their own way considerably more easily when they have a clear mental picture of what they want to do. Through the discussion, the child's general thoughts crystallize, become more lucid, plainer, and thus easier to put into form. It is the responsibility of the teacher to guide the discussion in such a way that every child will experience sharper focus of thoughts and feelings. By motivation the teacher helps the children to become conscious of their own ideas and experiences and relate them to the problem at hand.

When it seemed evident to the teacher that their remarks and behavior indicated that the children were ready to begin, she quickly drew the verbal expression to a close to give the children an opportunity to put their enthusiasm into art form.

As a result of such a motivation, Debby drew a much more complex, detailed, and interesting Christmas picture (Plate XIII). Instead of just the shiny balls for the Christmas tree that she had drawn in the first picture, Debby drew a Christmas tree decorated with balls and lights of different sizes and colors. The discussion helped her to associate the two. Before Debby came to art class she knew from her first-hand experiences with Christmas trees that the balls were placed on the branches, but she did not bring this knowledge into active thinking. With the help of recall and stimulation she was able to think of many ideas associated with looking at her Christmas tree and presents on Christmas morning. The gaily decorated tree and the bright red dress she is wearing in the second picture communicate her feeling as well as her ideas.

In the first example, without such stimulation, Debby made no such associations, nor did she show much evidence of the excitement and pleasure she felt in connection with Christmas. Without being helped, through motivation, to remember her thoughts and feelings, she participated in the art experience in a simple, barren way. She drew only one isolated idea because the teacher had said ". . . draw something about Christmas." Debby was impoverished by such limitations and her art work showed it.

Children need the suggestions that they gain from their classmates' statements as well as the stimulation of their own thinking through the teacher's questions. Each child takes, from what he hears, those suggestions that apply to the broadening of his own idea. As each child talks, the others are thinking about and responding emotionally to their own *different* ideas and planning what they will draw or model.

Debby drew herself in the second picture. The form at the top of the page is Debby. She colored her dress bright red with stripes. Red is an exciting color, and most children enjoy using it. In this composition she has associated herself with the color. She was stirred by the motivation and remembered how excited she was on Christmas morning. The stimulating discussion helped arouse her excitement. Debby transferred this feeling to her art. In drawing herself she included her blonde hair and strong arms and legs along with facial details. She was thinking deeply. When her picture was completed, Debby said: "This is me. I am looking at my tree on Christmas in the morning when I first get up. I got a dolly that walks and some other presents." The doll is in the picture, too, and so are some other presents in boxes decorated for Christmas. She included two of the same shaped tree decorations that entirely filled her first picture. Debby started to draw another form in her picture, but did not complete it, which children sometimes do for various reasons. One of these reasons might be a lack of time to complete the work. Debby worked hard during the art class, accomplishing a great deal and doing it well.

Debby must have felt quite a lot of satisfaction with this example of her art work. Every child in the group profited by the motivation. The completed crayon pictures showed it. When the teacher projects her enthusiasm for and confidence in the children through her reactions to their contributions during the motivation, the children catch the feeling. This feeling stirs thinking and promotes richer, more meaningful art.

These two examples show the effect of high quality teaching upon what each child is able to do. In each case, the two pictures were made by the same child, the materials were the same, the topic was the same. What made the difference was the quality of the teaching, the inspiration of the motivation in which recall and the imagination play important parts.

The way a teacher works to stimulate, to excite, to provoke, to incite, and to motivate children to express their own ideas in their personally unique way is an extremely important part of the art lesson and has a deep influence upon the children. Leading the motivation in art is a very important role of the teacher. The teacher *leads* the motivation. The children and teacher together *create* the motivation through the presentation of and response to the ideas presented orally before the drawing begins. Each child, to be sure of himself and of his ideas before the work begins, needs to feel the warmth and personal interest of the teacher in his ideas—in himself.

Children need to expand their vision beyond themselves and their own immediate concerns to include the tremendous world of other people, of nature, of the environment, and of the imagination. During the motivation the teacher can help children consider other things and extend their interests by including references to, for example, bridges, community activities, and probings into exciting imaginative worlds. Even when they center their ideas for art upon their own activities, this can also be considered.

Only those ideas that the children know about and that are a part of their life and experiences are suitable for art. As has already been said, the child decides upon his own topic for the art experience by choosing what is most meaningful and most important to him at that time. During the discussion the teacher may add suggestions of how the subject may be broadened or of something else the child can do with it, but these are to be merely other thoughts thrown into the melting pot of class discussion. The child should feel free to associate the suggestions with his idea, reject them, or ignore them. When children feel obligated to incorporate into their work ideas presented in the discussion by the teacher, then it is no longer a situation in which each child determines his course. When many examples of the completed art work show the teacher's suggestions, the teacher's influence is too strong.

> It was found that more creative drawings resulted from motivations concerned with unusual objects than from motivations dealing with familiar objects, e.g., the child himself. Therefore, a child's imagination can be definitely boosted by use of motivations wherein the child is encouraged to invent or imagine unusual forms, e.g., strange machines, environments, and animals. So many times it is believed that the *only* desirable motivations should include the child himself; however, the study reported on here strongly indicates that creative ability is promoted to a much greater degree by use of motivations concerned with novelty or fantasy.[3]

GUIDANCE

As the children begin to work with their art materials, the teacher participates in a less active way to allow each child to assume a leadership role of his own. During this period of the children's concentration upon their expression of ideas, the teacher quietly studies what each child is doing and observes his working habits. This is a period of intense concentration on the part of the children. Each is giving close attention to the ideas stimulating him. There is a complexity of tasks to be undertaken by each child: each

---

[3] Clarence E. Kincaid, "The Determination and Description of Various Creative Attributes of Children," in *Creativity and Art Education*, Lambert Brittain, ed. (Washington, D.C.: National Art Education Association, 1964), p. 115.

needs to keep in mind the idea and feeling behind his work, the control of the medium, the attaining of satisfactory shapes in the composition, and the management of his own partially developed abilities. Every form or shape already included in the art work regulates, to some extent, the shapes that follow it. As the art work progresses, less and less space or materials remain, creating a problem in the placement and size of other things that the child may want to add. Although art work is challenging, fascinating, and personally satisfying, it is not easy. While children are intent upon their purposes of expressing their flood of ideas and feelings, the teacher protects them from interferences and interruptions. As long as the children continue to work on the expression of their ideas, they should be permitted to do so undisturbed. The teacher lends support by standing by while the children are working. Her presence makes them feel confident. The stimulation from the discussion during the motivation carries the children through this intense concentration and work.

As a child continues to develop his art, problems sometimes arise that he finds difficult to solve. A child needs help and guidance. If he does not receive it, he may become discouraged or even abandon his work. By helping children as their problems arise, the teacher performs her guidance responsibilities.

Guidance in art is an indirect action. Through guidance the teacher leads the child toward:

(a) Definition of his problem.
(b) Consideration of possible solutions.
(c) Information that aids in a solution.
(d) Incentive to develop his art work to the extent of his ability.

Throughout the motivation the teacher worked with the children as a group. Even though she talked with them one at a time, many of the things she said were directed toward the group. During the guidance period, which follows the motivation, the teacher does most of her work on an individual basis. There are times, of course, when the group, or a large part of it, needs direction or redirection, but most of her attention, at this stage of the children's work, is given to each on a personal basis as individual problems arise. Since each child is working on a different basis from every other, his problems will likely differ from those of the others. Therefore, guidance will be most helpful when approached individually. Although the teacher discusses each child's work with him individually, it does not follow that only this child is helped by the teacher's assistance. Everyone who hears what is said learns something. The amount that each child learns is in ratio to the importance to *him* of the knowledge given at that time. It may be that the guidance and help being given to one child will be related to the difficulty another is having. As the teacher instructs or helps the first child to focus upon his problem, the other child listens, applying what he hears to his own work. If the child is interested in the guidance being given, if it has meaning for him at that time, he listens and learns. If it has no significance, he disregards it. Nevertheless, he does hear it, and when it is presented again it will be somewhat familiar to him.

Because the teacher gives help and guidance to children as they work in art, it is not to be assumed that she tells them what to do or shows them how to do it. This would be an infringement upon the child's right to choose, to express, and to organize. Neither does the teacher give the children pictures to copy because they say they cannot draw a certain thing. This work interferes with and damages the child's own creative concepts of a form. Children *want* to do their own work. They want and need the teacher's help but not her interference.

It is difficult for many adults to understand the highly imaginative, emotional, inventively stated, sensitive world of child art. Becoming adjusted to the characteristics of child art is one of the biggest factors in a teacher's preparation. The differences between what child art is and adult concepts of art cause many difficulties in art education. It is, of course, an error to "correct" child art, because children seldom, if ever, make mistakes in art. It is the adult who makes the mistake when she "corrects" it. It is always an error to correct something just because it is not understood. The more a teacher studies children's art, the more she understands and appreciates it. Help the child to know more about objects, about art, about life; that is the way to help him in art.

Some teachers feel that when a child needs help, their job is to take the child's work into their own hands and solve the problem for the child, explaining as they proceed what they are doing and why. Erroneously, they reason that this type of help given at that moment will carry over into other similar problems that the child may later encounter. What happens is that the child loses the personal feeling or the identity with his work. It is no longer *his*. He no longer wants it, and he has lost interest and pride in it. How can he, then, learn much by it? The child may form a distaste for his art work. If a child knows or suspects that a teacher functions in this manner, he may refrain from soliciting her help or even revealing that he needs help. He wants to protect his work against such an encroachment; he wants his work to be true and honest—to be *his*. Even though others may think the addition of the teacher's work improves it, *the child does not*. He does not feel "right" about it any more.

The teacher's role in guidance during the art work period is one of helping the learner toward understanding. She does this as she explains. Through talking, through questioning and discussing, she helps the child develop his ability to put his ideas into art form. In the first place, a problem arises because the child does *not know*. He cannot analyze. He has no clear or certain idea or plan of what he wants to do or how he might do it. Sometimes he does not even know the nature of his problem. He may sense that something is wrong or incomplete about his art and not even be able to indicate the reason for this feeling of dissatisfaction. He needs someone to lead the way. Since he is immature, he has only partially developed skills, a limited background of experiences, and needs and wants the leadership and advice of someone mature, skilled, and experienced. When given, the advice should be consistent with the child's age, mental ability, and purposes.

Children in the elementary grades need the teacher's guidance during the working period while their work is still incomplete, and they should receive it within a short time after encountering the difficulty. Children are

20

The teacher guides, encourages, and helps children with problems, but she *never* takes their art into her own hands to work on it.

21

Unless a child receives sympathetic help from his teacher when he needs it, he is apt to become discouraged with his ability in art.

not as patient as adults. If left to cope with a problem too long, they can lose the inspiration that keeps them working, or they might change the course of their art work, abandoning the challenge and substituting in its place a form or idea they can do or have successfully done before. This limits learning. It is of little help to a child to be exposed to guidance influences after his work is complete, for this tends only to create a feeling of dissatisfaction with his work. To a child of this age, confidence in his completed work is important. The child needs to feel that his work is accepted and his achievements appreciated. After the art is finished, the teacher leads the discussion of it on another basis, for another purpose.

There are many reasons why children need guidance as they work. The reasons vary with the children and with the problems. In modern art education based upon creative expression, every child's work is different from every other, and every individual's work varies from day to day. Each medium presents its special problems as well. Therefore, the teacher should bring an open mind to every problem, expecting it to be somewhat unusual. From conversation with children during the motivation and from observation during the working period, the teacher brings to the guidance knowledge of their feelings, ideas, and purposes. Although it is true that no two problems are identical, there are some common ones.

Helping a child to define his problem is one of the general areas of guidance with which a teacher deals. As was mentioned earlier, sometimes a child has a feeling of dissatisfaction about his work without being able to identify the reason. He may say: "I don't like it" or "Something's the matter with mine" or "I can't make it look right." If the teacher asks a question such as "What don't you like about it?" or "Why doesn't it look right to you?" sometimes a child may simply name a part of the art work in order to give an answer, which may not be the problem bothering him at all. Or he may answer in much the same way as he first spoke: "I don't know, it just isn't right" or "I didn't do it right." This state of discontent with a vague cause is frustrating and discouraging. The child needs to be led to see what his problem is. Such guidance is the first step in showing the child the way. The teacher might ask the child to put his art work a greater distance from himself and to look at it, or she might have him look at it in a mirror to give him a fresh view. Sometimes, then, he sees the trouble for himself. If not, the teacher can point out the area of success and ask him if any area is not as well worked out. From her knowledge of art, the teacher would recognize the difficulty. The easiest course would be simply to tell the child, but he has more to gain by learning how to discover it for himself. In much the same way as she conducted the questions in the motivational discussion, the teacher might also ask the child questions that will help him focus upon one aspect of the work at a time.

The teacher might also suggest that the child discuss or describe what he wants to work out, or she may describe details of it. Words help at times by becoming a bridge over which details, shapes, or combinations of things can be brought out of the vagueness from which imagery might emerge and into a clearer definition of ideas and emotions. At other times the teacher might ask a question to call attention to a problem but do it in such a way that the child makes the discovery, and thus not only sees the solution but is lead to a step further in analyzing other works of art. For example, she might ask: "Do you have a variety of widths in those spaces or are they a great deal alike?" or "Is there any part not unified with the rest? Does any part seem left out or by itself?" or "If the wind is blowing the waves like that, would it be blowing anything else?" Frequently as the child defines his problem, solutions come to mind. When this is the case, the child should continue with his art unaided. He *knows* what has been troubling him and what to do about it. His incentive to continue has been rekindled by this additional insight and purpose.

A child who has been led to recognize his problem may still not know what to do about it. Through further questioning and discussion of what he knows about art and about his subjects, the teacher guides the child to determine his own course. The teacher seeks suggestions from the child as to what he might do. If there is a class atmosphere of friendliness, she may involve other children in the discussion or in suggesting ideas. The use of this procedure depends on how the child might react to it. The better the teacher knows her students, the better she can help them. The first suggestion may be the solution the child is looking for, or several may be considered before he decides. The teacher may, from her more mature viewpoint and with her rich background of education, see solutions that are quite different from those suggested by the child; she keeps in mind that hers are right as adult suggestions, and the child's are right for his level of maturity.

In addition to helping the child to define his problems and to consider and decide upon possible solutions, the teacher guides the child toward information that aids in a solution. He may know what his problem is and how he wants to organize and continue with his work, but his lack of some technical skill may block his way. In this case, the teacher simply teaches the skill to him and to other children who may be interested in learning or watching. The child may want to form a particular animal and realize as he works that he does not know enough about it to produce a satisfying shape. Questioning him about the animal will draw out what he does know and point to what he needs to learn. The teacher refers the child to pictures of the animal. After he has studied them for a while, she helps him by calling his attention to points that are characteristic of the animal. In a giraffe, for example, she would point out the shape of the head, how the head and neck join, how the body slants, and the differences in the front and back legs. Knowing a few of the typical features would help the child form his own mental concept of a giraffe that would facilitate his art expression. He has *knowledge* to draw upon. From his own ideas, he creates, imagines, and designs as he works. He does not *copy* his subject.

There are other resources to which a teacher may lead a child in helping him add to his knowledge. Knowledge is one of the bases for creative art work—knowledge about objects, operations, or art principles. Knowledge, imagination, and emotion are the sources of and driving forces behind a child's art. In her guidance role the teacher encourages the children to use pictorial and textual material.

A great deal of the teacher's guidance work is in remotivating children to continue. In spite of a strong desire to put ideas into form, a child may stop working simply because his enthusiasm runs low. To rekindle it, the teacher herself should be warm and zealous as she talks to the child about what he has accomplished and what other related ideas he might consider. The teacher questions and draws out; the child thinks and develops. Sometimes the whole group needs to be remotivated, but often it is an individual matter.

As the teacher moves among the children while they work, she gives some word of encouragement or assistance to each child. Children are aware of their teacher's presence and want some bit of personal attention from her. Teachers are never neutral influences; what they say affects children. The fact that the teacher passes a child by without making some comment about his work, or without offering some incentive for him to go forward, affects the child. He may think that she sees nothing worthy of mention in his art, or he may feel left out. Each child is important. Each deserves some personal comment. Ruth Strang indicates how the teacher functions with students in the role of guidance in the art class:

> In no other classroom, perhaps, is there more opportunity for skillful, unobtrusive guidance than in the art room. There the teacher works almost exclusively with individuals. He brings out the student's ideas, waits for him to discover his difficulty, makes suggestions that enable him to complete his work successfully. Pleased by the teacher's praise and helped by his tactful hints, students work with increased effort and interest. The teacher can usually find something of promise in any piece of work and is resourceful in making suggestions for improvement: a shift in line, the addition of another color, a detail added for balance. Under skillful, unobtrusive guidance, students grow in creative ability and in personality.[4]

A teacher can judge when the art work is completed by the attitude of the children. When they seem to have developed their work to the extent of their interest and ability and are satisfied with it, the teacher should accept it. Her role changes again as she discusses the work with the children. She deals with the whole group again as she helps the children to evaluate the completed work.

> The teacher approaches the child and his painting with as free a mind as possible. He should know what he thinks would help the expressive quality of the painting, but his purpose is not to impose his superior knowledge on the youngster. His purpose is to first praise what is good and then to ask questions or make comments that will stimulate the child to visualize what he wants to do.[5]

EVALUATION

Evaluation, a vital process in elementary school art education, is a measure of the quality of the art—a search for value within each piece of art work. Quality is measured:

---

[4] Reprinted with the permission of the publisher, Ruth Strang's *The Role of the Teacher in Personnel Work* (New York: Teachers College Press), copyright 1946, Teachers College, Columbia University.

[5] Helen Merritt, *Guiding Free Expression in Children's Art* (New York: Holt, Rinehart and Winston, © 1964), p. 31. Reprinted by permission of the publisher.

(a) By the child as he works on his art.
(b) By the teacher as the child works on his art.
(c) In pupil-teacher discussion of the completed art work.
(d) In study of the exhibited art work.

Evaluation has deeper implications than grading, which may or may not be an outcome of evaluation. Because grading of art is in opposition to the purposes of creative expression, evaluation will be considered as a learning situation, since the children's art products themselves serve as a teaching aid through which *successes* are recognized. The teacher calls attention to the superior achievements of each and avoids giving attention to the inferior; by so doing, she shows the way of success and creation. The discussion becomes more like a good and helpful conversation among friends than a critical diagnosis by a superior, and should leave each child heartened and uplifted. Looking for a weakness always puts the other person on guard. Recognizing a strength creates a bond. Protecting the other person's pride is a vital point in opening up and developing strength in art expression.

There is no such thing as an objective evaluation in art, for art comes out of the individuality of each person and is greatly tied to his own intimate choices and feelings. Because of this, the child whose work is being discussed feels exposed and vulnerable as a person. Reactions to art and comments made about it are personal to the evaluator. He is reacting to his own preferences and prejudices which may actually serve to alienate him from the heart of the art. The evaluator needs to involve himself in the same way as the creator did, or he misses the very core of it. This rewarding projective approach to the evaluation of art, which adds dimension to art appreciation, requires guidance and experience and can, with practice, be learned.

Evaluation by the Child as He Works

The child's evaluation begins as he begins to consider an idea for his art: many ideas come to him, and he chooses the one he considers important enough to concentrate upon and that he judges to be valuable enough to absorb his attention. He gives consideration to each idea, evaluating its interest to him and its appropriateness to the materials with which he is working. Thus, before the child actually begins dealing with materials, he begins to evaluate. He continues to make judgments of his art work from that point until the work is completed and during the time it is exhibited. As a child works in art, he forms an opinion of every shape he creates, deciding whether it measures up to the standard he expects of himself. Before he proceeds, he also appraises the form he has created in relation to the dimensions of the background or the space around it. Every form and area he structures is evaluated in this way. As each form or area is added, the whole composition is also reevaluated. The more skilled the child is in making evaluations, the more proficient he can be in developing and improving his work. The child learns from making his own judgments. He learns many things by working them out himself, especially if his own experiences are supplemented by the help of a teacher who points out ways of making deeper or more appreciative evaluations of art work.

22
Teacher and children evaluate completed art work, discussing the strong points of each child's work.

Evaluation by the Teacher as the Children Work

In order to make the guidance period more significant, the teacher evaluates, appraises, and measures the child's achievements and problems by studying the child's art as he works. The children evaluate their own work as it moves forward, and so the teacher does also. The child's purpose in this constant appraisal is to create the best piece of art of which he is capable; the teacher's purpose is to help the child grow in his ability to express his ideas in art and to learn how to appreciate the work of others. Evaluation is an important tool in furthering both purposes. Another purpose of the teacher's evaluation is a general appraisal of the group's approach and partial achievements to ascertain what, if any, aspects of the motivation need to be reenforced.

Pupil-Teacher Discussion

After the art work is completed, further education takes place as this work is evaluated and discussed. As the discussion begins, the role of the teacher changes. Again she works with the group as a whole instead of with the children on an individual basis. Children have much to learn by hearing what is said of the strengths of their classmates' work. They see and hear an explanation of what each child has done and how he has worked it out.

It is important for the teacher to know some of the bases for making evaluative statements of children's art. Try to avoid confusing the development of skills with art quality. Sometimes adults look for such features as naturalistic representation, shading, perspective, or anatomical proportion. These are technical skills and do not necessarily contribute to quality in art. In fact, such work may have little or no art value. Essential to every work of art, child or adult, are vitality, imagination, originality, and feeling. In a work of art there seems to be a haunting personality, a wholeness, and a harmony of expression and purpose. Child art is full of these qualities. Look for them. Study the way a child has attempted to organize his art; comment upon it. Delicate, sensitive art should be recognized, for this is another kind of expression. Not all art needs to be large, powerful, or intense; some can be just the opposite, expressing delicacy. Encourage this flexibility and versatility.

The original idea, the fresh new expression, or the individual way of shaping a form, color relationships, and compositional structure should be mentioned.

Perhaps a teacher may at first feel at a loss for something to say about a particular work. Something as general as: "Nothing just like this has ever been seen before" or "You are the only one who has ever done anything like this." What a wonderful comment to hear! Practice helps as a teacher continues to look for strengths. Tact and graciousness are as essential to this relationship as they are to any other situation in which people work together. The evaluative discussion should benefit every child and not be reserved for the teacher-selected or group-selected elite. Comments made often bring to the attention of the child who created the art points of quality he may have missed because: (a) he is too sensitive to his own work to see it with a fresh eye, and (b) he may not have sufficient knowledge of art to recognize and verbalize about points in his art that he feels pleased with.

Occasionally, to help facilitate the pupil-teacher discussion, the teacher might write a specific positive comment on the back of each child's art. It is there for him to profit by, and for his parents to see, helping them understand and appreciate their child's art.

Study of Exhibited Art Work

As long as the art work remains on display and within view of the children, each child forms his own private opinion of the success of the project and of the relative quality of each child's work. Regardless of what was said of it during the discussion, a child is free to make his evaluation in terms of his own values, experiences, and emotional responses. Independently of the viewpoints of others, he admires certain works and studies them more closely. With no intention to copy the successes of others, he is further inspired toward his own achievements. Such evaluation can lead to improvement of his own art and to the development of a unique style. His personal preference is frequently for the work of those children who express their ideas as he does. Then he explores the challengingly different ones. He learns and is inspired as he studies the exhibition.

Purposes of Evaluation

Evaluation in art is a discipline through which the child:

(a) Learns how to make or to improve his judgments.
(b) Gains more art knowledge.
(c) Adds to his general knowledge.
(d) Understands the work of others.
(e) Learns what to look for in observing works of art.
(f) Learns how to talk about art products.
(g) Improves his own art expressions.

These advantages are the result of the child's evaluation both as he works on the expression of his ideas and feelings and after the art work is completed. Both the children and teacher have responsibilities in this vital educational process.

Evaluation constitutes the making of judgments. Children develop the ability to form opinions, to appraise, and to judge. The children's skill in estimating and selecting quality grows as the teacher guides and supplements their evaluations.

Through the pupil-teacher discussion of the completed art work, children gain more *art* knowledge. They look at each piece of work to see how they react to it, what particular element makes it interesting. Then they study it further to try to find out why they react to it as they do or why they find it interesting. They look for a spot or for an area they consider more successfully worked out than some others and attempt to ascertain *why*. Not every child will be able to do all of these things and should not be expected to. Neither should every child in the group be expected to come to the same conclusions. Evaluation should include an approach to the study of art. By evaluating, the child learns that art is something worthy of study. He discovers the rewards of such evaluative procedures and feels the satisfactions that come from closer association with a variety of types of art work. Quite often after closer study and more searching evaluation, the child discovers art qualities that he previously failed to notice or to understand.

As the child discovers what particular quality of the art expression causes his reaction, he associates this element with the emotion he feels. Therefore, he builds knowledge about additional ways of expressing and communicating feelings through art. Sensitivities are developed through every attempt to associate one's own feeling with that of the artist by the responses that must be alerted. This deliberate quickening of the senses helps the child become more responsive to art and to the reactions and feelings that the artist has expressed through his forms, colors, and organization.

Many of the disciplines of art are learned through the evaluation of works of art. As the children and teacher jointly discuss how a certain thing has been accomplished, they sometimes refer to structural principles of art. They may talk about how colors have been mixed to bring about particular shades and tints, and what qualities of these colors create a pleasant relationship among the groups of which they are a part. They are probing deep in order to learn why these certain colors are pleasing.

When an evaluation has shown that organization is a strong point in a composition, the teacher and children together discuss how this organization has been achieved. They want to see what there is about this particular arrangement of forms that makes for an organized grouping and how it is structured to give the impression of belonging together. Since every piece of art is different and every organization different, many such evaluation experiences help children to form criteria for making judgments about art.

As the child evaluates art work, he finds out about forms, ideas, and meanings unfamiliar to him. Other children have had experiences that may be unknown to him, or they may have reactions that differ from his. As these are expressed and discussed, the child adds to his general knowledge.

Through this new knowledge, the child also becomes more familiar with his classmates. He observes their work and listens to their comments during the evaluation discussion. As children discuss their own work and that of mature artists, they learn to appreciate the work of others and understand and enjoy a much broader range of expressions in art.

When evaluation of art work becomes a regular part of the art program, children learn what to look for as they view art. Since art is basically a visual subject, knowing what to look for helps people to enjoy it. They have criteria that help them to analyze the work. A viewpoint of evaluation based upon a search for achievement builds a positive attitude toward the approach to art. Children need to learn what to look for in a wide variety of art products. It is helpful in everyday living if they learn how to evaluate textile designs, appropriate and harmonious dress, and the products of industry such as utensils and furniture.

As the child learns what to look for in art by helping to point it out and hearing it discussed, he will grow in his ability to talk about art. He will have developed an art vocabulary and will have learned how to use it. He will have learned phrases that can be used to describe certain relationships in art, as well as how to describe the novel, fresh approaches to art with which he will, no doubt, come in contact.

One of the most important outcomes of evaluation is the improvement of the child's own art expression. From all the information that he gains as a result of his participation in evaluation study and discussion, the child is most deeply impressed by that which interests him most. He also learns many things that will be most helpful to any subsequent art experience.

It is unnecessary to conduct an evaluation discussion of everything that children produce in art. This is a valuable although time-consuming procedure. Children in the elementary grades want to *do* art. They will enjoy the evaluation if it is not done so frequently or so extensively that they begin to feel deprived of working with materials. Sometimes, however, an evaluation can be quickly done. Small groups of children may hold their art work up as the teacher and children simply make one brief value statement of each, or a general favorable statement can be made of the group of art work shown. The same is true when all the art is exhibited. One brief comment may suffice. Indeed, there are times when the work can be hung, looked at, enjoyed, appreciated, and evaluated by all who see it—without an accompanying discussion. Children may became somewhat apprehensive if they feel that *everything* they do will be discussed.

Some teachers may feel that an evaluation is not complete without adding to the positive comments a discussion of the areas that need improvement and suggestions of how the child could have improved his work. They feel that suggestions of this type will help the child solve similar future problems. Such reasoning seems logical to adults. The mature teacher may feel that *she* would gain more if an evaluation of *her* work were handled this way. Such reasoning is based upon adult thinking, purposing, and reacting. Children are not yet ready for such mature ways. Having one's shortcomings pointed out by his teacher and classmates in front of his peers and friends is a difficult situation defeating any educational purpose the teacher may be trying to establish, for the child is more concerned with his embarrassment than with the negative approach to teaching. It is necessary for the teacher to vigilantly avoid criticism and comparisons of children's art if the child is to survive in art. The withering effects of criticism destroy the art achievement in the eyes and feelings of the children. It eventually kills art. Its scalding effects leave scars on the child which are reflected in his attitude toward his ability in art and toward his response to art in general.

Neglect also has its own kind of cold, chilling effects on a child. When, during the discussion of their art, a teacher passes over a child's work without some mention of its quality, she fails the child at that time. If she does not mention any child's achievement, however, there is no slight to anyone. But if a few are singled out for favorable comment, or a few passed over, then discrimination is being shown. Comparisons are obvious.

EXHIBITION

A final rewarding part of creative art work is the showing of the completed art product. The opportunity to share his ideas and thoughts with others is important to the child. Therefore, some type of display of every child's work should be planned as a part of the art project. To have each work shown is just as important to one child as it is to another. Therefore, *every* child's work should be shown. To have all the work displayed without any indication of favor or disapproval of any individual child's work is also important. Hangings based upon the preference for one child's work or for a selected few children's work would be contradictory to the viewpoint stressed throughout this book. Every child is as important as every other. Every child's work is important to him. Therefore, every piece of art work produced by a group of children is important. Whatever is significant to the child should be of consequence to his teacher.

When all of the children's art is advantageously displayed, there is an opportunity for each child to take responsibility or credit for his art achievement, whatever it may be. Even though it may not be a distinguishing achievement, it needs recognition: even needing it more, because of this, to nourish educational advancement and further art expression.

Limited Display Space

The display space in some classrooms is, unfortunately, so limited as to make it impossible to hang every piece of work at once. In this case, the children should have their work hung indiscriminately and in turn, with no child's work being displayed twice until everyone's work has been shown once. There are many ways to deal with such a space limitation. As examples, the teacher might display the work of children who sit in groups together; or the boys, then the girls; or one portion of the class on Monday, another portion on Tuesday, and so forth.

When inadequate display space exists, the teacher should occasionally provide some opportunity for all the children's work to be hung together even though the exhibition is hung outside the classroom. The school hall is a fine place for this and frequently looks more colorful with children's art work filling up the empty walls.

Classroom windows are sometimes used to display children's art, especially during holiday seasons. This display has the added advantage of showing their work to the public. It also reveals the art education philosophy of the program. If the art displayed on the windows is all alike, the impression given is that art in that classroom in dictated: that there is little or no opportunity for creative problem solving or individual development provided.

Another example of a display of art can be found in Illustration 91 on page 226. There are many variations of ways of hanging and of background treatments that can add interest to a display and improve the whole group of work.

Suggested Bases for Display

Although a display hung according to someone's ideas of "quality" is difficult for children to accept, they approve of exhibits arranged on other bases if they understand how the selections are made. They can agree with exhibitions arranged on some basis that makes a more aesthetic appearance. Then, too, art exhibitions are more attractive and interesting when the arrangement of the exhibit has been so chosen. A few bases for more pleasing displays might be: pieces light in color shown alternately with those dark in color; or complex pieces beside those containing few large forms; or pieces of a certain size or shape arranged together; or pieces that seem related in subject matter or form shown together.

When children see an aesthetic exhibition of their art work and understand the principle determining the placements, they are adding to their art experiences and art knowledge.

There are times when a child may not want to have his art work included in the exhibition. He may have come to this conclusion because an experiment with the media, color, or form may not have worked out as well as he had anticipated. He tried it, but it did not work; he should therefore be free to dispose of the result if *he* so chooses. The initiation of the idea to withhold his work from the group display should come from the child (without the teacher's suggestions, subtle or otherwise) and should be respected by the teacher. If, however, such withdrawal becomes a habit, there is a different kind of problem.

Exhibitions Outside the School

An exhibition of children's art held outside the school is stimulating to children and gives them a sense of pride. It also creates public interest in children's art. Store windows are fine for art exhibitions, and so are the public library and empty storerooms. The exhibition should be hung in spots easily accessible to the public. A little imagination in considering the community resources may lead to some excellent locations. Keep the exhibition simple. Do not undertake too much or let it become burdensome so that the pleasure is gone and the initiative to do it again dulled.

Mounting and Backgrounds

Mounting the art work appropriately adds to the beauty and effectiveness of each piece. Displaying it against a background that brings out its unique qualities adds interest to a piece of art work. A light directed at the three-dimensional art pieces is simple to install and can be so placed as to cast shadows in any direction or to elongate them. The shadows, cast against a background, add interest to the art work and become a part of the exhibition. Children find such a simple device fascinating. Mounts for flat work should be selected to bring out the unique quality of the art work; they can vary in color, or can be all white, grey, black, or any neutral shade suitable to the work.

23

The way art is mounted can add greatly to its attractiveness.

The background area for the display can be changed to emphasize the various types of work exhibited. Textured materials such as corrugated paper, wire, string stretched in a pattern, or strips of colored paper are a few suggestions. Children will have other ideas to offer. Appreciate their suggestions. Let them work some of them out and hang the display. When participating, children feel more responsible for and more personally involved in the exhibition and in its relation to the whole classroom appearance. Often, children's art work needs nothing more than to be displayed. Although mounting it or arranging special backgrounds enhances it and adds to the appearance, neither is necessary. Child art is attractive just as it is.

Change of Exhibitions

As soon as a new exhibition of their art work has been arranged, children study it intently. With each succeeding day their interest in it wanes. The younger the child, the more quickly he has exhausted the potentials of the exhibition. His attention span is shorter than that of older children, and he has not yet acquired the background of knowledge necessary for deeper study. Then, too, the art of young children is less complex than that of the older child, containing less material for study. After two or three days children in the primary grades have lost interest in an exhibition. Children in the upper elementary grades do not lose interest as quickly, but after a week, at least a part of the display of upper-grade art should change. Large projects upon which the group has spent possibly several weeks can be more permanently shown.

The teacher thus concentrates on creating a facilitative climate and on providing resources. He may also help to put students in contact with meaningful problems. But he does not set lesson tasks or assign readings. He does not lecture or expound (unless requested to). He does not evaluate and criticize unless the student wishes his judgment on a product. He does not give examinations. He does not set grades.[6]

SUGGESTED ACTIVITIES

In order to empathize with children's sources for ideas in art and to broaden your own awareness of them, think through and list your experiences and emotions during the course of one day that might motivate art.

Make a list of questions that a teacher might ask children to stimulate original thinking during the motivational discussion.

---

[6] Carl R. Rogers, "Learning to Be Free," *Art Education*, National Art Education Association, Washington, D.C., LII, No. 3 (1963), 29.

4

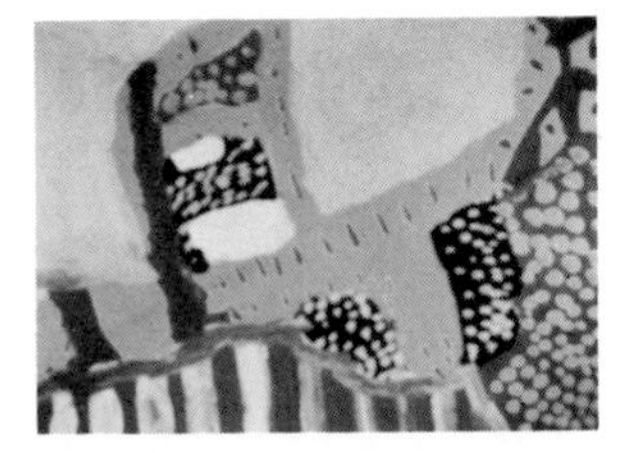

Teaching Toward Creative Art Expression

There is a certain definite series of actions that constitutes the role of the teacher as she motivates, guides, evaluates, and exhibits the work of the children in her group. In order to free the children to create, the teacher needs to proceed in such a way as to inspire each child's confidence in his own ideas and ways. So as not to interfere with the individually different intentions and purposes of each child, the teacher works in a general way with the group and on an individual basis with each child.

The art processes the children use and the teaching processes the teacher uses are interdependent. If the teacher wants the children to work in a free and independent way she must be permissive in letting them choose their own ideas, improvising and creating as they go. They need to feel this continual operation of her inspirational influence, her confidence in them, and her appreciation of their work. The children take their cue from the teacher; she takes hers from them.

The example of how a teacher functions with children in creative expression constitutes the major part of this chapter. This is a method that teachers may use with children without in any way interfering with the child or directing him in his work. It is a method designed to free the child, to stimulate him, and to give him confidence. It gives help where help is needed as well as instruction and information at the time least likely to influence a particular art product and most likely to contribute to the child's knowledge and creative ability. It is a procedure that each teacher can adapt to her own personal way of teaching. In creative art expression, there are individual ways of teaching just as there are individual ways of working in art.

24

Children should have art experiences with a variety of materials and processes to provide challenge and stimulation. New processes using familiar materials can add interest, just as art can be further personalized by bits of attractive materials brought from home.

The entire process of teaching art to help children toward creative expression can best be shown through an illustration of the way one teacher functioned with the children in her third-grade group. The same procedure is applicable to children of any age. Because of the individual differences among teachers, no two would conduct the motivation, guidance, and evaluation in exactly the same manner. Each would ask questions with different phrasing and content. The example in this chapter is not intended as a pattern that teachers should copy verbatim.

To present a pattern of teaching to be copied would bring results as barren and limiting as expecting all children to copy the same picture. The inclusion here of a specific example of the teaching of modern creative art serves as a basis for a better understanding of how this teaching method is put into operation with children. Teachers need to have some idea of *how* to teach it, *what* to say, and *when* to say it. Reading and thinking through one example of an art lesson can serve as a guide to inspire teachers to think of other approaches, other ways, *their own* phrasing, and *their own* responses and questions. Each teacher knows her own group of children better than any other person does. She is aware of the personality of the group and of each child within the group. The example that follows is a presentation of the actions and conversations that took place in one situation. The example and its accompanying comments, however, represent the method that serves to draw from each child the expressions of his unique thinking. Such a process of teaching inspires children, helps them recall events, motivates imagination, and excites and challenges them without interfering with their intentions.

MATERIALS AND PREPARATION

Preparing and making available the materials is a part of the pupil-teacher work that precedes the discussion. In addition, procedures for obtaining paper, paints, and other necessary materials are determined by the children and teacher together. The children should know where to put their completed paintings to dry, how to clean up after their work, and what to do in case they finish before the others. Such preplanning before the motivation discussion begins frees the child to concentrate upon his ideas and to create. An example of the way one group of children handled the problem of tempera paint gives a basis for considering other desirable ways of procuring and sharing paint and facilities.

25

Felt and pinking shears were new to the children, and the motivation from the introduction of something new stimulated this and many varied compositions of fabric.

Before any discussion began the tempera paint was mixed and stirred and placed on a large table on one side of the room. A brush was put into each jar so that the children would not carry color from one jar to another by using the same brush for each nor dilute the paint by cleaning the brush between each color.

All the jars of paint of different colors necessary to complete a painting would require a great deal of space. For that reason, the children decided to get one or two jars of paint from the table just as they needed it, then return it so that the others might use it. This procedure gives the child an opportunity to move around. The physical freedom contributes to freedom of thought. The children have already put their names on their papers and have accomplished all other details ahead of time so that they are ready to begin to put their thoughts and feelings into form as soon as the discussion is over.

One child may already have an idea and seem ready to begin, but since he is such a quick thinker, he would contribute to the discussion. Participation in the pre-work discussion will likely broaden his ideas as well as enrich and stimulate some of the other children.

If some children begin to work before the discussion is over, it distracts those who have not yet chosen an idea or have not become emotionally stimulated enough to begin. The latter group may feel pressured by the fact that some of their classmates are getting ahead of them and, consequently, they may start to work before they have had time to think about painting or to decide upon what they would like to do. Conversely, the continued discussion may disturb those who have begun to paint, so it is better for all the children if everyone participates in the entire discussion.

Some people feel that to be wholly creative the child must not only be permitted to choose the subject matter for his art, but he should also have the choice of any medium he wants. This should be done as far as possible; however, a free choice of materials has some problems with children of elementary school age, especially very young children. In the first place, some of the children may repeatedly use the materials with which they feel some familiarity or have had some success. Then, too, the length of time for art activities in the elementary grades is usually shorter than with older children. If a variety of materials had to be distributed according to individual needs, it would consume a disproportionate amount of the time allotted for art.

Children of this age change their minds. They think they want a certain material until they see a classmate using something else. If the teacher helps these children make the change, more time is taken. If there is an arbitrary rule that a first choice must be the final one, some children will be unhappy because they are unable to change their first selection for another; this unhappiness is not conducive to creative art work.

If children are to have free choice of any materials for the work period, all materials must be prepared and placed in a convenient location for easy accessibility. There must be quantities of each in readiness, for it would be difficult to predict how many children will want to paint or work with clay. If the clay is not all used, it dries and hardens. Other materials that have been prepared and placed in an available location for the children require handling. All this varied preparation uses teacher and student energy in an amount disproportionate to the value of such a procedure.

In the elementary school, working habits and procedures are being established, and with various materials and under different circumstances, this takes time and effort. Until such habits are built, constant reminders need to be given and supervision provided. Children need to know how to get clay, where to put the finished clay piece, and how to clean up. When this is well in mind, children are free to give thought to their work. It takes many repetitions of this procedure to establish the habit. Children in the elementary grades have not yet mastered the various procedures with different materials. They still forget and need to be reminded.

26

The establishment of good work habits and a clear knowledge of routine procedures helps to facilitate freedom of thinking in such media as finger paint.

Therefore, it often works more satisfactorily for a group of children to use much the same material at the same time. This in no way interferes with their right to choose their own ideas and work them out as they desire. A variety of materials presented, each at different times, develops flexibility and ingenuity with children and is good for the educational development of the child.

MOTIVATION

The teacher might begin by saying: "Some of you already have some good ideas for your painting. What would you like to paint? What is one idea you might use for a painting?"

ALICE: "I'm going to paint about our summer camp where we go for our vacation. There is a lake there and we go swimming. I'm going to paint us in swimming. Our dog, too. He goes."

TEACHER: "Is your summer camp in the woods or near the lake? What is the place like?"

ALICE: "It is right by the lake. The shore is right by our cabin. But there is a kind of woods there, too. There are some trees. No other cabin is very near ours."

TEACHER: "How does it make you feel to be there? Are you glad or how *do* you feel?"

ALICE: "Well, it makes me feel glad. I like to go there. I get excited when my mother tells me we are going to go. Then I can hardly wait. We have fun, Mary and me. [Mary is her sister.] We can just play and don't have to watch out for cars or anything. It is kind of cool feeling by the trees and in the cabin. But the sun is good, too."

By asking the location of the camp, the teacher encouraged Alice and the rest of the children in the group to think about the other objects and feelings associated with the topic. The question was pointed to Alice, but many others would realize that it would make their picture fuller, more interesting, and more informative if they thought about the landscape and the objects and people near or associated with their ideas. The question was a cue to the children to think about emotional responses to the subject each had chosen. We all react to every experience we have. This reaction is a part of the experience. Recalling the reaction is part of the motivation for art. The experiences (real or imaginary) that children have plus their reactions to the experiences determine their art. It is not necessary for the teacher to question each child specifically about his feelings because the answers of one or two children will serve to remind the others.

TEACHER: "Who has a *different* idea for a painting?"

JOE: "My Dad took us to the airport. We watched the planes go up and land. Some were refueled. The gasoline trucks went right out beside the planes. There were big planes came in while we were there, and people got off."

TEACHER: "You have lots of interesting things to put into your painting, Joe. Exciting things happen at the airport and to planes while they are flying."

Although the teacher did not question Joe about his emotional reaction to his visit to the airport, she sensed his feeling of excitement from the way he told about it. From this cue she said: "Exciting things happen at the airport and to planes while they are flying." The second part of the sentence, ". . . and to planes while they are flying," broadened the topic and may have inspired Joe further or set other children thinking about exciting things.

TEACHER: "We don't always have to paint or draw about things that are exciting or amusing. Other kinds of things happen to us, too, sometimes. What might be one of them?"

HELEN: "Getting scared. Sometimes at night I get bad dreams and get scared. But I'm not going to paint about this for my art. I already have my idea."

TEACHER: "You can paint about anything you want to. Can anyone think of *another* feeling we sometimes have besides fear and being happy?"

HAROLD: "I get afraid sometimes when I have to go home after it gets dark."

Since this was a different experience, but the same emotional reaction, the teacher did not comment on Harold's contribution. She simply accepted it with a nod of her head.

TEACHER: "Can anyone think of *another* feeling we sometimes get?"

DORIS: "When I have to practise my piano lesson, I get mad. I don't want to do it. It's always when I have started to do something important or something."

TEACHER: "Yes, we all feel that way at times. You could paint about how you feel, or you could paint about some idea you have—a real or an imaginary idea. You don't have to choose any particular thing."

By making such a statement, the teacher was trying to free the children from any obligation of being expected to paint about a feeling or emotion, specifically as such, just because attention was focused upon it briefly. It is the responsibility of the teacher to help children to think broadly about many aspects of their ideas for art. She added the suggestion that they could paint an imaginary composition, "a real or an imaginary idea." At the same time, it is also her job to help them keep in mind that the choices are *theirs*, that there is nothing in particular that she expects of them, and nothing that she will be looking for as a result of their discussion.

TEACHER: "Who has a *different* idea for his painting?"

JACK: "Baseball."

TEACHER: "What about baseball, Jack? What will you put into your painting?"

The other two children who had presented their ideas seemed to have not only a subject in mind but also an experience associated with the subject. They mentioned action, people, and environmental objects associated with their idea. Jack's contribution to the discussion lacked such broad associations.

JACK: "Me, hitting the ball."

TEACHER: "What other players were in it, too?"

JACK: "The pitcher."

TEACHER: "Anyone else?"

JACK: "The guy catching."

TEACHER: "Anyone watching you?"

JACK: "Yes. There were some other kids."

TEACHER: "Where were you playing, Jack, in the street or in a field?"

JACK: "Behind Fred's house in his yard."

TEACHER: "How would I know this when I look at your picture?"

JACK: "I could put in the house."

It is clear that Jack is not very vocal and thinks about his idea only one step at a time. There is much more that the teacher could have developed with Jack. She could have brought into the discussion other children who would have other ideas, and often this is a good practice. The teacher would not always wish to function in the same way with Jack nor with the other children in the group. Although Jack knew all the things that the teacher talked to him about, they were not in his active thinking at that moment. He needed help in making associations and in thinking through his idea about baseball. He also needed practice in vocal as well as graphic expression.

The teacher's more detailed discussion with Jack served several purposes:

(a) To help Jack broaden his concept into a whole composition that included more than just one person holding a bat. Although simply one person holding a baseball bat could make a strong and vigorous picture, the teacher, knowing Jack, realized that one of his personality characteristics was to draw just one thing or say just one or two words. She felt he needed this developmental process of learning how to think deeper and of making more associations.

(b) Jack has a tendency to think only about himself. This interrogation pointed toward the inclusion of others, especially those who cooperated in helping him play ball. Because Jack is shy, the teacher included the question "Anyone watching you?" to suggest to him that he was a person worth watching. In so doing, the teacher developed the personality of the child as she developed ideas with him that would improve his art. Both took place at the same time.

(c) The teacher's probing of more and more ideas that Jack might include in his art made other children think more deeply about their own ideas or else concentrate on Jack's whole idea from *their* viewpoint. This is a learning situation in which *every* child benefits directly or indirectly.

At *no* time did the teacher make any suggestions to Jack of what he might include in his painting. She was, in her questions, sensitive to him, taking her cues from what he said and from what she felt he needed as a person.

TEACHER: "You have lots of interesting things to put into your painting, Jack."

JACK: "Yes, and trees were there in the yard. I could put a tree in."

Jack was stimulated to the point of thinking independently about objects and ideas associated with baseball.

TEACHER: "Who has a *different* idea?"

JANICE: "Could I paint about last summer?"

TEACHER: "Of course, Janice. What do you think you might paint about last summer?"

JANICE: "About the baby pigs. Last summer at my grandma's farm their pig had baby pigs—lots of them. I could make them in my picture."

The teacher nodded approvingly at Janice, who indicated by the tone of her voice a feeling of emotional excitement about the little pigs. It was not necessary for the teacher to stimulate Janice further; her own emotions did that.

The teacher makes the children feel at ease during the discussion by talking with them on their own level, omitting academic or professional phrasing but at the same time being grammatical.

She also helps put them at ease by accepting *every* idea presented without either a hint of criticism or a suggestion that certain contributions might be more important, more imaginative, or better in any way than others. These two ways of dealing with children are keys in encouraging participation in discussion.

TEACHER: "Who else has a different idea?"

By this time in the questioning several children raised their hands, indicating that they had an idea for art that they wanted to tell about. Just because some children, however, do not volunteer to talk about their ideas before they begin to paint does not mean that they have no ideas. They may have been thinking in terms of form and color and about the painting of *their own* ideas. They are not interested, at this point, in discussing them orally. Children are different in this respect; they function, as all artists do, according to their personality demands.

MIKE: "I'm going to paint an abstract."

TEACHER: "All right, Mike. What are some of the things we have discussed that help to make abstract paintings more interesting?"

MIKE: "Not to make everything alike."

TEACHER: "Yes. What else?"

RACHAEL: "Make some large things and some small—all kinds of things."

SAM: "Just make it up as you go. You can tell what to make next when you look at what you have already done. But don't make it like the one you've seen or like one you already made before."

TERESA: "Make your picture all over your paper."

ANDREW: "When we were looking at those pictures painted by real artists, we saw that the colors were put in different places in their paintings. They didn't put all the red in one place. They distributed it around."

MIKE: "They used light and dark colors, too."

TEACHER: "Can anyone think of anything *else* you could paint—a different idea from those we have talked about?"

DOMINICK: [excitedly and with lots of gestures] "I'm going to paint airplanes—fighting and getting shot at by the soldiers and with people watching them."

JERRY: "I'm going to paint a war picture with airplanes fighting."

TEACHER: "That's Dominick's idea, Jerry. What other exciting things do airplanes do?"

It may seem at first as though Jerry were avoiding the responsibility that freedom of choice places upon people. It is often easier for a child to take the idea suggested by another than it is to concentrate upon selecting an idea meaningful to himself. Because a certain way is easier does not mean that it is better. In this situation, the teacher has several points to consider: (a) this is Dominick's idea, and he has a right to it without having someone copy it, (b) Jerry's apparent dependence, (c) the possibility that Dominick's suggestion may have precipitated a feeling for which Jerry was trying to find form. Since it is difficult to know the intention of the child from this brief conversation, the teacher should avoid a statement based upon a quick conclusion which might embarrass or discourage one of the children. The teacher said gently, "That is Dominick's idea, Jerry." Her tone indicated no reproach; it was just a reminder that someone else had thought of the idea first. Her next question, "What other exciting things do airplanes do?" was intended to help Jerry think about a little different type of activity that he might deal with in this exciting topic.

The teacher did not embarrass Jerry, for embarrassment causes a child to become self-conscious and sometimes emotionally confused. Such procedure would not have been conducive to his further and more independent thinking. Neither did she insist upon an immediate answer to her question,

"What other exciting things do airplanes do?" Some children may have a ready answer, and others might require a little time to reflect upon it. She did not tell him that he could not paint an airplane war. She merely tried to encourage him toward more independence.

Since creative expression gives every child the right to make his own decisions and to use his own ideas, it also implies, to a great extent, the right of a child to the protection against having his ideas used or copied by another. The teacher stepped in immediately when Jerry repeated Dominick's idea to communicate this thought to both children. She wanted Dominick to know that she *knew* that it was his idea in the first place. He would realize with satisfaction that even if someone else used the idea, the teacher credited him with originating it. She wanted Jerry and the other children to remember this, too.

In the few seconds required for these two questions the teacher did a great deal of teaching. She was not only talking to the two boys about this practice of using the idea of another, she was also teaching fairness to all of the children, which would help in character development. Every child in the group heard and was reminded that each is privileged in creative art expression to express his own individual personality, that each should think for himself, and that each idea is accepted and is important.

Although it seemed to the teacher that enough discussion had taken place to motivate every child, she decided to ask one more question so that the last impression of the motivation would not be the situation of two boys with the same idea. Throughout the discussion the emphasis of the teacher had been upon the *different* ideas that children think of. Consider how many times she used the word *different* and the emphasis she placed upon it every time. Creative expression in art richly provides for individual differences, and the teacher stressed this during the motivation.

TEACHER: "Does anyone else want to talk about what he thought of to paint?"

PATRICIA: "I was thinking I might paint mine about the Indians. How they lived before the white people came here. You know, what we have been learning about."

TEACHER: "Yes, you could make a painting about Indians. Stories we read give us lots of ideas for art."

JANICE: "I could paint about Bill and Jean going for a ride in the train. Our reading story is all about the train ride."

Children get many ideas for art from the vicarious experiences in the stories that they hear and read, and also watch on screens. The most meaningful and exciting correlation of art with another school subject is that which comes from the suggestion of the child himself. Patricia, apparently, had been interested in Indians, since her group had studied about early American life. She thought about it and was still emotionally involved in the subject when art class came, so she chose that subject for her art idea.

Patricia's discussion of her idea plus the added assurance of the teacher that other stories might also provide subject matter for art gave Janice the inspiration to paint a picture based upon a story the children had been reading together.

During the discussion, as often happens in a class, two different ideas for painting were presented by one child. Some children are more imaginative than others, and some are more vocal. Some may express two or three ideas, while, at the same time, there are other children who will not enter into the discussion at all.

Even though a child may talk about an idea, he may paint something entirely different from what he describes. Children have wonderful imaginations when encouraged to use them.

By the time Janice volunteered her last comment, it was evident to the teacher that the group as a whole was motivated to begin to paint.

TEACHER: "All of you seem to have lots of good ideas. Why don't you go right ahead and paint them without discussing them any more?"

THE WORK PERIOD

After such a stimulating motivation, the third-grade group of children were eager to begin to paint. With this last suggestion from the teacher the children began the wonderful *outpouring* of creative expression that is the very core of art work. The teacher took the lead during the motivation; now each child takes the lead for himself. For the next several minutes the children work intently. The teacher steps aside but does not withdraw from the group. During this first beginning period of intense personal expression the children work in a concentrated manner, usually quietly, trying to get all their ideas into organized form.

Because there is no active work for the teacher to do at this time, she may be tempted to fill in the time by doing some other work such as reports, correcting workbooks, or preparing work for another class. When she does, she withdraws from the art activity. There are few other situations in school in which the child feels so much on his own as he does at this time. The child needs to know that he has the support of his teacher while he is working so hard. The teacher should be in a position where the children can see her and where she can give an encouraging smile and nod of her head to anyone who looks to her for some little indication of her support. Her role, although an inactive one, is important to the children.

This period of outpouring is the basic, vital core of the art lesson as far as the child is concerned. The child depends upon the teacher to protect him from interruptions. Any break in the child's concentration could mean a discontinuance and lack of contact with his creative art activity. An interruption, even a temporary one, can displace, with another emotion, the feeling he has already associated with his art. Such interruptions can change the course of his work or disturb the child so that he finds it difficult, if not impossible, to continue the intense outpouring at this stage of his work.

GUIDANCE

After the initial stage of expression, children work more slowly and less intently but just as seriously. They were pressured by their desire to put feelings and ideas into form. This, when partly accomplished, often results in a slower pace of work. The child is mentally active in probing deeper into his subject and into his feelings for material to complete the expression of his ideas. Relationships between what has been done and what else he decides to do must be established. Not only are ideas associated with his original subject included and put into a meaningful relationship or organization, but what the picture needs from an aesthetic standpoint also receives consideration. The child may decide to put a tree in a certain spot simply because it would make the picture look better, or he may decide to omit something about the subject that he recalls. He may think, "I could put all the bases and the fielders in this picture of myself batting a baseball, but if I do they would all be too small and my picture wouldn't show up well." He may consider one possibility after another before deciding what to do. He may be influenced in his thinking by color. He may think, "In this picture of Larue and me taking a walk in the woods I could put some more trees over in this corner, but it might make too many trees the same. I could just color it green for grass, but the trees are green. I might have too much green. I could put in a house or a stream of water or rocks."

This evaluation is best done by the child without adult or any other interference as long as the child can carry it alone. His decisions will be based on previous learnings.

During the first intense outpouring of creative expression the child feels alone. He is concentrating deeply upon his work, which is unlike any other. After the first flood of expression is over, his first reaction may be to re-establish contact with his group. Children approach this differently. Sometimes a child looks around at his neighbors just because he has felt alone for a while and likes to see that they are still working at their art, too. Another child might want to show his work to his neighbor for a bit of approval as encouragement to go on. Another may hold it up for the teacher to see.

Now is the time when the teacher becomes more active. She moves among the children doing little more than looking at their work. During this period of self-evaluation and decision, children need the teacher's support. Although the teacher may plainly see room for improvement in much of their work, she should refrain from offering suggestions based on her adult judgment. As a teacher, she should project her thinking into every child's different problem and try to see and to understand what each is doing. Children want to solve their own problems; they also want to know that their teacher is right there to support and to help them over a difficult spot (as was explained in Chapter 3, pages 60–66).

During the time the children have been making decisions and working from their self-evaluations, the teacher has been studying their work, trying to understand each child's purpose. This familiarity helps her respond more helpfully to their questions. Children become ready for guidance at different times; some may want none of it, having solved their problems to their own satisfaction. All children need stimulation and encouragement, but the teacher can sense which children are self-sufficient on that day from the manner in which they work and otherwise conduct themselves. (The same children who work in such a confident manner today may need more teacher help at another time.)

As the third-grade teacher works among the children, she meets some of the problems in this way:

TEACHER: "I am interested in this blue area you have here, Mike."

MIKE: "This is my abstract painting, and the blue I just put in there."

The blue was a strong dominant spot on one side of Mike's painting that seemed to overbalance the pale colors on the other side.

TEACHER: "Put your painting up on the chalk tray, and let's look at it from here. Sometimes we see our picture from a little different point of view if we look at it from a distance." [Mike put his painting on the chalk tray, walked back, and stood beside the teacher.]

TEACHER: "The blue does look well, doesn't it, Mike? It shows up very well."

MIKE: "Maybe I should make some more blue in it."

Mike felt proud that the teacher had made such a favorable comment about his successes and so he wanted to build more onto what his teacher admired.

TEACHER: "Where could you put it?"

MIKE: "In between those places on the other side between the white and the pink."

TEACHER: "That's a good idea. It usually helps to use a color in more than one place."

Mike could see that repeating of the blue would add strength to the other side of his composition. As a final remark the teacher had stated a general art principle that applied to Mike's problem. Mike thus learned that repeating or balancing or distributing color is a good way to make a painting look better. He would remember this principle, because it had applied directly to his own work. Mike had learned something that would help him better express his ideas in art, would give him more satisfaction in his finished art product.

Probably some other children in the group were interested in looking at Mike's painting on the chalk tray and hearing the conversation about it. They, too, would learn something about color distribution, but probably would not remember it as well as Mike did because at that moment it was not their personal problem.

The teacher led Mike toward seeing for himself what he needed to do. Through pointing out his achievement to Mike she helped him focus upon the strong point in his painting. Although the teacher could plainly see that his painting was out of balance, she did not approach her discussion with Mike from this adult and negative viewpoint. She spoke to him of the strongest point in his work. Because he knew that the bright blue area was a strength, he realized that another area of his work needed more strength. So Mike suggested that he put some blue on the other side. There are more mature ways in which this problem could be solved. There are many more solutions that the teacher could think of. Perhaps Mike's suggestion was not what the teacher had in mind as she considered his painting, but she was quick to grasp and to approve Mike's solution.

We cannot expect an eight-year-old boy to solve his problems as a mature adult would. We cannot expect a graduate of the second grade to solve a problem as a college graduate would. We cannot expect *any* other person to solve his problems as we would. The teacher is the one who should reach out to the child. She should adapt her thinking to his and not expect him to try to fit her pattern of thinking.

Mike did not carry the solution of his problem very far as he and his teacher looked at his art together, but he did make one step in learning. He made a suggestion as to how he might bring the other part of his painting into somewhat the same strength as the blue area. This is enough to expect from a child in one art class. Even though the teacher and perhaps other children in the group could see areas they would change, the suggestion of such "help" could make a child feel he had not accomplished very much and that it was not satisfactory. A child needs to feel that he has succeeded, and that he has built and can build upon his successes.

Jack's hand was urgently signaling to the teacher, and she went immediately to the distress area. As she approached him, Jack said: "I can't draw it."

TEACHER: "What can't you draw?"

JACK: "Me hitting a ball. I can't draw it."

TEACHER: "You want to make a picture of yourself hitting a ball, and you can't draw the arms. Isn't that it? [Jack nodded his head.] I can see that you have drawn yourself very well, but I can also see that you have been trying to draw yourself holding the bat."

JACK: "I don't know how to draw the arms."

TEACHER: "You know how to bat a ball, though."

JACK: "Yes, I know."

TEACHER: "Take this yardstick and show me how you do it."

Jack knew very well how to bat a ball. He had done it many times, but now when he came to draw a picture of the action, he had difficulty. When he held a bat in a ball game, he concentrated upon the action and not upon the actual visual appearance of his arms. The teacher asked Jack to hold a bat this time so he could focus upon the position and action of his arms.

TEACHER: "Look at your arms. How do they bend?"

JACK: "They bend up."

TEACHER: "Do they go straight up from your shoulders?"

JACK: "No, they go down then bend up."

TEACHER: "One crosses over your body. Do you see where it crosses over in front of you? Do you see which hand is the upper one on the bat? Is your right arm close to your body or far away?"

JACK: "The arm halfway down is close, then it goes out to the bat."

TEACHER: "Now let Kenneth hold the bat, so you can see how it looks when someone else does it. Do both arms bend alike?"

JACK: "No, the one that goes across his body is wider. Now I know how to do it." [He successfully continued his drawing.]

Jack was led, through the guidance of the teacher, to a deeper knowledge of the way his arms and hands function and look in holding a bat. The more a child knows, the more intelligently he can express his ideas. One of the keys to better creative art expression is knowledge about objects, people, activity, and the general principles of art.

The art education program evolves around the child and his ideas, imagination, and problems. Teaching develops as an outgrowth of these problems. As the problems confront the child, he is ready for the learnings that facilitate the solution of the problem. Knowledge gained at the time of most intense interest or need is remembered longer. Children not personally involved with the problem would gain little if required to give their attention to it, and would only lose interest in and contact with their own art activity.

Not every child is ready to learn the same thing at the same time. The guidance procedures that accompany creative art experiences provide in a very real way for individual differences. Every teacher knows she cannot explain a thing once and have every child learn it, because only those who are ready to learn will remember. The teacher will doubtless be called on by another child at a later time for help with just such a problem as Jack had in drawing himself holding a baseball bat. The problem may be that of someone holding a broom, or a little girl holding her doll, with essentially the same arm positions. By helping another child toward more specific knowledge the teacher will be repeating her teaching. Some who may not have paid much attention to the first explanation may listen and learn. Some who remembered the first explanation to Jack will profit by the repetition. To the child who asked the question the answer will have a familiar sound and be more easily remembered. Everyone hears, but those most personally involved learn most.

TEACHER: "You're getting along fine, Maxine. Keep right on going."

Maxine looked up and smiled in response to her teacher's remark. She was having no difficulty at the time and seemed to be self-sufficient. The fact that the teacher recognized this and seemed pleased by it was encouraging to the child. Maxine received a challenge toward further achievement or broader development of her idea when the teacher said, "Keep right on going." Every child needs help. Every child needs encouragement. Every child needs a challenge to stimulate him to the extent of his ability. The gifted and the independent can become indolent if not challenged.

Just because she seemed not to be faced with a difficult problem at that moment was no reason why the teacher should pass Maxine by. Certainly it is important for the teacher to help those children who are having difficulty, but it is important for the teacher to help the others as well. *Every* child is important. Since we provide for individual differences in American education, we provide for the capable as well as the less able. We provide for the self-sufficient as well as the more dependent ones so that each can be helped toward fuller development of his abilities. The range of maturity within a group broadens with every new experience.

Judy had stopped working on her painting and was still looking at it and apparently thinking about her work when the teacher approached her. In the center of her page, Judy had painted a picture of a girl jumping rope and had added nothing more. Judy had held the paper in a position that gave it much more width than height, so there was considerable amount of empty space on each side of the girl skipping rope (31). Judy had thought about one person doing one thing and not about any other people who might have been involved in the activity or about any environmental relationships.

TEACHER: "You did a good job of painting this girl jumping rope, Judy. The rope is swinging over her head, her arms are out to the sides, and she is holding the rope with both hands. Where is the girl, Judy, in the town or in the country?"

JUDY: "In the town, on our sidewalk."

TEACHER: "How would I know this when I look at your picture?"

JUDY: "I could put in the sidewalk."

TEACHER: "Yes, you could. What else could you add that would tell more about where she is jumping?"

JUDY: "I am jumping rope by my house, so I could put my house in."

Remotivation is a part of guidance—perhaps the most important part. The teacher realized that Judy had concentrated on her painting and on representing herself doing what she liked to do, and that she needed to think more deeply about related ideas. This is not true of every child who paints one figure in her picture and stops. Sometimes the one figure so fills the area or is formed in such a way that it satisfies the feeling being expressed, and nothing else needs to be added. Such a judgment has to be made by the teacher before she comments. The teacher makes this judgment from the depth and maturity of her experience with art. She probably decides that the page looks empty, that the figure is not in relationship to the size of the space on which it is drawn, or that one figure alone on the page would have been better related to the space if the paper had been held the other way.

However, the teacher does not say these things to the child. In elementary school the child is concerned with his own purposes. He has yet to learn much art knowledge that will help him see further possibilities in the development of his own work, so the teacher refrains from imposing her own judgments upon him. Rather, through comments and questions about his intention and ideas related to it, she guides him toward deeper and broader thinking about his ideas. The teacher studies the child's work from the child's viewpoint, trying to understand his purposes. She then communicates with him in terms of his own understandings that are consistent with his purposes. That is why the teacher questioned Judy about where she was and included a need for environmental relationships. Such a question as "Where is the girl, Judy, in the town or in the country?" seemed logical to Judy. The question was an easy one for her, and the answer was quite obvious. She sensed immediately the need to tell more, to think more deeply, and to relate her idea to other objects. Such insights help the child to better understand how to express his ideas. Through his own attempts and through understanding of the relationships as they apply to his own work, the child learns some valuable things about color, composition, and expression. The terms used are within the vocabulary of the child and are consistent with his purposes on that day for that problem. The teaching has been personalized to him during the guidance.

When the teacher first began to talk to Judy about her art, she referred to the figure in the picture as "the girl." The last statement made by Judy revealed that her real intention was to draw a picture of herself jumping rope: "I am jumping rope by my house." Children frequently put themselves into their pictures. They are more interested in their own activities than in the activities of others, so it is natural for them to choose for their art the subject in which they are most interested. In an oral discussion the child does not always reveal this intimate involvement. He is sensitive to the intimacy and is afraid of exposure and possibly being hurt by the reactions of others to his ideas and the way he has expressed them. Therefore, he often discusses his art in the third person. It was only after friendly teacher interest was established in this particular picture that Judy felt sure no embarrassment or hurt would come to her. She felt confident in her trust of her teacher. This trust carries over to some extent to the next dealings that Judy has with her teacher but may not entirely replace her caution about identifying herself with ideas and feelings that she feels are personal or intimate. A new situation is faced by Judy every time she undertakes a new art problem. Trust in her teacher and in her classmates is built slowly and can quickly be destroyed. We all learn this as we grow up. Judy, like all of us, is cautious.

TEACHER: "Are any other people with you or near you?"

JUDY: "No, I was by myself."

The teacher, feeling that Judy had gained something by individual attention, moved on to another child.

TEACHER: "Are you finished, Harold? [Harold nodded his head.] Do you want to get another sheet of paper and paint some more?"

Harold did not answer. He liked to paint, so he immediately put his completed painting in a safe place to dry and got another sheet of paper. There was, he felt, no need for conversation on this point. It seemed as though he was just waiting for his bit of attention from the teacher. He also wanted further assurance that he could paint some more and that there was time to do it. Not all children work at the same speed, of course. Some will complete two paintings while others are still working on their first, as mentioned earlier. Then, too, some children attempt a more difficult subject or carry their idea farther than others do. Through guidance, provision is made for problems arising from individual differences as they occur.

The teacher noticed that several of the children were using the same paint brush with different colors. The outcome was that colors were beginning to be mixed in the large jars of paint. When the class had started, there was a brush put into each jar of paint in order to keep each color in its original hue. Provision was made for mixing paint by making available the small water pans used in water-color painting. The child could mix paints as he chose. Several of the children were using more than one jar of paint and, instead of using the brush found in each different paint jar, were using one in the red for a while, then putting the same brush into the white, and then into the yellow. As a result the white was turning pink and the yellow becoming more orange. Since several children were involved, the whole group needed guidance at this point.

TEACHER: "Children, I think many of you are forgetting about keeping each brush in its own color. Some of our colors are getting mixed and are more difficult to use. Some of you who are putting the same paint brush into different colors really don't want to mix colors. You are just forgetting to change brushes. [The teacher went over to the table where the paints were. Picking up one jar, she said:] See, this was plain green when we started, and someone has put a brush with black paint into it. [Showing the paint to the class, she said:] If anyone were looking for green, he wouldn't want to use this jar. Try to remember to use the brush that is already in the paint in order to keep the paint a clean color for yourself and for others."

This procedure is group guidance. The teacher is not telling the children what to paint or how to paint it. She is helping with the use of materials. It is the responsibility of the teacher to give guidance to children in ways that will help them express their ideas more freely and more to their satisfaction.

VIRGINIA: "I can't find any blue."

TEACHER: "Does anyone have any blue paint that he isn't using at the moment? Virginia needs some."

JERRY: "I have some here, but I'll need it again in a minute."

TEACHER: "Will you need to use it for very long, Virginia?"

VIRGINIA: "I just want to paint the sky. Then I'll bring it right back to you, Jerry."

The teacher should help the children learn how to share, as she did with Jerry. She should also suggest that a child not take advantage of this sharing and generosity by saying, as she did to Virginia, "Will you need to use it for very long, Virginia?"

JIMMIE: "See, I painted a boat in a big storm."

TEACHER: "Yes, you did. You made it a very frightening storm, too. The lightning is all around the boat. Is your painting finished?"

JIMMIE: "Not yet."

Although this was simply a picture of one object in the center of the page as Judy's painting of a girl jumping rope had been, the effect was quite different, and the way the teacher functions with the children would also be different. Judy's composition looked as though it needed related objects to make the expression more meaningful, so the teacher in her guidance role remotivated the child in this direction. Jimmie's picture of a boat seemed most effective alone on the big sea with the lightning flashing all around it. The very loneliness of the boat made it seem more helpless and more acutely affected by the storm and big waves. The teacher, realizing this as she looked at Jimmie's painting, commented upon his achievement, simply leaving him to complete his painting.

Illustration 27 is typical of the way two children, who sit close to each other, become interested in each other's art work. Although children do take an interest in what their friends are doing, they are not looking around for ideas to copy. If the teacher has placed a premium upon originality, each child will want to persist with what he has undertaken regardless of what his neighbors are doing.

In the photograph both second-grade children have chosen different colors of paper to begin with and continue to make individual selections and decisions throughout the working process, creating very different art work.

The next photograph (28), taken the following day when the cut and paste compositions were completed, shows the same boy with his completed art. He has made some of his figures perpendicular to the base or background, giving his work a sculptural effect rather than a two-dimensional effect that most of his classmates achieved.

In guiding children, the teacher avoids interfering with such friendly communications between children unless they are disturbing others. She does, however, come to the aid of a child who has trouble with such technical parts of his art as supporting vertical figures so they stand erect, for example. Her suggestions, in these instances, do not interfere with the free flow of creative thinking; nor do they impose her ideas upon a child. They do, in effect, facilitate the children's creativity and prevent discouragement.

JUDITH: "This is the fire truck. It has just been shined. The firemen keep it in the place across the street from our house, and I often watch them working and fixing it, and once they gave me a ride. I was away up on the high seat, and I was afraid at first, but it was good. This is the fire truck."

TEACHER: "What are you going to do now that your painting is finished?"

JUDITH: "Maybe I could paint another picture of the fire truck."

TEACHER: "How would this one be different? [No comment from Judith.] What could the men be doing to the fire truck?"

27

Children are interested in many things, including what others are doing. When teaching emphasizes originality, children do not copy even though they take an interest in each other's ideas.

28

The next day when the cut paper compositions were completed, each showed the original ideas of the child who created it. Bill (also pictured in 27) gave his figures a three-dimensional effect. He said, "This is a man talking to a bird, and there is a snake coming to join the conference."

The teacher asked this question to help Judith see more deeply into the problem, to guide her away from the possibility of repeating the same subject in the same way, and to associate the action and purposes of the men with the truck. Action and movement make pictures more interesting, and knowledge of this principle of art, when understood and applied, helps children to improve their art work. The teacher indirectly pointed this out to Judith but without undue emphasis, since she knew that good teaching involved many repetitions with a variety of situations.

JUDITH: "Oh, I know. I could make the men shining it. No, I will make the men fixing it and folding the hose. Or I could make them giving me a ride."

Judith was full of ideas and inspired by the excitement of her subject. She needed no further help from the teacher.

TEACHER: "Go right ahead, Judith, and start your painting. But there isn't much time left. Do you want to start it and finish it another time or do something else for a few minutes and save that painting idea for some later day?"

The teacher's reminding Judith that only a few minutes of time remained confronted her with the problem of an unfinished painting. The choice was Judith's. The teacher did not follow the easier course of making the decision for the child.

JUDITH: "I guess I won't paint my idea now. Could I draw it with my crayons on a little paper? Then I could keep it in my desk and do it in the mornings or something."

Judith made a decision that seemed to serve her best at that time. Children will and can make intelligent decisions when given an opportunity to do so.

TEACHER: "Boys and girls, there are only a few minutes left to complete your painting. Those who have finished can read their library books or get a piece of drawing paper at the end of the table and draw or cut."

The foregoing conversations and comments about guidance give an example of how the teacher functioned with every child in the group. She did not bypass any child. It is not necessary to spend much time with each child, but it is important to personally contact each and to give him some help and inspiration. Personal attention to individual and group problems is the purpose of guidance.

EVALUATION

Much of the teaching of aesthetic qualities, color and form relationships, and of the understanding of individually different approaches to art expression is done through the evaluation of the completed art work. This is the time when the teacher and children discuss together the strong points in the art products and analyze why they are considered successful or what qualities and relationships make them interesting. It is important for children to recognize qualities that give a piece of art work its strengths, unity, interest, emotivity, consistency, and appeal. It is also important for the child to understand *why* certain art works are regarded as having one or more of these qualities. *How* the artist has achieved these results is vital if the child is to understand the work and gain knowledge and insights that will help him more adequately to express his own ideas.

29
Children can be creative with stencils when they design and cut their own and use them in new ways.

A recognition and analysis of achievements is enough for children of this age. As the child grows and matures through secondary school there is time enough to include an attitude and approach of how weaker areas might be improved. He must feel confident in achievements before he can accept a discussion of his shortcomings. Comments should be carefully made, be worthwhile educationally, and be inspirational, for these statements influence growth and direction in art. A child may not be aware that something he has done in art has quality until someone points it out to him. Consider the exhilarating, far-reaching effect of this teaching process alone. The evaluation should be a joint discussion guided by the teacher to:

(a) Keep the discussion moving.
(b) Keep the discussion on a positive level.

(c) Recognize the work of every child.
(d) Add to and fortify the children's learnings.

The finished art products need to be seen as they are evaluated. There are different ways of doing this. They can be hung or held by the children as they are discussed. In this particular third-grade class all the paintings were hung indiscriminately in a place where each could be seen well by every child.

TEACHER: "Your paintings look very attractive. Let's talk about them a little while before we begin our next art project. What makes them so attractive?"

SAM: "They are all different. That's why."

SANDRA: "You have to look a long time to see each one."

TIMOTHY: "Every time I look at them I see ones I didn't see before or something different."

ALICE: "Let's hang them out in the hall so the other rooms can see them. I want my brother in the fifth grade to see how well I can paint—how well all of us in third grade can paint."

TEACHER: "How many would like to have these paintings hung in the hall when we finish talking about them?"

The teacher, following the lead of one child, let the whole class decide whether or not to accept the suggestion.

TEACHER: "The paintings as a group are interesting, but so is each one by itself. This first painting is Dominick's. His two airplanes, shooting at each other, are just about ready to crash. The two planes fill the whole paper. Nothing else was needed to make a strong, exciting picture. Because there are not a lot of unrelated things to distract your attention, and because of the action and position of the planes, you feel the excitement and disaster that is about to happen. The bright, intense colors also help to show this feeling."

By the type of statements she makes about the first two or three paintings the teacher sets the tone for the kind of remarks she hopes the children will make when she involves them in the discussion. The discussion period is also a time for the reemphasis of some of the points brought out during the motivation.

Since the expression of emotion is vital to art, the teacher in her comments about the airplane picture explained how the placement of the two planes and the colors helped to communicate excitement and danger. She indicated *what* emotion had been expressed and explained *how* the child had shaped and colored the forms to express it. She also commented upon the directness of the work by saying that the two planes filled the page and intimated that the child had been wise in not adding more to his composition.

TEACHER: "I am sure you all notice the beautiful, big, blue lake in this picture. It shows up well because Alice has painted it a dark color and painted the sandy shore and grass around it a very light color. The light yellow sandy beach and light green grass make us feel the warmth of the day. The fact that she has painted the sun large with rays coming out from it also helps us feel the warm day. It makes the cold blue of the water more inviting."

ALICE: "That's our cabin back by the pine trees. The lake water is cold when we first get in. Then it feels good to get out in the sun."

In Alice's painting, the blue lake was the dominant object. It could be seen from any part of the classroom. The teacher called attention to its strength. Her explanation of its size and dark blue color, which was surrounded by a contrasting light color, helped the children understand *why* it had such a strong appearance. As she mentioned the warm light colors of the grass and beach in addition to the size and shape of the sun, she indicated *what* the feeling of the picture was and *how* Alice had been successful in expressing it. Alice was quick to appreciate her teacher's comments. Her statement about the physical effect the water and sun had upon her was almost a repetition of what the teacher had said, only interpreted into her own personal experience. Alice wanted to identify herself with the comments of success made by the teacher about her art.

Alice and all of the children learned something about the effect of light and dark colors through the teacher's comments and by seeing how Alice had worked it out. One explanation of an art principle or knowledge will provide only an introduction. Many repetitions are required before most of the children learn and understand it.

TEACHER: "What do you find interesting about Jack's picture?"

After setting the example to children of how to approach the discussion of art, the teacher gave the children an opportunity to take an active part in the evaluation.

DORIS: "The batter is big and you can see him easily, but the part I like is the way he made the crossing line for wire way in the back to protect the people watching. It looks kind of lacy."

SAUL: "That red ball suit on the batter looks nice. It makes him show up."

TEACHER: "The red does help make it show up because it is such a bright shade. The wire fence helps the picture because the parts are small in size beside the large player. A variety of sizes and shapes makes most art more interesting."

Doris knew what made the picture attractive to her, but she was not able to analyze how the child had accomplished it. To recognize the area of success is a valuable achievement for a third-grade child. The teacher, realizing that it takes much more knowledge and deeper insight to decide why it is interesting, added this information herself.

To supply new information is part of her role as a teacher. Children's own art provides excellent examples for the teacher to use in teaching.

30

Sometimes the expression of an emotional reaction motivates a child's art. Margaret said of her work, "I was sled riding down a hill last night. It was snowing all around, and the wind was blowing so hard, I just screamed."

Children hear her talk about it and see an actual illustration of it. Being more interested in their own work than in that of others, children pay more attention to the discussion of it than they otherwise might do. This fortifies learning.

ANDREW: "I like that next picture about jumping rope. It looks like a girl jumping rope, but I can't tell what the other parts are. They look more like just a design or something. It all looks kind of like an abstract. I thought it was at first. Now I am sure that is a girl jumping rope. Anyhow, I think it looks good."

Andrew's observations and judgments were based upon his appreciation of the total effect of the beauty of the work. He was not coerced by the teacher to say why he liked it. At times this can be a difficult question even for an adult to answer. The teacher knew this. She also knew that children would begin to explore reasons as their knowledge grew. Andrew was beginning to make judgments based upon aesthetic qualities. From other experiences in art, he had learned that it was not important to be able to name the objects in art work.

TEACHER: "Judy's painting is an interesting one because it has such a variety of interesting things in it."

JUDY: "After I painted the girl jumping rope, I made the door to her house. Then I thought I might paint more houses and people, but I felt I would rather make dots and blocks. I just wanted to. I like them."

TEACHER: "Yes. They add an interesting pattern. Everything doesn't have to be real."

The teacher, realizing that it is normal for children to express ideas and feelings both naturalistically and in abstract designs, accepted the fact that Judy had done both in the same picture (31).

SAM: "That next abstract painting makes me feel dreamy if I look at it for a while. I can't help looking at it. I keep looking at it more than some of the others. The lines are all wavy and it makes me feel the same as when I watched the waves at the ocean beach last summer."

Sam could identify himself with Teresa's painting because of a former pleasant experience with waves. To more fully appreciate and enjoy a work of art the observer needs to bring to it his own experiences and a willingness to make some effort to understand it.

TEACHER: "Another quality of Teresa's painting that helps you feel that way is the light, bright coloring. These lines in her picture are

31

Judy must have felt the permissive atmosphere the teacher tried to establish in the art class, for she painted both naturalistic and free-form shapes in this one composition.

grouped, and the spaces between the others are not even. Variety adds interest—variety of spaces between objects as well as variety of shapes and colors. Grouping helps to hold parts of a composition together and gives it some organization."

JOE: "Why did Nancy, in that next picture, make all the trees alike along the road? I think it would have looked better if she had made them different."

TEACHER: "Maybe it would, but they look very attractive this way. Nancy has drawn and painted the road almost like a border pattern or a design. We have some famous paintings made with a row of trees along a road. In fact, there is a print of one such painting in our school near the drinking fountain. It is called 'The Flamingos' by the artist Rousseau. Probably you have noticed it. Along the edge of the water Rousseau has painted a row of trees. They are almost identical. Notice them the next time you look at the picture."

Joe's statements were negative. From the beginning, the teacher had attempted to establish an approach toward recognition of achievements. To reestablish this point of view she immediately identified Nancy's intention with successful works of famous artists. When comments begin to move in a direction inconsistent with the best learning situation, the teacher needs to redirect it.

DOMINICK: "Well, you said a couple of times that variety was good. So I thought we should never make things alike."

Children misunderstand at times. They are also sensitive and eager to do what is expected of them. The examples of work discussed thus far in the evaluation showed variety as a quality worth mentioning. Therefore, it seemed to Dominick that perhaps it was always a desirable element in every case. As he and others hear many such discussions, they will understand that there are various ways of solving every problem in art and that the qualities of every piece of art need to be appreciated in relation to the idea or emotion the artist was trying to express.

TEACHER: "Variety is important, and Nancy has it. She put in the farmhouse, the lane, the barn, and a car. Sometimes repeating the same object can also add interest in another way. You could remember that we mentioned in Judy's picture of a girl jumping rope that the row of dots and blocks helped make it look better. These blocks and dots are just another row of objects that present a pleasant repetition or pattern as Nancy's row of trees do. Repeating an object in a picture can add emphasis. We have to make many decisions as we work to express the ideas and feelings for each different picture."

This discussion provided a good chance for the teacher to remind the children that an art principle did not always hold true in every situation. What is good in one situation may not be in another, and to learn this fact in art as in all other aspects of education requires many reminders in a wide variety of situations and circumstances.

32

Holidays and special events motivate ideas for art. Parts of this Halloween mask are three-dimensional.

33 *(right)*

Speculation about life on other planets interests children, and they sometimes use these imaginative ideas for art, as this child has done.

TEACHER: "I see that the next painting, Patricia's, has some Indians. What impresses you about her work?"

LEROY: "The idea of the Indians around the fire came from our reading-class story. We were reading about how they put war paint on and danced around a fire."

TEACHER: "We sometimes get ideas for art from things we read, and Patricia was successful in expressing her ideas."

Calling upon the group in this way not only varied the approach to discussion, but also involved all the children in the participation of recognizing the most evident area of Patricia's success. By way of such interchanges they see the effect of appreciation upon interpersonal relationships, feel the personal satisfactions and confident feelings that are developed, and also enjoy the friendly attitude that is promoted among their classmates. Such an approach to a discussion of children's art has values for the art education of the children. It also has deeper values of building understanding among people.

TEACHER: "The last painting is Jennie's. What do you like about it?"

MARGARET: "It's so plain. I can see all of the edges. She didn't let the colors run together. She kept the edges neat. You have to work carefully to get it so neat."

TEACHER: "Her colors are clear, too. She kept her brush clean. If we don't clean the brush after each color, they get mixed. Of course sometimes we purposely do this in order to mix colors. We can do different things with paints. Colors can be mixed, or they can be kept bright by cleaning the brush after each use of color."

After each child's work had been commented upon, a committee of children was selected to hang the paintings in the hall.

Seeing their art work displayed in a place where many other children and teachers see it is stimulating and satisfying to children. They enjoy the attention of older and younger children to their work. Children's creative art work improves the appearance of a school. Its colorful quality brightens a room or hall and makes it look more cheerful. The fact that each piece is different makes it interesting.

During the process of working with children in creative art, the teacher sometimes functions in a general way with the whole group and on an individual basis with each child. The teacher needs to develop enthusiasm as she motivates, guides, evaluates, and exhibits their art. Through her questioning, she stimulates their ideas for art. By sensitively projecting her thinking into studying their art, she approaches the guidance of their individual problems. As she guides and provides comments during the evaluation, the teacher is educating the children through art. Appreciation for the achievements of the children is the foundation upon which the teacher builds the discussion of the completed work. Since art is visual, it needs to be seen to be appreciated. Sometimes it needs to be viewed several times to be understood or enjoyed. Therefore, every child's work should be exhibited in a place that makes such study possible.

SUGGESTED ACTIVITIES

1. *Discuss his art with an elementary school child. Try to discover:*
   - (*a*) *His attitude toward art.*
   - (*b*) *His attitude toward his ability in art.*
   - (*c*) *What he likes best about art.*
   - (*d*) *His feelings of inadequacies through what he avoids or feels that he does not want to attempt.*
   - (*e*) *Why he enjoys his art work.*
   - (*f*) *Whether he does any such work at home.*

See if you can learn any or all of these things through a friendly discussion. Try to make the discoveries indirectly, if possible, without pointed questions.

Plan what steps you might take as a teacher to broaden this child's knowledge or increase his interest in art. What specific art activities would you provide for him?

2. *By referring back through the chapter to statements made by the teacher and children, identify the purpose in each by listing them under the following headings:*

   (a) Incentive.
   (b) Recall.
   (c) Emotional association.
   (d) Association of ideas to materials.
   (e) Broadening of knowledge.

5

Teaching Toward Creative Art from a Topic to Interpret

A METHOD of teaching art centered around a broad topic to be individually interpreted was presented in Chapter 1: described and explained on pages 7–9 and evaluated on pages 11–13. When this approach to an art experience is used, the teacher needs to critically examine the contributions made during the motivational discussion and guidance to avoid suggestions that might constrict thinking and narrow choices. There are certain situations in art in which the children profit from a group focus of attention on one general subject or activity such as: the discussion of the works of artists, making their own Halloween costumes, exploring ways of showing depth in their art, experimenting with ways of joining parts of a construction project together, or a broad subject to interpret.

Focusing the art lesson around a specific topic to interpret is usually done only when the teacher has some specific educational purpose in mind: (a) some particular art knowledge to introduce or reenforce that the group needs to give attention to at this time, or (b) to open up a new area of interest to the children. If assigned topics are used as a continuing basis for art, the free open ways of intellectual freedom and individual choices found most abundantly in creative expression are limited. Art education needs freedom from imposed limitations to remain closely related to the nature of art as it is and has always been through the ages, and to apply, as almost nothing else does, the basic educational aim of individualizing instruction.

Expanding the base of children's knowledge and skills which enhance opportunities for (a) improving their art work, (b) deepening their resources for creative thinking, and (c) building independence and confidence can often be done best when focus of the pre-work discussion and the following experience with art materials are directed toward one thing at a time or one aspect of the total art experience. This is especially true with older children.

Often an art experience centered around a topic is more in the nature of a practice lesson that leads to eloquence in art than a fully creative art expression. Even so, the pre-work discussion can contain the pointed teaching aim with the following work experience being free of pressures. The topic chosen should offer the fullest possible spread for individual options and be one through which a child can find personal feelings and ideas of his own. It should also be one which branches in different directions, releasing thinking in expansive and intimate ways, and one with which it is possible to associate a variety of emotional responses.

Sometimes through her evaluation of the on-going art work or of the completed works, a teacher decides what emphasis needs to be given to an art concept or skill and what teaching-learning situation would best implement it. If the explanation and conversation about a particular topic facilitate the purpose of the lesson and at the same time offer depth of intellectual freedom, an assigned topic is educationally useful.

Regardless of this apparent need for specific art educational focus, every art work experience must remain free enough to include opportunities for departure to any degree in any direction. If a child wants to depart from the topic chosen and use a different topic, the teacher accepts and encourages it in this as in any art work.

Three-dimensional art work often focuses around a particular theme or topic, in a very broad way, such as the creating of papier-mâché masks, wire sculpture, mobiles, or puppets. The teacher and children share new and helpful information about the subject, first studying together a variety of types of successful examples. They then consider appropriate materials and working processes. During the next work session the instructive conversation might well include the many kinds of shapes and individual interpretations possible with a mobile or puppet as the teacher helps them bring into conscious thinking the recall of knowledge and its associated emotional responses. This brings to bear imaginative possibilities for further exciting realization of their ideas, as described in Chapter 3 (pages 54–55) and illustrated in Chapter 4 (pages 82–88).

In the case of two-dimensional art, the teaching-learning attention might be given to the problem of the improvement of drawing or shaping the human figure, for example, followed by creating compositions including people to provide opportunities for strengthening concepts about the human figure and to give practice in the skill and facility of shaping them. However, children remain free to use any people in any kind of situation. When the topic can be interpreted from many angles and each child be free to organize and to express the content for his art, the art experience is closely related to creative expression and is educationally sound.

An assigned topic is best used as a tool to implement a learning situation that helps children move toward fuller use of their powers and enables them to create art on a plane consistent with their growing abilities in other fields. If a child may always select his topic, he may avoid certain subjects or processes because he recognizes his inadequacies.

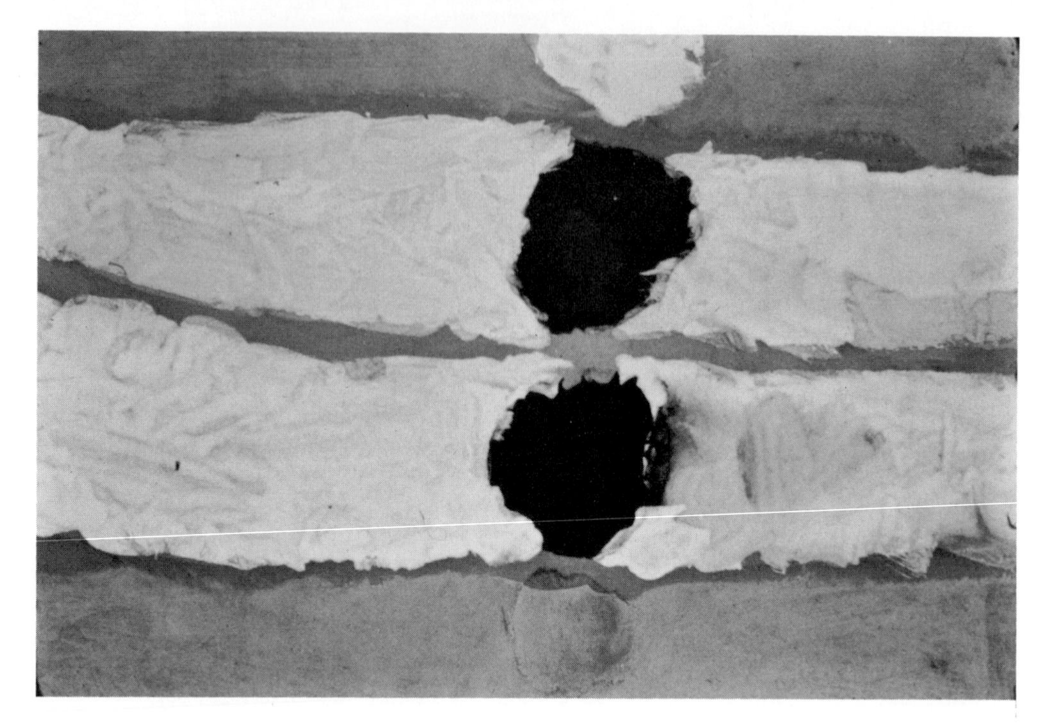

34

35

After seeing and discussing some works of artists that showed strong design quality, the kindergarten children painted, and these are two examples of their efforts.

The examples of child art shown in this chapter illustrate, in each case, how two children, within the same group, differ in their interpretations of a topic common to the group. These same examples illustrate not only differences in children's interpretations but also suggest to teachers other subjects and materials that might be used as a basis for stimulating children toward highly individualized directions.

In addition to these examples refer to and study Illustration 5 in Chapter 1 and the two examples of printmaking (Plates VIII and IX) that reveal not only each child's aesthetic judgment but also his way of using or combining materials and arranging his block printing into a pattern.

The preponderance of drawings and paintings used as illustrations in this book reflects the fact that elementary school children do more drawings and paintings than any other type of art work. Regardless of whether or not we may feel such experiences deserve priority, they outnumber other art activities. Children need many art activities other than flat work. They can easily visualize three-dimensional forms. Children seem to realize that every object occupies its own space, and their flat work often shows indication of this reasoning.

Since the previous chapter dealt with painting and with the younger age group, this chapter will illustrate how a teacher might function with a group of older children who are about to begin a three-dimensional project using materials less frequently used by younger children. Although mobiles can be made by young children, such a project is better suited to the interests and needs of older children. Working out the problems involved in the delicate balance and movement of mobiles fascinates children who are older. Such an art project takes time to execute. Even the introduction of the subject and the discussion of materials and techniques may take several class periods, but older children can continue a project for several weeks if there are new and interesting things to learn and to do.

MOTIVATION

In spite of the fact that mobiles are sculptural forms that are increasingly used, many children may be unfamiliar with them. Some of those who have seen them may not entirely understand the principles of movement and balance that are basic to their structure. For this reason, it would seem desirable to preface the work with either actual or pictured examples of mobiles.

Motion pictures serve especially well to show the grace, balance, and movement of mobiles. The children should have an opportunity to study and to enjoy them by watching them. After this experience, the teacher could call attention to the ever-changing pattern of forms and shadows as the mobiles move and twist and as the light changes. The greater variety of mobiles that children see, the better they will understand the many materials that might be used and the limitations and possibilities of materials as they contribute to balance and to free graceful movement. The teacher might then explain the materials used in the examples and why lightweight substances are necessary. Together the teacher and children should talk about balance, its principles, and how it is achieved. They might also study together the suspension materials and the way the artist has formed the joinings.

Focus on Materials

If the teacher has on hand some interesting and colorful materials from which mobiles might be made, children will want to work with them. There are also many materials that children may have at home and will want to bring to school to use in their project and to help give to it their personal touch. To have children depend upon themselves for some of their structural supplies as well as for their ideas will help them develop resourcefulness. To have them depend entirely upon themselves for all details of materials and equipment may be expecting too much of children of this age. Children in the elementary grades are still dependent on adults and feel secure when they can see that provision has been made for them.

In showing materials to children it would be helpful if the teacher would relate the materials she has provided to the examples of mobiles that the children had seen during the introduction of the project. Showing a sheet of lightweight copper, for example, and pointing to that part of a mobile that had been made from copper, would help children to see the possibilities in that material.

CLARK: "That doesn't look the same as the copper in the mobile you showed us."

GEORGE: "No, the copper in the mobile is shiny. It looks like other copper I have seen. Couldn't it be polished?"

TEACHER: "Yes, but it saves time if we wait until the metal is cut and shaped before we polish it. Why?"

GEORGE: "Because it would only become tarnished again as we handled it. Copper is easy to polish, though. My mother has some good copper polish she used on the bottoms of our cooking pans."

GERALDINE: "If we use that copper, how do we get it cut into the shape we want?"

GEORGE: "Easy. You use metal shears. My dad has a pair I can bring. He lets me use them."

TEACHER: "I have a pair of metal shears right here. Are these like the ones you use, George?"

GEORGE: "Yes, something like that."

As children begin the study of an art project that utilizes materials and tools, such as the copper and metal shears, they should learn something about their equipment before begining to work. When we say in art education that children are free from teacher direction and should carry through their own ideas in a manner personal to them, we do *not* mean that no teaching takes place. When children are taught to use tools safely, to respect them and to take care of them, they are being taught skills and habits that free them to give concentrated attention to the creative part of the job. When children are shown the unique properties of a material and are shown some of the ways it can be used as well as some of its limitations, they are learning in a short time what it has taken mankind many years to learn. They are also saved the discouragement of learning these things by trial and error. They see a skilled teacher bring beauty into a piece of metal, and they are inspired. The teacher does not cut a piece of metal and have each child cut an identical piece in order to teach such a technique. She shows them and lets one or two try cutting a piece, which is enough to give the others the idea of how it is done. They will have a general idea of how to do it and will be ready to try it themselves. As they work with the metal, she helps the children with their problems and teaches additional skills as they are needed.

TEACHER: "Would you like to try cutting a piece of the metal, George."

If the first child called upon to try the new materials and process is one with some experience with it, he is likely to succeed, thus giving the others confidence.

Although there are other things that the children need to learn about metal, at this point the children were just being introduced to a variety of materials.

TEACHER: "I see some of you looking at the rolls of wire. There are different kinds of wire there. One of them is copper, the same as the metal. Which one is it, Jean?"

JEAN: "This one."

TEACHER: "What has this wire been made from?"

NICK: "Iron."

TEACHER: "This one?"

JEAN: "Aluminum, and I think it would be the lightest. Aluminum is not as heavy as other metals."

TEACHER: "Some wire is thicker than others." [She showed the children two different gauges of wire.]

The teacher explained wire gauges and used the word *gauge* repeatedly in her explanation in order to help the children build an art vocabulary and to understand how the word is used.

TEACHER: "What could wire be used for in the making of a mobile?"

ANNA: "The horizontals that the pieces are hung from could be made from that heaviest wire. They have to be stiff enough to hold their shape, and they have to be strong enough to hold the pieces hanging from them."

AL: "They can't be heavy, though, or the air won't move them."

TEACHER: "Is there anything else that we could use wire for?"

ANNA: "Some other parts could be made from it. I was thinking we could make shapes like we did in wire sculpturing and hang those from our mobiles. If we made them from that real thin wire they would still be light enough to move."

MARVIN: "Some of the mobiles had shapes made out of wire, but it looked like they were soldered together. We couldn't do that because we have no stove to heat the soldering iron."

The conversation about the use of the various materials has progressed so smoothly, with suggestions and ideas coming from the children, that it might seem as though this group of sixth-grade children is well informed on such matters. Actually, only a few children in the room had any background at all in using such materials. The teacher brought these informed children into the conversation and used their knowledge and experiences to help with the teaching. It served also to give recognition to these children's achievements. To most of the children in the group the whole idea of working with these tools and equipment was new. For most of the children such words as *solder, gauge,* and *mobile* were new, and the processes were unfamiliar.

SALLY: "Some of the metal in the mobiles was red. Is there red metal or was it painted, or was it even metal?"

TEACHER: "Yes, it was metal that had been painted. Why did the artist do that to only one piece of metal among the many in his mobile?"

The teacher used Sally's question as a cue for calling attention to an *art* aspect of a mobile.

FRANCIS: "It calls attention to that spot in the mobile. That must be what he meant as the most important spot in his mobile."

RALPH: "It keeps it from being too much all the same. You see that spot first when you look at the mobile. Then you see the rest of it."

TEACHER: "Sometimes an artist uses color spots in just that way—to carry your eye from one area to another. We have talked about this in regard to paintings. Mobiles are art compositions, too. Some of the same principles apply. Allen asked a question about soldering a minute ago that we didn't answer. Since we have no heat we will have to use solder that comes in a tube. Solder is used on metal to secure parts together, as paste holds paper together. It would require a great deal of expense and work to prepare this room for heating the other kind of solder. Our fire laws require safety installations before an open flame can be used in a classroom, so we use tube solder."

Safety is an important part of all teaching. In the use of any tools and equipment children need to be reminded constantly of safety measures, and they also need frequent explanations of why safety measures are necessary. The children need to understand the use of the tools before they begin to work. Since they are about to use them, this is the most effective time to teach the skills, techniques, and processes involved. When their interest is high, they want to learn. Such knowledge frees them to create. They know enough about the use of their materials and equipment to work with them, to see what they will do, and to deal directly with the materials as they create.

Each child needs to be given a piece of metal to try out to see what it will do and to acquire some mastery with the tools and metal; he should then be allowed to work with a piece of wire. Since soldering is a new experience, some practice with it should also precede the actual creative total work. A certain mastery with tools and processes allows a child to concentrate on ideas, shapes, organization, and aesthetics as he works. It would be both unnecessary and lengthy to describe procedures for teaching the use of each tool. Teachers do not need detailed instructions about how to teach specific skills; they do need insight into teaching processes involved in art and competence and familiarity with the art project. A teacher must know how to do it herself before she can teach it.

An example of teaching toward creative art through a topic to be interpreted as it is described in this chapter is meant only as an example to be studied, for teachers will develop their own ways. Neither is it desirable to set a pattern for teaching. Teachers do, however, need to study teaching procedures, to evaluate them, and to draw from them whatever help they may find.

TEACHER: "There are some other materials here that could be used in making mobiles. This is balsa wood. What is one feature of balsa that would make it usable?"

ALDEN: "It is much lighter than other wood. Model airplanes are made from it."

TEACHER: "I also have a box of pieces of brightly colored glass."

ALDEN: "The fish mobile we saw had pieces of colored glass inside."

BRUCE: "This white stuff is what we use at Christmas to make decorations. It is certainly not heavy."

TEACHER: "It is called Styrofoam, and these are pieces of colored plastic that you may use."

AL: "Those pieces of colored cardboard. Could we use them, too?"

TEACHER: "Yes, and there are many other materials not here that we might think of to use. What might be one?"

CLARK: "Corrugated paper."

THELMA: "I was thinking about how we made the heads for our marionettes out of papier-mâché. They were lightweight, and we could make it in any kind of shape for our mobile."

TEACHER: "In order to help us think of the many things we might use, let us make a list on the blackboard. We will start the list now, and as you think of something else, write it on the blackboard yourself."

Such a device stimulated thinking and research. It kept changing, growing, and adding interest and knowledge.

TEACHER: "I am going to leave these materials on the table for the next couple of days. You can inspect them and think about how you

36

Jo Ann's drawing of herself wheeling her doll comes from an experience common to most second-grade girls. It looks rainy, so both Jo Ann and her doll have umbrellas, which helps to express an emotional tie between Jo Ann and her doll.

37

Another girl expressed the same subject differently. The main forms are unified by the tree, pole, and wires, and the wires themselves have an unusual pattern of forms.

might use them. You can also consider what you might bring from home to use. The things on this table can be used by anyone who wants them."

By giving the children several days to examine the materials and to collect others, she was also allowing time for ideas and thinking to mature. Children of this age like to plan and will do research when interested.

TEACHER: "These books I have on mobiles will be on the table, too, for you to look at. I have asked Miss Sands to have whatever materials she has in the library ready for you."

Individualizing the Project

TEACHER: "Did you notice in studying the examples of mobiles last week that each one was made with a certain idea in mind? Each had either a theme, a subject that you could identify, or was an abstract. [Showing some of the pictures of mobiles again.] This one is a fish. It is not intended to be an exact form of any particular fish but is a design in wire and colored glass to suggest a fish."

The teacher's statement was the beginning of a discussion about the motifs of mobiles. As the children restudied the examples of mobiles to consider the theme, they mentioned factors about materials and construction not previously noticed.

In spite of the fact that the teacher had shown the children how to use certain materials and tools, they may still be curious about how each artist has achieved particular effects. Since the children, however, are relatively unskilled with tools, they will need help and reminders throughout their work on the project.

ANNA: "In magazines I have seen mobiles that were made for a holiday like Christmas."

TEACHER: "Those are very often made of shapes and materials suggestive of Christmas. Of course, they can be made for any holiday or special occasion. You could make one for a birthday that would have shapes to suggest the interests and the personality of the person having the birthday."

It is the responsibility of the teacher to add ideas to broaden the thinking on a topic. By doing so once or twice during a discussion, she stimulates the children's imagination.

BARRY: "I was talking with my parents about it over the weekend. They had some good ideas, too. My dad is a fisherman, so he was thinking that different fish shapes or even different kinds of trout flies might make good ones. I wouldn't want to do a fish one because one of the mobiles we studied was like that, and it wouldn't seem very original. My mother had an idea I have been thinking about. She said we could hang mine in the stairway because there is a draft there. She said it might be made to go with the living room, and take suggestions from the things in the room—the drapery design and things like that. I was thinking about trying it. We have brass lamps. Maybe I'll use some brass shapes."

Children frequently discuss their school work with their parents. This is part of their independent study before work begins. Barry had several good ideas. The teacher should take advantage of these cues and develop them further without belaboring them, but with just enough comment to stimulate thinking.

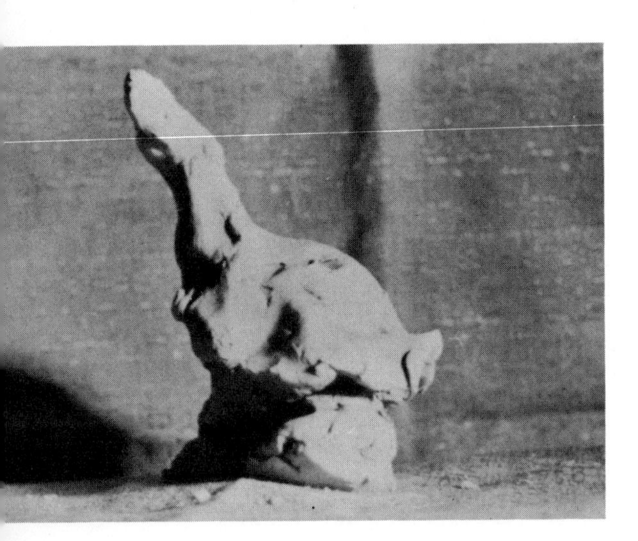

38

The topic for the first-grade class was clay animals. Walter captured the form and gesture of the seal he shaped.

39 (*right*)

Another child in the group modeled a dog. Before the work began, the teacher had guided a discussion of animal forms and movements.

TEACHER: "If we make any art form for a particular spot, it is a good idea to consider the forms and designs already there, so that our art work will be in harmony with its environment. A stairway is a good spot for a mobile because of the air currents. There are always places in every house where the air moves more than it does in other places. These places are fine for a mobile if it makes an appropriate decoration there. It should be hung where it *looks* well as well as where it functions well. What might be another reason why we want to consider the space where it will hang before we make it?"

MARVIN: "The size. In our stairway you would hit your head on it. If we put a mobile in a high place, we can make it to hang down more than if it is in a lower spot. Then how far it reaches out is important, too. It can't bump anything."

TEACHER: "Barry mentioned that he might not like to make a fish mobile because one of the examples we looked at had a fish motif. I see no reason why he could not use the same theme as long as he created the mobile very differently. Does anyone have another idea for a mobile?"

JONAS: "I have a little sister. I could make one to hang on the ceiling in her nursery. She likes to watch things that move. I could use toys for ideas for figures or even nursery rhymes or animals."

ARABEL: "I was wondering how the artist made the holes in some of the pieces of metal he used?"

TEACHER: "You might all like to watch while I do it to see how it is done. Then I can help you individually with it as you work. Why would an artist want to put a hole in a metal form for a mobile?"

PATTY: "I think it makes it look better."

TEACHER: "Why?"

AL: "The hole is a good shape. It isn't just round."

TEACHER: "How can you tell how large to make the hole?"

SIDNEY: "According to what looks well in the shape of the metal you are using."

VICKY: "That might throw the whole mobile out of balance."

MARVIN: "It might be just what you need to bring it into balance. You could do that if you wanted a big piece on your mobile and didn't want the big piece to be heavy."

SALLY: "It must look well. It can't be decided just by balance."

ALDEN: "It has to be decided by balance or the whole thing won't work."

TEACHER: "You must consider both. At every step of the way we must consider how well it looks and whether or not what we have done improves its appearance. At every step of the way we must consider balance and movement, too, or the mobile will not function or even look well."

ANNA: "If it gets out of balance, you just have to figure out some way of balancing it again. That's all."

TEACHER: "There are several things that you might use to suspend your mobile. Think about it in relation to your own problem."

NICK: "The string isn't a very important part of a mobile."

ARABEL: "It is so. Without it the mobile wouldn't stay up."

NICK: "Like that, it is important. But not as a part of what you look at. Like a watch, the works are the important part, but they are closed in a case. You don't see them. Some parts, even if they are important to how a thing works, are not important to how it looks. I think the strings of a mobile are like that."

The teacher felt that the children had reached the point where they were ready to leave the discussion and begin to work with the materials. She also felt that there were some things they needed yet to learn. From her experience she knew, also, that some of the processes discussed and demonstrated would be forgotten or only partially remembered. Many of these things would need to be retaught as the children faced their problems during the working process.

Since many of the materials were relatively expensive, the teacher and children talked about being economical by first planning and cutting trial shapes out of paper.

TEACHER: "There is something else, too, that I think would add interest. Among your books and magazines at home may be articles on mobiles and the artists who create them. We would all profit from hearing some of the interesting things you find. Could we start each art work period with a brief report by one or two of you?"

BARRY: "My mother gets magazines on interior decoration. They often have pictures of mobiles that I could bring."

TEACHER: "Let's use our bulletin board for mobile information from either pictures or short articles."

As the discussion ended, the children began the exciting and wonderful adventure of trying their own strengths and abilities in a new field. Each, with plans and ideas of his own, began working them out. Some were drawing plans, some cutting paper shapes as explorations of possible forms for their mobiles, while others examined supplies and resource materials: each attacking the complex undertaking according to his personality demands at that time.

GUIDANCE

The teacher's responsibilities in guiding the children's on-going work from a topic they are individually interpreting follow the suggestions given for guiding creative expression on pages 60–66 in Chapter 3. To relate the teacher's guidance role to the example of creating mobiles described in this chapter, a few suggestions for guiding it will illustrate this important responsibility which varies as individual problems arise.

The differing character of the materials creates challenges and problems as do the tools, which are new to the children. Sixth graders attempt complex projects. For these reasons, the problems arising as they work are apt to be somewhat involved, and the teacher must be ready for almost any situation. The teacher's responsibility may not be as demanding as it sounds, but her job is to analyze a child's work and, by means of discussion, help him focus upon one phase of the problem at a time. The teacher's role is to guide the child toward seeing his problem in a clearer way, to help him understand it better, and to encourage him to suggest his own solutions. It is also the teacher's duty to help him evaluate his solutions in terms of his purpose, materials, taste, and the accomplishments he has made thus far. The teacher does this through skillful questions and comments. However, the teacher must judge the extent to which she can follow this course by the reaction of each individual child to it. If a child seems to have been struggling with a problem to the extent of impatience, it saves him from further discouragement if the teacher simply points out the problem expediently. Identifying the difficulty is a relief. Discussion of a solution can follow.

For a while, at the beginning of the work period, the teacher becomes less the leader and more the adviser as each child becomes engaged in his own creative enterprise. The teacher, following the lead of the child as he meets and faces problems, becomes a resource. During the work period, which in the case of the making of mobiles will cover several days or weeks, the teacher's major role is that of giving help, but she must also motivate, evaluate, and exhibit, *always teaching* as she works.

INA: "Miss Gray, see, I brought two stones from an old bracelet to use in my mobile. I am going to make mine about my cat and dog. They are always chasing each other around the house and all over the place. I thought I would make a shape of my dog out of metal, and all over it I would cut out little triangles and curve them to make it look like her curly hair. My cat I will make out of wire and stretch gray yarn back and forth over it to make it look woolly. I might even put a mouse in to balance it if I need to. The cat and dog could move back and forth and maybe up and down and look like they're chasing each other, if I can get it. I don't know how to get this green stone in for the cat's eye and this blue one in for the dog."

TEACHER: "One way would be to wrap thin wire around the stone and fasten it once or twice with that wire to the heavier wire that the cat's form would be made of. I have some pictures of stones set that way. You can look at them and then have a better idea of how it looks."

As the teacher explained the operation, she demonstrated it to Ina. In helping Ina with her problem, the teacher proceeded directly toward the solution, because the teacher felt that the setting of a stone was an experience new to the child. Ina was not ready to deal with the stone-setting and would not be for some time, but she felt it necessary to see the entire scope of her project and to understand the solution before she could begin. The teacher did not invite other children to hear the explanation because she felt that few would encounter this particular problem.

RALPH: "When I cut the metal with these shears, it gets curly at the edges. See?"

TEACHER: "The metal can be straightened. [To the class.] How many of you have had some trouble with the edges of this thin metal curling a bit as you cut? [Those who did raised their hands.] You might come up here and watch while I help Ralph straighten his metal. Anyone else who is planning to cut metal can join us if he wishes."

The problem Ralph encountered was one the teacher thought others might meet, so she invited all those interested to watch as she demonstrated. Children who were not facing this problem could continue to work without interruption.

CLARK: "I am using some of this balsa wood, and I want to make a hole in it. How can I get it started?"

As the teacher introduced tools and materials, she demonstrated the use of a hand drill in the boring of wood and had one or two children from the group try it. This procedure was helpful because it gave the children the knowledge that such a thing could be done and an idea of how to do it. However, it was only an introduction to such a technique. Learning takes place best as the actual work is done by the child in relation to his own problem under the guidance of a competent teacher.

TEACHER: "Let's go up to the workbench and try it."

The teacher invited those interested in this particular problem to join them, thus involving the children in the teaching process. The specific teaching-learning situation that followed is typical of the many that arise as the teacher guides the children's work through an art project.

TEACHER: [To the whole group.] "At the end of each work session, you will want to store your materials in a place where you can easily get them when you want to work on them. If you have free time during the day, you could work on your art if you want to."

Provision for additional work time is good because it:

(a) Gives the children who work slowly an opportunity to keep up with the others.

(b) Supplements an enrichment program of education.

(c) Gives those especially interested in mobiles an opportunity to do more.

(d) Gives the children a choice of one more interesting thing to do in their free time.

TEACHER: "From one work period to the next, put all of your mobile tools, materials, and plans in a large container and put it on these shelves."

Definite storage and clean-up information can aid the child in his work and will avoid classroom confusion and untidiness.

PATTY: "I can't hold mine and stretch this string at the same time."

TEACHER: "Ask someone near you to help. [To the class.] It may be that your work will be easier if you help each other. Why don't you work together as you need to?"

As children work on an art project such as mobiles—using tools, metal, and other materials—there is, understandably, a certain amount of noise. The teacher's suggestion that children help each other will occasion some conversation. These sounds are typical of any group of children working in a situation in which they are, to a great extent, on their own. Work noises can be expected. However, the teacher needs frequently to remind the children that handling of tools and materials as quietly as possible will add to good working conditions, as will a minimum of conversation in low tones. Since a responsibility of the teacher is to guard children against interruptions as they work and to protect their right to work without disturbance, she must deal with children who engage in disturbing activities. The fact that art activities involve freedom of decision and of action does not mean that children's behavior breaks down. Courteous, considerate behavior is especially desirable in such a situation.

EVALUATION

In any lengthy individualized art project a great deal of evaluation is done by both the teacher and the children as the work progresses. Much critical judgment goes into each child's choice of theme, materials, shapes, and composition. When the teacher notices an interesting and original piece of work, she often calls it to the attention of the class, explaining why she believes it is interesting.

TEACHER: "Ina has finished the cat form for her mobile. See how the interweaving of the gray yarn has given a fur effect. You fixed the eye in very well, too."

INA: "I am going to try to make her claws move, too, if I can—and maybe her whiskers."

Whenever she found the opportunity, the teacher praised or called attention to some child's work, explaining *why* it was interesting. Therefore, since evaluation took place to such an extent during the working process, less evaluation of the completed art was needed, lest it be repetitious. When the work was completed, the teacher and children appraised it, calling attention to those features of the mobiles that had not previously received recognition.

EXHIBITION

The final major responsibility of the teacher in art is to display the children's completed art. Since art is appreciated through visual activity and emotional sensitivity, exhibiting it is a necessary part of the cycle of activity involved in any art project. Children enjoy the creating of an art project, and they also enjoy their completed work. They want to share with others a part of what is so vital to them. Realizing this need and desire for recognition, the teacher should plan to display the work of the children in whatever way best suits the particular art product.

Most art work can be successfully and attractively displayed in the children's own classrooms, school halls, assembly rooms, or cafeterias. Mobiles, however, present a different problem. Since each requires a certain volume of space for its own movement, few can be shown in the classroom at one time. In the situation that has been discussed in this chapter, exhibition outside the classroom seemed desirable. The class discussed the problem, making several suggestions, and finally deciding to place the mobiles in store windows. The children reasoned that their mobiles would not occupy much of the merchant's valuable window space if they were suspended from the ceiling. They also suggested that the movement of the mobile might call attention to the window display. The children, acting through a committee of their classmates, found enough store windows, and each child hung his own mobile.

During the committee's investigation of available shop windows, the children decided to write articles to present to the local newspaper. They decided to describe mobiles, explain their uses, and summarize the educational values inherent in this project. Their writings included the names of the children who had made the mobiles, identifying each with the particular shop window in which it was displayed. Valuable public relations resulted from the newspaper article that appeared. Some of the outcomes were:

(a) Public recognition received by the children for their work.
(b) Wider dissemination of information on art education.
(c) Better lay understanding of the educational values of an art project such as mobiles.
(d) Closer school and community relationships.

For a more complete discussion of this subject refer back to the section on "Exhibition" in Chapter 3.

The teacher has active and changing roles during the teaching of an assigned topic in art. When she introduced the topic of mobiles to her sixth-grade class, she used a variety of visual materials and led the motivational discussion. Since the work period for this complex activity extended over a few weeks, the teacher had many opportunities to help children on an individual basis with their problems as they arose. She evaluated their art with the children as they worked, often calling the attention of the group to successful and interesting achievements. When the work was completed, attention was directed toward successful areas of the art that had not previously been mentioned. Each child became responsible for exhibiting his own art. Children of this age can and want to assume responsibilities. They want to work independently, to be on their own, and to be grown up.

Art is not an isolated activity that children do in school as a recreational relief from their more difficult academic subjects. Art, as a vital part of children's daily school activities, is related to other phases of school life as well as to other experiences that the children have. Art is just as difficult as any other school subject, but the types of creative thought-provoking problem-solvings involved differ from those in other subjects and thus strengthen its educational value.

Having thought through the mobile project in this chapter, adults can well understand the complexities and difficulties arising in art work. Indeed, this challenge, combined with the independence, the working freedom, and the individual personal expression made possible through art, is responsible for children's enjoyment of art.

SUGGESTED ACTIVITIES

1. *Plan an art project suitable for children in the fourth or fifth grade. Include:*
    - *(a) Some general art aims or objectives to be gained through this project.*
    - *(b) A list of the materials needed.*
    - *(c) Ways of introducing the topic.*
    - *(d) A few questions you might use in the motivational discussion.*
2. *Referring back through this chapter, list the conversational statements that help children learn more about art by building their knowledge and judgments about the* art *qualities of their work.*

6

Art of the Young Child

THE ART that children create from their own ideas and feelings has charm and quality. The characteristics of children's art are different from those of adults' art. To study and understand these characteristics is very rewarding, for additional areas of appreciation and enjoyment are opened. Children's art is, in fact, a true and meaningful art when it is a sincere expression of the child's own personal ideas and feelings.

The type of art with which most people are familiar is found in periodicals, billboards, and newspapers, and is unlike children's creative art work. This type of art, often naturalistic, is frequently in our line of vision; it looks like real objects, and frequently is idealized in style. We become so accustomed to seeing this type of art that the imaginary, creative, design-centered art of children seems "strange." Many people feel that because naturalistic art is so frequently used and because it is what they have learned to accept as art that it is superior. They tend to measure other art expressions by this standard. When we begin measuring children's art or any artist's work against such a background, we are applying a limited kind of adult standard. Children do few things as adults do them. They do art work differently, too. Realizing this difference is the first step toward understanding and appreciating the characteristics of children's art.

The younger the child, the more spontaneous and direct his art work is. His methods of working are direct, and the finished art product he creates gives the appearance and impression of directness and freshness. The young child quickly becomes stimulated by an idea with which he has had some emotional relationship. Any experience that carries with it an emotional reaction is remembered longer and is apt to be the idea he chooses for his art. The stronger the emotional reaction, the stronger the urge to express it.

In order to assure the child's freedom to create, the teacher needs to maintain in the classroom an atmosphere of understanding. Feelings and emotions do exist, and the child's talk about them and his expression of them should be accepted. Feelings and emotions are sensitive, tender spots and, when exposed, must be treated gently. If not, the child tends to hide them and so cannot face his own feelings and emotions. When this happens, his art work suffers because it has to be deeply personal and meaningful to the creator to be expressively done. When the child feels free to discuss his feelings without shame or ridicule, when less socially acceptable emotions are felt, discussed, and expressed in organized form, he feels safe in the adult and sometimes bewildering world in which he finds himself—a world he is trying so hard to understand. The wise and understanding teacher leads him to express his ideas and feelings in art and praises his achievements. In this way the child becomes confident. He faces his ideas and emotions, going directly to the core of an idea and expressing it.

The young child who is just beginning to paint and to work with art materials works rapidly. He creates several paintings or drawings, while a child of six or seven might be doing one. The child of nursery school age is eager to begin. Preplanning has no meaning for him. He paints as he goes. He dips his brush into one color and covers an area of the paper with it. Then he either makes another form or changes to a different color or both. The young child is fascinated with the exuberance of painting. He enjoys the *doing* of it. This does not mean that the forms, marks, or lines he puts on the paper result entirely from the chance physical movements of his arm and hand. Watching the young child work and seeing his seriousness of purpose indicate that there are some mental decisions involved in the process. He seems to decide what color he will use, where he will place his brush on the page next, in which direction he will move it, and when to stop working on each form, as well as eventually deciding that each painting is completed.

There are both physical and mental processes involved in art work. They are both going on at the same time. The child must be concerned about each as he works. For the young child one limitation will, of course, be the extent of his ability. At three years he has less motor control than a child of seven or eight. He also has less ability to create an involved composition because he has had a much narrower background of experiences from which to draw. He also has a shorter attention span which causes him to tire quickly of working on one piece.

Young children, in addition to creating nonobjective art, attempt to draw, paint, or shape people and objects with which they are familiar. They maintain an interest in both forms, often combining them, unless they feel pressured toward art content that can be named and discussed. Because vocal expression is given to objective art and because any attempt to describe nonobjective art seems inadequate, children tend to feel more attention is given to objective products. The child wants *his* art to receive the same attention and appreciation that his classmates' art receives. To gain attention a child may change his style of expression. Teachers must guard against such subtle and indirect influences.

Many adults think that much of what young children do in art is random scribbling. In fact, some give the name of "scribble" to these early art experiences. To those who observe children, however, these early attempts are much more than marks made by random physical movements. Children make some kind of choices of color, vary sizes and shapes, and make some attempt at organization, crude and childish though it is. Some people not only consider children's early attempts at art as "scribble," but they frequently have this same attitude toward the mature nonobjective art of our day. Although the young child creates immature childish free-forms, there is no reason to regard them as insignificant or to intimate that representational objects are more desirable or that they always emerge from such beginnings. Early attempts at representational art are also immature and often difficult for adults to recognize. But the two are different in purpose and meaning for the child as they are for the adult artist. Favorable comments and reactions to both have powerful and long-lasting effects upon a child's feelings to maintain the freedom so necessary in art expression. They also encourage his growing interest in free-forms and his flexibility in moving from this to other ways of art expression.

To help children become more aware of and learn more about the concepts and structure of art, which they need as they need that same knowledge in other school subjects, the teacher takes advantage of the countless educational opportunities to point out areas in their art that show design and color qualities. Even though the accomplishment may not have been done consciously by the child, it is nevertheless there and can be recognized by the trained eye and pointed out by the alert teacher. An important element in child art is this intuitive aspect.

The child whose interest in many types of expression has been kept alive by teachers will have a well-rounded and balanced appreciation for art and more widely developed ideas. During the discussion that precedes creative painting, some child will always say: "Can we just paint?" or "I'm going to paint a design" or "We could do abstracts?" Welcome the idea; your tone of voice can be influential. Art that is simply representational can be dull and lifeless.

In order to draw out a verbal expression of the children's thinking about this type of their art, one teacher had a conversation with some of the children in the primary grades. On the following pages are some of their statements:

TEACHER: "Why do you like to paint these abstract pictures?"

CAROLE: "Whenever you draw an abstract you are drawing something that isn't real. You are thinking, 'I'll just put in some dots or some shapes or something,' so you can do it any way you like, but if you are making some people or dogs you have to make them like they are."

SARA: "Well, I like them because they are not real and you don't have to be real careful to draw it like what it is and worry about staying inside the lines you made, or you don't even have to make lines first. You can change it if you want to. If it is a real picture, it wouldn't look as well when you don't keep in the lines, and you would spoil it."

PATRICIA: "Sometimes when you have a good idea you get good designs in your picture and then you get a real good picture. I like to do them because you can think your ideas any way you want to."

PAMELA: "You don't always have to make a design for a picture. You can make whatever you want to."

BOBBY: "I think they are fun because they are not real. I like to draw the other kind, too."

TEACHER: "How do you feel when you are painting these abstract pictures?"

CAROLE: "Your hands feel loose and it is different from crayons and real. Crayons you hold something like a pencil, but a brush is softer and you go along smoother. I think it feels looser. Painting the abstracts goes the same way."

PATRICIA: "It feels better sometimes to do an abstract because you have to keep in and do what it looks like if you are painting something real and if you are not you don't have to worry about anything like that."

BOBBY: "It feels just freer because if you smear the paint with your hand or something then it spoils what you drew. But in an abstract you can make it into something maybe even better if you try hard. Just sometimes you can do it with the other kind of pictures. And I think your hands are freer because they don't have to be so tight to try."

TEACHER: "How old are you, Bobby?"

BOBBY: "Almost eight."

TEACHER: "Where do you get your ideas for these paintings? What tells you what to paint?"

DAVID: "Your mind. Only sometimes it doesn't come out as right as you want it to."

PAMELA: "As I go along I decide and sometimes I decide my ideas before I start."

TEACHER: "How old are you, Pamela?"

PAMELA: "Five."

CAROLE: "When you start maybe you thought it would look pretty in your mind inside, and then you make it that way, and sometimes it is the other way around. It gets different in your painting and then you see it and you like it or you make it so you do. That's how you get ideas for these paintings."

RICKEY: "You don't get ideas from anyone else or anything. You are free and you can do what you want to do because you just want to do it."

ANN: "I think in an abstract you can be real easy and you wouldn't have to do it real hard or worry."

TEACHER: "When do you paint best—when you worry or when you don't?"

BOBBY: "When you don't worry."

NANCY: "Well, I say it would be best if you worry because when you worry you are just thinking about what you want and you would be thinking it so hard it would come out just the way you want it to."

TEACHER: "Are thinking and worrying the same?"

NANCY: "No. Whenever you think, you know what you might want to do and you do it. But if you worry you are scared and it does not come out right. You get nervous."

TEACHER: "How do you know when your abstract pictures look right?"

BOBBY: "Whenever you see them after they are done then you know they look right."

SARA: "Whenever your page is full and you don't want to make more in it."

The above conversation, recorded in a study of the sources of children's ideas for art, was taken from a tape recording of a classroom discussion between a teacher and a group of children.[1]

There is a wonderful freedom about these nonrepresentational paintings. The child seems to be guided by his own judgment as he works. He feels a new kind of enjoyment in using form and color as they are needed in the composition or as his personality directs their use.

> Without being sentimental about childhood, it seems fair to say that children's thinking may have a freshness, an imagery, a creativeness, which the adult does not always achieve.[2]

> One remarkable characteristic of the art work of most very young children is its extremely high aesthetic quality. . . . Part of this high aesthetic quality is believed to result from the young child's inherent sense of design and the tendency of his early concepts to reduce various subjects to their structural and ideological essence.[3]

CHILDREN'S INSECURITY

Young children are highly sensitive in their early school years as they begin to take their places as responsible individuals in public life. They desperately

---

[1] Blanche Jefferson, *Art Experiences in the Primary Grades: A Presentation through Color Transparencies with Accompanying Script* (Project, Ed.D., Teachers College, Columbia University, 1954).

[2] David Russell, *Children's Thinking* (Boston: Ginn and Co., 1956), p. 305.

[3] Howard Conant, *Art Education* (New York: Center for Applied Research in Education, 1964), p. 61.

I

Sometimes a child paints in a visual manner, at other times emotionally. Linda has painted her house with warm, glowing colors to suggest how it feels to her at night.

II

When a child is free to choose his own subject and to make his own associations, unusual combinations sometimes result, such as Donna's Christmas tree among valentine forms.

III

Since creative expression gives to each child the opportunity to choose for his art the topic that is most meaningful to him at the moment, such diverse work as shown in this group can be achieved. Mary Sara's new dress excited her, and she chose this object as her topic for art.

IV

Jackie experimented with lines and colors in his rich and bold painting.

V

Suzan's two vigorous trees show a full feeling for and a confidence in the expression of her subject.

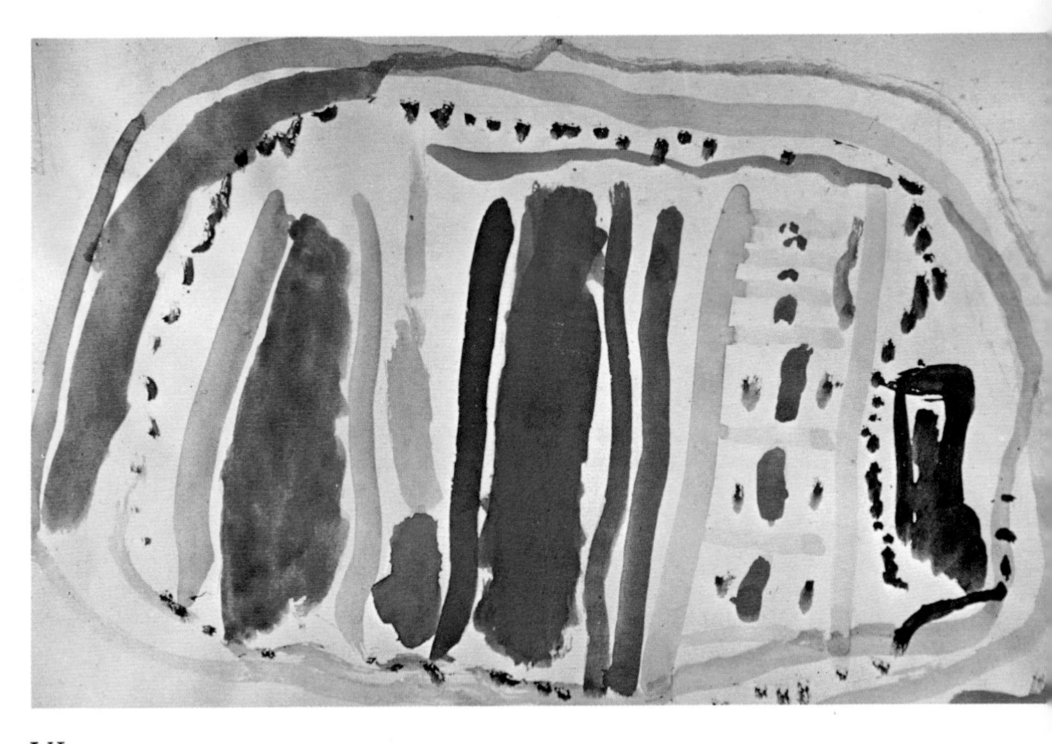

VI

Although children often have difficulty in verbally describing or explaining their abstract art, they create it freely and confidently if they feel their teacher is as receptive toward it as she is toward other forms of expression.

VII

Classroom windows are better suited as display areas for some types of art than for others. The light added a luminous quality to this display made from colored tissue paper.

VIII

These two examples of printmaking resulted from freedom in the choice of ideas for design and in ways of using and combining materials upon which to print.

IX

X

XI

Children's art work often reflects the teacher's stimulation or the lack of it. The first example of Donald's art (X) reflects the lack of stimulation as the topic "The First Thanksgiving" was given to the second grade to interpret. The second example of his art work (XI) shows the influence on his expression of the same topic when a lively motivation and recall discussion preceded the work.

XII

Debby's Christmas tree ornaments (XII) resulted when her kindergarten teacher, in motivating the art, simply said, "Draw something about Christmas." The second drawing (XIII), done later, resulted from an exciting exchange of ideas preceding the art work. Quality teaching inspires quality response.

XIII

XIV

Pam's embroidery reflects her aesthetic judgment and sense of color and design. Children have an innate feeling for color and design, and their art work reveals this quality when they are strongly motivated by what they are doing.

XV

Bob's water color painting characterizes the mood of a rainy day: few people about, dreary colors, and a soaking feeling.

XVI

The excitement of being the center of attraction motivates children and gives them drive to create amazingly complex forms as Sheryl has done in this picture about her birthday party.

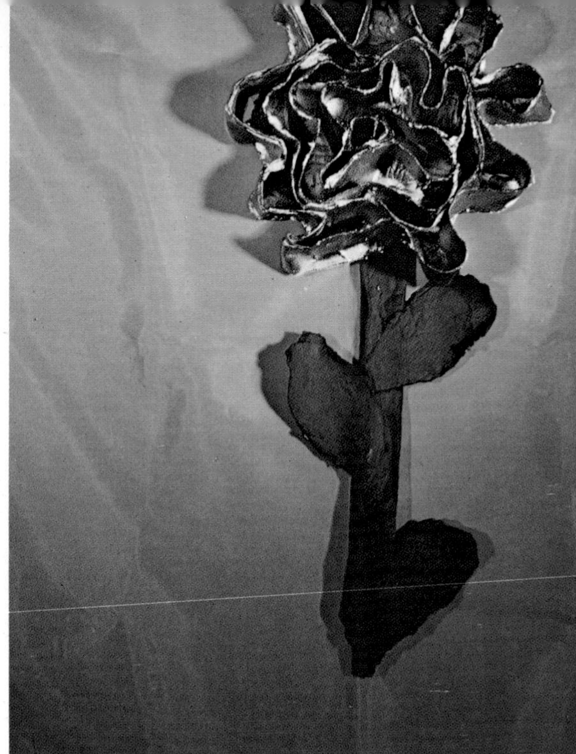

XVII *XVIII*

Large flowers made of paper was the topic from which these two very different examples resulted.

XIX

This child's landscape has many childlike and appealing features. The sun not only has design and form but is a dominant force in this piece of art as it is in our lives. The house windows have pattern and rhythm, and the whole work is an art expression of the out-of-doors.

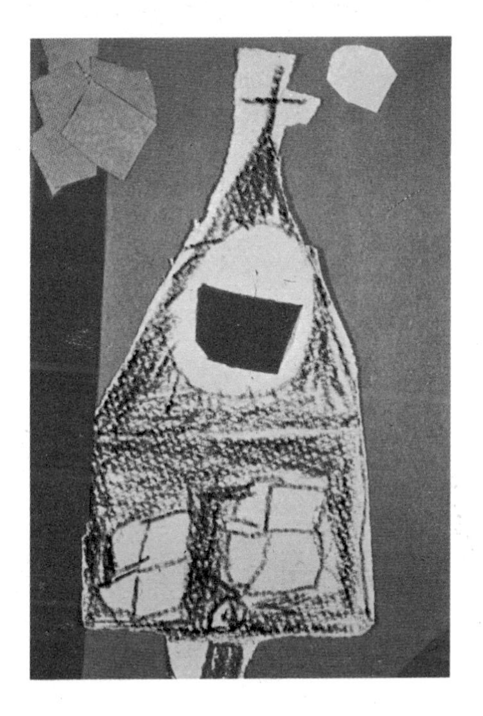

XX

A kindergarten child combined media to achieve this strong and attractive work. An important element in this and all art is the expression of the artist's sensitivity for the subject.

XXI

The irregular edges of torn paper lend a character to this first-grade child's art consistent with the emotional atmosphere of Halloween.

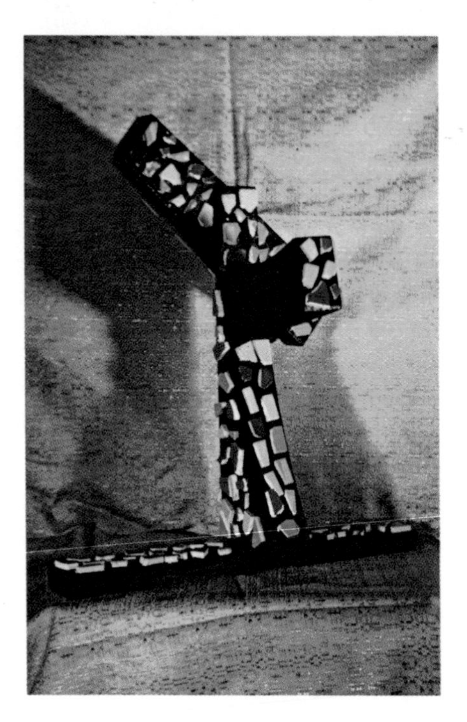

XXII

When a variety of art materials is available, children often combine materials to complete satisfying art forms as this fifth-grade boy has done by gluing mosaic tiles onto his painted wood sculpture.

XXIII

An older child can often achieve more in art than younger children because of a longer attention span, more knowledge to draw upon for ideas, and more patience to work out such effects as the transparencies that express the supernatural quality in this crayon work.

XXIV

Torn or cut pieces of paper assembled as mosaics gives children an opportunity to develop and use texture in their art. Judy's art expresses the lush feeling of summer.

XXV

Even though all children in the group worked with paper mosaics, there was complete freedom of choice in the selection of colors, ideas, and ways of organizing their art work. Dennis' use of colors is unusual as is his composition.

XXVI

Her dog, Boots, "helped" Susie shovel snow. Knowledge and awareness of winter is shown by the snow on the roof of a car, warm red mittens, and the tracks Susie and Boots made in the snow. Rhythmic lines define varying heights of the snow accumulation.

XXVII

Aesthetic and emotional qualities are shown in Kenneth's painting of a mother bird feeding her young. The branches create a design especially against the sun.

violet

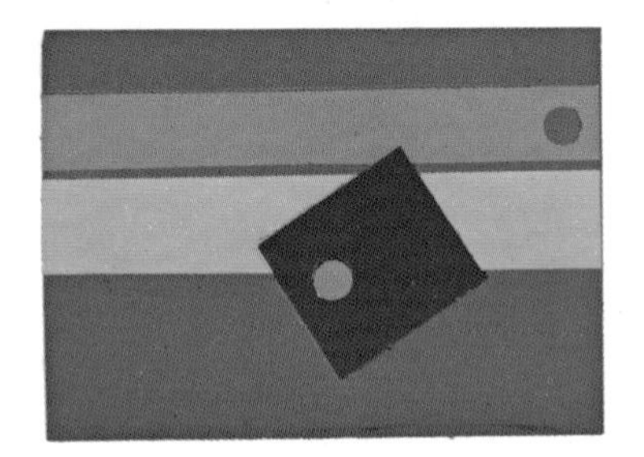

blue

green

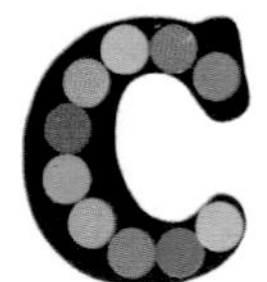
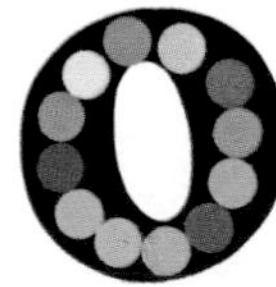
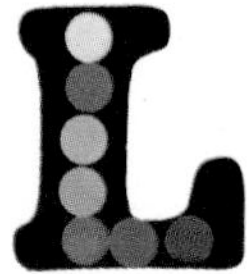

yellow

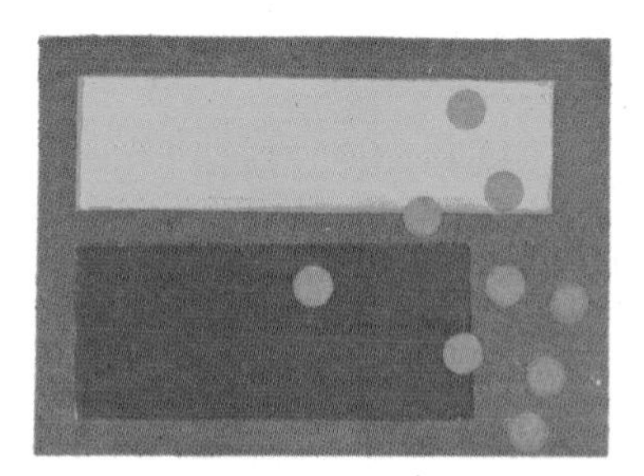

orange

red

XXVIII

Children learn about colors from seeing them and working with them. (Page 65 from *My World of Art*, Book 1, by Blanche Jefferson. © Copyright 1963 by Allyn and Bacon, Inc. Reprinted by permission of the publisher.)

XXIX

Three-dimensional art appeals to older children. As they learn more art knowledge and processes and explore a variety of materials, their skills improve and so does their art.

XXX

After an enriching teaching-learning situation, some children are so aware of the new knowledge that they encounter difficulty in using it immediately. Later they may use it to create well-designed art, as this child has done in art he created at home.

XXXI

Other children react differently and put the new knowledge to work then and there, as this boy did.

XXXII

Older children set high standards for themselves and critically evaluate their own work as it progresses. This self-motivation helps them achieve art work of a higher quality than might be achieved on the basis of an imposed standard.

XXXIII

When older children preplan and have a thorough understanding of the overall processes of tie-dying before it is undertaken, they have little trouble attaining such satisfactory results as Dimitri's work shown here.

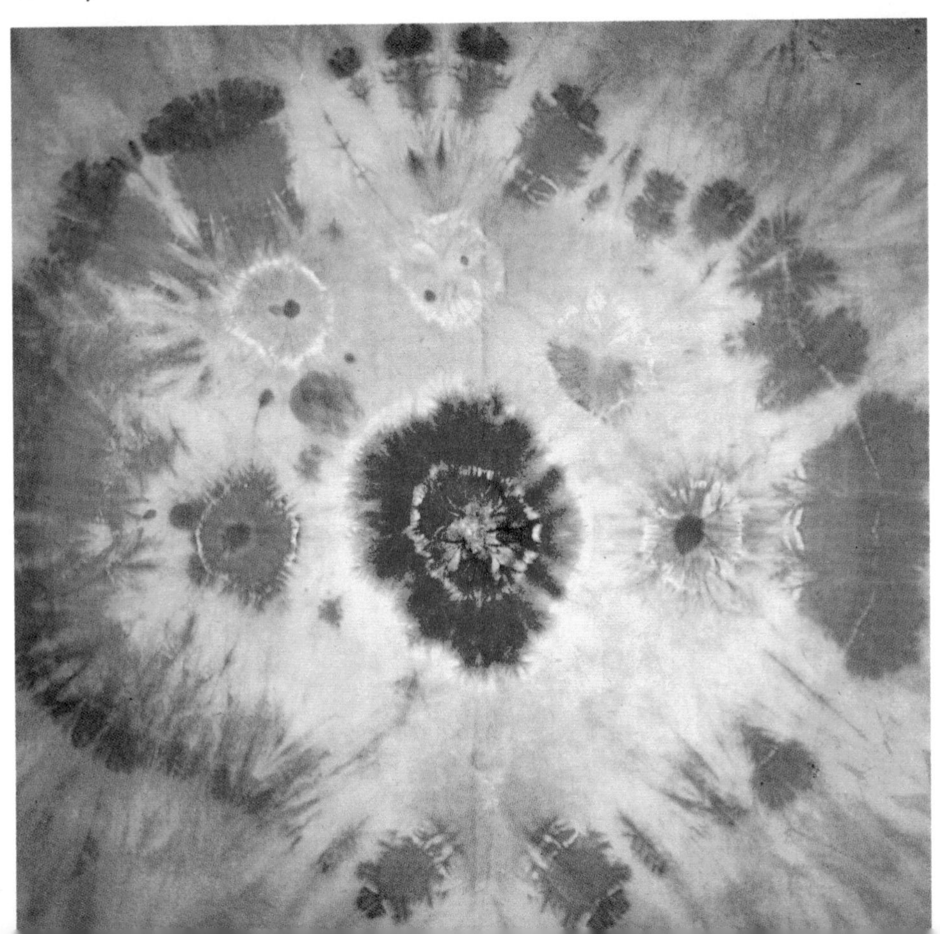

XXXIV

Not all young children like to carve, for it is a slow and time-consuming endeavor. Julie is using a ceramic tool to carve her plaster.

XXXV

Notches cut into the edges of cardboard provide a base upon which a child may create design with yarn. Every placement of the yarn and every color choice requires a decision which affects the appearance of the art.

XXXVI

Experiences a child has or imagines are always potential subject matter for his art. The textural effect of the starry sky contrasts with the plain colors in this eight-year-old boy's painting.

XXXVII

Children realize their aesthetic potential in art through freedom, an intense experience, concentration, and judgment. This water color was painted in the fourth grade.

XXXVIII

Children may be looking at the same thing and react to it differently. This child enjoyed the outdoor sketching and said so; his art reflects this feeling.

XXXIX

Another child working close to his friend who drew the previous work reacted to the destruction of the lawn and flowers, saying, "Boy, they're sure tearing it up out there."

XL

Children's out-of-school life affects their ideas and emotions and helps to determine their art. A change in these conditions can often be detected by a change in the child's art expression. Two entirely different feelings are expressed in these two samples of the same girl's art.

XLI

XLII

Janet concentrates as she works on her stitchery. Some art projects move slowly, such as this one, supporting interest over a long period; but children also need an occasional fast-moving art experience as a change of pace.

XLIII

A seven-year-old child painted this work in the studio of an artist friend. He wanted to paint with the same oils and knife used by the artist. Both painted abstracts, each very differently.

XLIV XLV XLVI XLVII XLVIII XLIX

To make value discriminations among these paintings (first grade) violates the premise of individuality.

L

The shapes, colors, movements, and organization in Corneille's "Where the Pavement Ends" help express feeling and character in art. The viewer should look for these qualities in all art and carefully consider his reaction to them. (Courtesy of Museum of Art, Carnegie Institute, Pittsburgh, Pa.)

want to succeed. Away from the security of home and parents and in a strange place, they undergo shifts of self-confidence and need a teacher's support plus a curriculum in art in which they can feel successful.

When this temporary feeling of insecurity and helplessness becomes a block, when the child says "I can't do it," he profits from his teacher's sympathetic help. In some cases suggesting a few topics is supportive, or just giving him some reassuring personal attention is enough; in other cases the need is deep and requires more than one such conversation.

By the second or third grade, if the art program has been a creative one and each child has developed his own strengths, the children have overcome these feelings of insecurity. They have wide interests, and their art is colorful, vigorous, exciting, and aesthetic.

> Most teachers have encountered the problem of the child who says, "I can't draw it," or "I don't know how to do it." This plea for help is accompanied by agitation and discouragement and sometimes by tears as well. The child needs understanding and sympathy as much as he needs help and guidance. When a child says he can't draw or model a form, it means that something has happened to discourage him with his work, perhaps because adult art has been held up to him as a standard or people have found fault with his products. He thinks that if he makes the "right" shape—something more photographic or naturalistic—he will win approval.

40

In this portrait of her family, including her grandfather's picture on the wall, Sergay has drawn herself twice: once as a member of a family of five children and again as an individual standing near her mother.

The only way to cope with this problem is to rebuild the child's feeling that his way is the right way for him. What he says he wants is just the opposite: he asks someone else to show him how to draw or copy a form. Talk to him about what he is trying to draw or shape, and help him to form a definite mental image of it. Explain that many mature artists create shapes of people and animals that are not naturalistic; show him examples of this kind of art. All this takes time and tact; it cannot be done with one casual remark.

Sometimes the children who are suffering this kind of discouragement turn to abstract art and do it constantly. You cannot let abstract work become an escape for those who do not want to face the task of creating identifiable forms. Teachers should constantly foster flexibility by guiding children from one type of art expression to another.[4]

NAMING OBJECTS

Pressure to create the more objective type of paintings can be exerted on the child in subtle and indirect ways by persons who think they are helping him. Adults, anxious to see the child paint or draw something that can be named, frequently ask a child, "What is this?" or "Tell me about your painting." This indicates to the child that he is expected to draw something that he can talk about, or makes him feel that he is, at least, expected to *name* the objects in his picture. This is extremely difficult to do, if, indeed, possible at all with the free, spontaneous, abstract type of art that children do in such abundance. Since the child feels that the parents and teacher, from whom he learns, want him to name and to discuss his art, he abandons this type of art in favor of forms he can name and discuss. Just through such a seemingly harmless question as "What is this?" the intent, interest, and purposes of the child can be influenced and directed.

Asking the child what he has drawn, even though he may be drawing people, houses, and objective forms, also indicates to the child that his art is so poor as to be completely incomprehensible to us. This causes the child to feel a sense of failure. He tries so hard to be successful and needs encouragement and praise for his work. Put yourself in the child's place. Assume that you have tried hard to make something to the best of your ability. How would you feel if asked "What is it?" Such an insensitive approach can destroy a child's self-confidence and may ultimately discourage him from painting. He expects his parents and teachers to be able to recognize what is so clear to him. Instead, accept his art with some appreciative comment, hang it up, and show it to others.

There is no reason why art should require or depend on an explanation. Art is a visual area. The enjoyment and appreciation of art depend on looking, seeing, and reacting. It is through *art* that we are teaching children. Art has its own powers and can stand on its own qualities without dependence on another form of expression.

If a child wants to talk about his art, give him your attention. He may bring it to you or begin talking about it when you come near where he is working. Some children have many interesting things to say about their art;

---

[4] Page 14 from Teachers' Manual to *My World of Art*, Book 1, by Blanche Jefferson. © Copyright 1963 by Allyn and Bacon, Inc. Reprinted by permission of the publisher.

other children have few, if any, comments about their work. The individual differences among children make them feel differently about their art and about explaining it. Sometimes a child may make interesting comments about his work because he was illustrating a particular action in which he had taken part; he had thought about the sequence of activities and the places and people related to it. This narrative type of art activity lends itself to oral narration, but not all experiences or ideas do—some are based on feelings and reactions. It is difficult for a child to put such experiences into words. It is even more difficult to discuss abstract or free-form art. It cannot be named, it has no story to tell, and so does not lend itself to verbalizing.

When we try to encourage children to draw something we can name, is it because we, ourselves, lack sufficient understanding of the beauty of expression found in free-form art? We should be careful not to deprive or direct children because of the limitations of our own knowledge of modern art. The more the teacher knows and the better she appreciates present-day and historical art, the richer the children's experiences and the better her guidance of their art experiences will be.

Sometimes an adult might be curious about a child's art and want to understand more about it. Simply give the child an opportunity to talk about it. When talking to the individual child, the teacher might look at his art and say, "This is a lovely blue area, John," or "I like what you did here." If the child wants to talk about his art, he has been given the opening without feeling an obligation. If he does not, your comments are encouraging and carry no indication of your inability to see for yourself what the picture is.

Some people try to influence a child toward more adult concepts by asking him to draw certain objects before he is ready to do so. Children pass gradually from immaturity into maturity in their art expression just as they do in physical, emotional, and mental growth.

When the young child first begins to name objects in some of his paintings, he should be permitted to name them and draw them as he wishes. These attempts need to be accepted by his teacher, no matter how incomprehensible they may appear. The child's first attempts in drawing should be treated like his first attempts in speaking. When a child first begins to speak the names of objects, he is encouraged and his parents proudly urge him to display his new ability. They do not mention the obvious fact that this may not sound like "dog" or "water." Neither do they feel called on to point out that he is just learning and, of course, he will speak plainly when he is older. Such procedures, if carried over into the child's art education, would greatly encourage him to build upon his successful achievements, to want to try different ideas, and to be eager to experiment with new materials. This positive method helps children form an attitude of enjoyment toward art and helps them grow in their ability to express their ideas.

SPONTANEITY

Children in the primary grades work with a great deal of spontaneity. They approach their work with enthusiasm and vigor and want to get on with it. Each child quickly grasps an idea and goes to work on it. Children of primary-grade age work in much the same way as children of nursery school or kindergarten age, but because of their maturity they can spend more time on each piece, for the following reasons:

(a) Their concepts and ideas are more fully developed.
(b) They have had more experiences and have richer imaginations.
(c) Their maturity gives them more drive to carry the project further.
(d) Their attention spans are longer.

Most children of this age will spend the duration of the entire art period (usually about 40 minutes) on one piece. They begin to be interested in objective shapes. Their interests are wider.

41

Finger painting is a fast-moving art medium that lends itself well to children's spontaneous ways of working in art.

The feelings and emotions that inspire the ideas children use for their art are responsible for that quality of spontaneity that makes the art of young children so appealing. Each child will express these feelings differently. Frequently, spontaneity results from the urge to give form to intense emotional experiences.

When the child is free, he approaches his work in a spontaneous way. Since with young children spontaneity is a characteristic of their art, teachers, aware of this quality, will recognize and accept it.

INDIVIDUAL EXPRESSION

The intensity of the inner drive a child feels often determines the extent and complexity of his art production. Sheryl was still so excited by her birthday party that the next day she asked her first-grade teacher for a L A R G E piece of art paper, spreading her arms out to indicate an unusually large dimension. The extraordinary power and influence of her motivation coming, as it did, from her emotional reaction to her party exalted her ability and kept her going through the strenuous task she had undertaken. It was as though she were impelled by some special force beyond her usual drive.

Her birthday cake is in the center of her composition with the words *Happy Birthday Sheryl* and candles on the top (Plate XVI). Her birthday party guests are all around it. The whole composition is well organized. It is clear in meaning, content, and purpose, and the excitement she felt as she worked is communicated to those who look at her art. Whether the artist is a child or a professional, strength and clarity of individual expression come from emotional stimulation and are reflected in art work communicating the artist's feeling.

Another example of individual expression in art is shown in Plates XXXVIII and XXXIX. Two boys, drawing from the same out-of-doors subject, produced two different expressions of the power shovel. As the text in Chapter 11 describes, the boys had different feelings about what was happening. Their feelings permeate their art, communicating their different reactions to other people who see it, and who, in turn, react in their own way to this difference between the boys' art.

One composition is not "better" than the other. Each child has been successful in expressing his ideas and feelings. If the same standard were required of each child, such personal highly individual expressions would be impossible.

The teacher looks for and tries to understand the differences in creative expression of children. Even when the reasons behind certain ways of creating seem hard to understand, the wise teacher will recognize and accept them.

> Because no two children are alike, it is impossible to place them arbitrarily in categories. Many children at three will paint like five-year-olds and vice versa. Some children at four will resemble three-year-olds in painting while their clay modeling may be like that of a five-year-old. This does not mean that if a four-year-old exhibits the achievement of a three-year-old he is retarded or that he is superior if he does work in advance of his age level. It merely shows that children's art expressions vary according to their experience, perception, and maturity.[5]

PROPORTION

In their urge to express their ideas children shape the forms they make and determine their relative sizes without much consideration for the visual appearance. Other factors often determine the shapes and proportions of the

---

[5] From *Art of the Young Child* by Jane Cooper Bland, copyright © 1968 by The Museum of Modern Art, New York, p. 13.

people and objects that children draw. Children seem instinctively to realize the importance of the imaginative and emotional qualities in art and seem to be only partially concerned with the naturalistic. Since art depends so closely on the imagination, this quality should be not only recognized and accepted but also encouraged.

Since the invention of the camera, artists have been freed from slavish representation. Before the camera was used, the artist was greatly limited in what was expected of him. His job was, largely, to reproduce likenesses. The camera can, of course, record much more accurately, in more detail, and quicker than is possible for the artist to do. The artist is therefore no longer responsible for recording likenesses and is free to create as he chooses.

The urge to create forms that do not depend on a realistic basis seems common to artists of all ages and stages of maturity. We see the wonderfully free abstract and nonobjective paintings and sculpture in modern art galleries. They dominate current exhibitions. We see this same freedom from naturalistic representation also evident in the work of children.

Visual Proportion

One interesting characteristic of children's art is the proportions that they use. The relationships that exist among the objects in their compositions are not always determined on the same basis. Proportion in art, as most adults understand it, means that the relationships shown in the sizes of the forms depend on their naturalistic sizes. The way something appears to the eye is the basis of proportion most frequently understood. The house is taller than the man, and the man is taller than the chair. This is visual proportion. Children use visual proportion. In Illustration 42, Ellen, eight years of age, painted this composition of herself and her family on Christmas morning. Ellen's father (still wearing his dotted pajamas), her mother, and Ellen have come downstairs to see the icicle-laden tree. The relation of sizes among the objects is based on visual proportion. The father is just about as tall as the tree, the mother not quite as tall as he, and Ellen is small in proportion to her.

Emotional Proportion

In studying children's drawings it becomes evident that other bases are frequently used by them for determining comparative sizes. Children sometimes draw the sizes of objects or parts of objects according to their emotional significance instead of according to the way they appear to the eye.

The drawings that children create on the basis of emotional proportion are not distortions, as some people may think. Persons who make such judgments do so on a visual basis, disregarding any other guiding purpose that the child may have.

Children often draw largest the object to which they attach the greatest emotional significance. The objects or parts of a person or object they care less about at that moment are drawn smaller or omitted altogether.[6]

---

[6] Viktor Lowenfeld and W. L. Brittain, *Creative and Mental Growth*, 3rd ed. (New York: Macmillan, 1957), p. 143.

42

Visual proportion shows in the naturalistic relation between sizes of objects as Ellen has painted them in this picture. She said, "My mother and dad and me came downstairs on Christmas morning to see our tree. It was covered with icicles. My dad had his pajamas on."

43

Emotional proportion is expressed when the child determines the ratio of sizes according to the way he feels about objects at the moment he is creating them.

Illustration 43 is a painting made by seven-year-old Linda. She has painted herself large and dominant in the center of the page. Her drawing of herself is the biggest form in the composition. She is larger than the house and larger than the tree. For this drawing at this time such a relationship among the sizes seemed most real to her. In order to express her feeling about the person and objects it seemed appropriate to draw them in this ratio. She was concerned with herself at this moment and thinking so intently about herself that she painted the form of herself first and made it as large as she could on the page. Then she thought of her house and made it smaller in accordance with the less important status it held in her thinking *at that moment.* Then she added a tree to complete her composition.

The objects in this composition are not drawn with the same purpose in mind as Ellen's picture of her family Christmas morning. Ellen depicted the scene as it had looked to her. She remembered and expressed her visual impression of it. Because this was the purpose in her mind on which she concentrated as she worked, the proportion of sizes existing among the objects is visual.

Linda's purposes and feelings were different. She was having an emotional experience about herself. She was thinking about herself and feeling excited about being alive. She had a sense of well-being and a healthy regard for her own importance. These feelings and reactions were filling her mind and emotions as she began to paint. Because this was her emotional state at the moment, it determined the idea for her art. It also influenced the size and shape of the forms that she drew. The girl is big and strong, with sturdy arms and legs, and fills the center of the page with importance. When feelings and emotions are dominant, the relationships of sizes existing among the forms are determined on that basis.

Emotional importance determines not only the ratio of sizes but also the parts of an object or person that are exaggerated in size and those that are minimized in size and detail. Children do not consciously reason through the determination of proportion as they work. Had Linda consciously reasoned about the relative sizes of objects, her picture would, no doubt, have been quite different. Linda *knew* she was not actually taller than her house. She could see this very well, and she knew it from moving about inside her house. She has not drawn this composition on the basis of what she has learned from seeing, but rather on the basis of what she has learned from her emotions and feelings. She feels that she is more important than the house or tree. No doubt if you were her parent, you would feel the same way and very well know, too, that she *is* more important. The emotional significance she attached to herself at this moment and for this painting was the guiding purpose that determined the size of the objects.

Gold tempera was a new addition to the paints that day, and Linda, impressed by its novelty and shining color, used it to paint her dress. Not only the largest form but the most impressive color was chosen to express emotional importance. Linda was not wearing a gold dress and very likely did not have one, but this is a painting—this is art. It does not have to be a duplication of what actually exists. Artists are free to determine the size and shape of forms and to color them according to their own desires and feelings. Linda made her judgments on the basis of her feelings of emotional importance.

Functional Proportion

The relative sizes of objects are sometimes determined on the basis of the work they have to do. The functioning of an object determines its size in proportion to other objects. The child might draw the leg of a football player who is kicking the ball much larger than it naturally is because that is the part of the player doing the job. One arm of a girl picking apples might be considerably longer than the other because it has to be long enough to reach up into the tree to pick the apples (44). Regardless of the fact that this arm might be longer than the girl's total height, to be functional, to do the job, it has to be long enough to reach the apples. This seems logical to a child because if you are going to pick apples, you have to reach them. Another way a child expresses functional proportion is to draw small or omit altogether an object or part of a person not necessary to the action going on in the composition at the moment. In drawing the girl picking apples, Linda greatly exaggerated the size of the arms in order to make them reach up to the branches and do the work, but she omitted altogether drawing feet and legs because they were not needed to do the work pertinent to that idea at that moment. The child knows, of course, that people have legs. She is well aware of her own legs. It is not a matter of not knowing or of forgetting. Linda was not concentrating on her knowledge but rather on the action. She was thinking about the doing and not about how it might visually appear to an onlooker. She was mentally involved in the business of picking apples; she was not an observer. It takes concentration and imagination to create such personal involvement.

For a teacher to indicate in any way that such exaggeration or omission should be corrected shows her lack of insight into the child's purposes. Children are not the only ones who use nonvisual size relationships. One has only to look at the work of contemporary artists to see many examples of it.

A child is confused by any suggestion from another person implying that he should correct the proportions in his drawing. He realizes that the critic fails completely to understand his meaning and intention. Children are sensitive, and such suggestions tend to make them discontinue nonvisual proportions; hence, such suggestions tend to discourage meaningful and personal art expression. The imaginative, the inventive, and the expressive are vital parts of art, and to discourage them is to discourage art expression.

In other areas of expression, children are apt to relate function or action to their subject and describe the object or person functionally. Ruth Krauss is sensitive to children's oral expressions. She quotes these definitions that children have given:

> "A hole is to dig."
> "A face is so you can make faces."
> "Snow is to roll in."[7]

---

[7] Ruth Krauss, *A Hole Is to Dig* (New York: Harper & Row, 1952).

44

Linda's arm needed to reach the apples in order to pick them. Feet were not needed to do this particular job, so they were simply not included in the composition.

These are function-centered instead of description-centered definitions. Children enjoy the doing, the action, the effort, the movement, and the work involved with a subject. Watch a child, and you will see how concerned he is with activity. The attempt to keep a child still for a while will be proof enough. No wonder they so readily express function verbally and graphically. Since action is so normally a part of childhood, functionally proportioned art will at times be emphasized, too.

SPACE AND DIMENSION

Young children seldom draw or paint one object in front of or behind another object. They have difficulty understanding how to represent in two-dimensional art the three-dimensional concept of one form partly concealed by another that is in front of it. Children can readily see and understand space concepts if they are making a construction project to be displayed on a table top or on the floor, because the three dimensions are immediately apparent. Since a drawing or painting is a two-dimensional art form, the partial concealment of one object by another means that the concealed part of the one form has to be omitted. In drawing one girl standing partly behind another, only a part of the girl in back would be drawn; she would have only part of a form. Such concepts are difficult for young children to accept. They know that no such people exist and feel that such a form is not whole and would not be "right." A great deal of the art work done by children is flat, two-dimensional work. At this young age such a translation from three-dimensional concepts to flat paper is done by children on their own level of understanding. In spite of this problem, children need two-dimensional art experiences. Adults need to try to understand and to enjoy the characteristic way in which children solve these particular art problems.

Children devise their own ways of representing three-dimensional ideas in two-dimensional art work. Generally, they solve this problem in a way that is harmonious with two-dimensional materials. Realizing that everything exists in its own space, they draw and paint each form accordingly. Frequently, when children paint rain or snow falling, there will be no raindrops or snowflakes falling in front of the people because a child feels the person is in that space. That spot on the paper has already been taken. A well-known law of physics stating "No two objects can occupy the same space at the same time" seems to be a truth sensed by children. Putting one form on top of another seems objectionable to most children in these early grade levels. They draw one form and then place the others beside or around it.

Children, aware of the obvious fact that their paper is not a three-dimensional material, proceed to treat it according to its flat two-dimensional nature. Many professional artists also respond to materials in this same way. They feel that the artist operates best when he works in harmony with the nature of his materials. Children in the primary grades sense this and are not concerned as yet with devices such as perspective for showing depth on a flat surface. That is one reason why some shapes in children's art look flat. That is why children sometimes draw a table as a straight line or flatten out the legs to conform to the flat surface.

The spaces left between objects in a drawing or painting determine the size of other forms the young child adds. The child has little difficulty placing the first one or two forms in a drawing or painting because the whole space of the paper is fully available to him. With the addition of each form, the remaining bare spaces of the paper become more limited in size and in shape. Since, to the young child, every form exists fully in its own space in art work as it does in nature, the child often changes the sizes of the objects to fit the space remaining after the first forms have been placed. According to adult standards, such differences among the sizes seem distorted. To the child, such size variations are of little importance. The child realizes that the limitations of the space he has to work in determine the size of the objects he draws. He also does not forget that this is art and expects the adults, who are more mature and better educated, to understand this, too.

Bill's picture of a covered wagon, inspired by his history lessons, shows how the sizes of the people were determined by the space left after the central idea had been expressed (45). Bill first drew the pioneer carrying his gun, then the covered wagon beside him. The size relationship between these two forms is based on visual proportion because Bill was thinking about how they looked. He had seen pictures of them at school and on television. He conceived this unity between them and their resulting sizes on a visual basis. The driver's seat, however, provided a small space, so Bill drew the driver to fit the space. An adult artist would have provided a seat for the driver and kept in mind, as he worked, the size of the other people. But Bill is not an adult. He solved his problems as an eight-year-old would solve them, and he did it in an interesting manner. The driver was carefully drawn with clothing details that indicated the approximate historical era. The woman walking behind the wagon fills the space available in that area.

45

Bill's picture shows how a child shapes the forms to fit into spaces as he finds them. The driver's size was determined by the size of the seat area. The woman walking behind the wagon could be larger since there was more space for her.

The young child disregards, to a great extent, attempts at perspective. He finds it difficult to understand that houses which are far away could be drawn smaller than any other houses in his art work. Although a child can accept the fact that houses vary in size, he finds it difficult to believe that the size of a house should purposely be changed by him just because it was built in a location some distance from him. In trying to teach this concept of showing distance by a change of size, one teacher took a child to the window and pointed to a house on the opposite hill, saying, "See, Jimmie, how small the house looks way over there." Jimmie looked at his teacher with a puzzled expression, possibly wondering if she thought the house really was smaller, and said, "But it isn't smaller; if you went over there, you would see that that house is just the same size as the ones here." Space gave the illusion of smaller size that the child was too immature to accept for his art expression. Some children in the intermediate grades begin to be interested in ways of showing space concepts in their art.

KNOWLEDGE AS A BASIS FOR ART

Have you ever noticed that young children paint or color the sky as a strip at the top of their drawings and paintings? This is such a universal way for young children to represent the sky in their art that persons at all familiar with children's art notice it. Sometimes they curve the sky or add a cloud or two, but it always stays high overhead, up above the other things in their pictures. The reason for it is very simple: that is exactly where the sky is. Children paint it high up because they *know* that that is where it is. Children frequently draw from their knowledge rather than by their vision. Later, in the study of geography, children learn about the horizon's being the line where the earth and sky appear to meet. As more mature persons they see it this way when they look at it. One beginning teacher, understanding this concept as an adult, thought that all she had to do was point out to children the very obvious fact that the earth and sky meet, and they would immediately understand and draw this way. When she saw some of the children put the sky in as a band across the top, she called their attention to it and showed them the sky and the horizon. One little boy said, "But Miss Miller, if you rode over there in your car the sky would be just like here, way up above. I know because we were over there once." The teacher learned. There is no place where the sky and earth do touch! Children know this, and they draw from what they know.

Children conceive the colors in their paintings and drawings in relation to the color of the paper they are using. If a child colors people, houses, and trees with the white paper in mind as he selects and applies the color, one can readily see how it would change the whole color relationship if he colored a blue sky behind the objects he had already completed. For example, the green trees, looking dark and sharp against the white, would lose some of these qualities if a blue sky were filled in between the objects and down to the ground.

As you have learned from psychology, young children have not enough motor control to do such tedious and precise work skillfully. The rough edges and the accidental overpainting affect the quality of their work and discourage children. Filling in the background with sky seems unnatural to children and often detracts from their art.

As you look at and study children's art, you will find many instances in which it was determined by a child's knowledge rather than by the way the objects looked to his eye.

In drawing a picture of her house, Nellie, who lived in one of a row of attached identical houses, drew on the basis of her experience with her house rather than the way it appeared to the eye (46). In her picture each house is drawn separately because her experience with the houses in the row influenced her in this way. Even though Nellie frequently saw that the houses

46

Although Nellie lived in a row of attached houses, she drew each house separately because she knew they function as individual units.

were attached and were all built of red brick, she knew that every family had a separate home. She had heard people talk about the homes of each different family, and by visiting in them, she learned that they were not at all alike as homes. In her art the houses are separate because they function that way. She painted them differently to show their individuality. Children create art from their knowledge and feeling about things and their functional relationships with them rather than from the way they appear to the eye. This is one of the characteristics of child art that makes it so interesting.

EMOTIONAL REACTIONS

The art work of the young child is at times characterized by the impact of an emotional response the child has had. Sometimes the most impressive thing about an experience is the way the child felt. When the child begins to put such an experience into form, he concentrates on the feeling he had. At the same time he associates this emotion with the object involved. Usually this form is the first to be made, with objects of lesser involvement being included later, if at all. The strength of the emotional reaction determines the subject matter for the child's art. It can also influence the size relationships within the composition, as was explained earlier.

Kenny made a drawing of one event from his summer vacation that shows the effect of such an influence upon his art (47). He had told his teacher about his family's camping by a place in the creek where they could swim. One day Kenny went down to the swimming place and saw a snake in the water. In the region of the camp the water snakes are small, grey, and harmless, but seeing it in the water surprised and shocked Kenny. He was still impressed by it after the vacation was over and school started. When he drew it in art class, the snake was almost as big as the pool and was larger than Kenny and larger than the tree. He colored it brightly with black and orange. It is evident that the factor characterizing that piece of his art work was his emotional reaction to the snake.

Repetition of Forms

The repetition of forms that interests a child, that involves him emotionally, or catches his attention is often repeated by him as long as this personal attachment lasts. Children (and adults) do this same thing when they repeat again and again the same song. Then suddenly it dies. There is something about the rhythm of repetition that satisfies us. When we have had enough of it, our minds turn to something else. Just as suddenly a child stops repeating a familiar form in art when, for some reason, he has had enough of it. It is more acceptable for a teacher to encourage a child to vary the repeated form than it is for her to interfere with his right to repeat it.

In the permissive atmosphere of modern art education, the child's right of self-determination in this, too, needs to be protected. Within the healing

47

Kenny drew his water snake large in proportion to other objects because of his emotional reaction to it.

atmosphere of acceptance and appreciation that is basic to the teaching of art to children, there is a good chance he will proceed to other ideas in time. The stress placed on a variety of ideas when an art activity is introduced in itself helps each child stretch his imagination toward other ideas. After this beginning, however, if a child returns to repeating a familiar form, his need to do so is greater than his need to try a new one.

There are, indeed, certain satisfactions in looking at repetitions of the same form, just as there are in making them. For example, the patterns in wallpaper, rugs, or fabrics are pleasing to the eye.

This tendency to repeat forms is not limited to the art of young children, but carries through all ages. Artists of different cultures and times have derived satisfactions and advantages from certain repetitions of forms or styles. They gain inner strength from whatever gains they make during this period of apparent standstill. Many artists work through certain "periods" then almost suddenly turn to other forms or ideas.

SUGGESTED ACTIVITIES

1. *Study the examples of the art of young children that are found in the other chapters of this book to see how many instances you can find of each of the three types of proportion mentioned and illustrated in this chapter.*
2. *Study examples of the art of young children done at home or in school with the following objectives in mind:*
   - *(a) See if you can identify the bases for the proportion you see.*
   - *(b) If there are no or very few examples of emotional or functional proportion, what might be some of the causes?*
   - *(c) If there are no abstract pieces among them, what may have caused this limitation?*
   - *(d) How would you the teacher proceed to encourage nonobjective or free-form art?*

7

Art of Children in the Middle Grades

A BROADER DIMENSION is added to their art as children progress from the primary grades into the intermediate grades. However, this change is not made abruptly but varies with individual children. They now have a critical awareness which influences their art and affects the spontaneity of their approach to art.

INFLUENCE OF INTELLECTUAL DEVELOPMENT

At this age children have a growing tendency to want to control the forms they make: to shape and compose carefully, accurately, and in detail. Whether they are attempting representational or abstract art, they seem more concerned with form than with expression, or at least with the type of expression shown in their earlier work. They are no longer satisfied to accept whatever forms and organizations result from a spontaneous outpouring of feelings and ideas. They want to see a change in their work away from impulsively created art toward what they consider to be more adult art.

The art, particularly drawings, of children in the middle grades is often characterized by a certain quality of stiff and somewhat inflexible looking forms, especially of people, and carefully calculated organizations. Many adults become concerned about it and feel that since children have lost the spontaneous approach of their earlier work, that corrective measures should be taken in the art class to overcome this reversal from free spontaneous expression to controlled deliberate expression. Much has been done to sensitize adults to the charm and quality of the art of young children, and less to help them appreciate the particular qualities of the art done by children in the middle grades.

The philosophy of acceptance of children's sincere attempts in art, as described throughout this text, applies here, too. What appears to be stiff and rigid is no more a fault than what appears to be inaccurate and careless in the work of younger children. It should not be "corrected" either, but accepted and used as a base for still further change and development. It is true that a certain freshness passes from their art as children try harder to control what they do, but a heartening concern for discrimination and improvement develops.

48

Knowledge is a sound basis for improving art: knowledge about actions and objects as well as knowledge about art. This sixth-grade boy's picture of a drive-in theatre shows both.

The fact that children in the middle grades tend to draw and erase, try shapes in clay or sculpture or cut paper before they are satisfied with them, shows a continuing interest in exploring, testing, and evaluating: all important art processes.

> Though a child's art expression becomes increasingly less spontaneous as he grows older, he continues to produce art work of surprisingly high aesthetic quality. . . . He will, for example, more or less automatically locate a tree, a person, a house, a bird, an abstract design element, or a lump of clay in what the professional artist might call the "perfect" spot in a given composition.[1]

[1] Conant, *op. cit.*, p. 65.

Growing Tendency to Reason

Children of this age seek understanding and want their art to reflect it. Most children in the middle grades plan their work in a general way before beginning considering cause and effect at that time and as they work. This preplanning does not preclude changes, additions, and deletions during the working process—nor should it. Artists of every age need to feel free to evolve and develop the expression of their ideas and feelings during the working process in art. As they work, they make aesthetic judgments of form, arrangements, and color. What results is a translation of mental images into art form. Limitations and possibilities of the art materials also play a part in defining each work of art. However, older children, individually or as a group, feel a need to have a mental concept of the entire project before beginning. They work more confidently and purposefully if they can visualize and foresee the effects of their decisions and if they understand the total problem and have in mind the general overall plan.

The extent to which a child plans and the nature of his planning should be left to his decision. Realizing that older children feel a need to plan, some teachers insist that they make drawings or small models of an art project before undertaking it. The teachers reason that children can thereby correct any mistakes they might make, and that they can visually appraise and evaluate their idea before putting it into final form. This argument may seem logical to adults, but it fails to take into consideration the fact that children become bored by executing the same project twice in succession. When a child has put his ideas into form once, he has little inspiration to repeat the same thing. Children want change; their play shows how much they need to move from one type of activity into another. This urge to express an idea and then to move on to something different is part of the rich, creative power common to children.

Preliminary sketches made with one art medium are difficult to compare with the same idea expressed in a different medium. Therefore, the purpose in making the preliminary sketch is lost. Differences in size also affect the result. A design composed and colored on a small surface may lose some of its qualities when enlarged. Children want to and should be encouraged to work directly with their art materials. If a child feels uncertain about how one part of the costume for his puppet will fit, for example, he could try cutting paper shapes until they fit the puppet before he cuts into the textile. The decision to do this should rest with the child, depending on the need he feels.

Concern with Naturalism

Naturalism in art stresses the conformity of art to nature in its quality, rendering, and expression: to depict the subject as it visually appears to the artist. Concern about naturalism in their art is a characteristic of older children and one with which all persons who deal with them soon become aware. They swing from one extreme to another in their attitude toward wanting to express their ideas in art. Young children are more concerned with emotional or functional expressions of their ideas; older children are concerned with the visual. Certain forces in their lives have been operating to condition their thinking this way.

Pressures of Photographic Illustrations

The photographic illustrations in the literature that children are learning to read and have long been exposed to before they could read have a tremendous influence on their thinking. Children see these naturalistic pictures of objects and people, and by the time they have reached the intermediate grades they begin to see the difference between what they have been creating in art and the pictures they see in newspapers, magazines, and most books. A child measures his art against this type of illustration and decides that the world cannot be wrong and he right. He sees the naturalistic art in the periodicals that adults publish, illustrate, buy, and read and concludes that this is the adult way, and his ways then appear childish to him by comparison. Seeing little or no abstract or design-based art in this environment, he concludes that perhaps he should abandon that, too, and turn toward what he considers to be a more mature style of illustration—the naturalistic. Quite often the only imaginative works of artists a child sees in newspapers and popular magazines are the comic strips and cartoons. A child begins to feel that in the adult world the serious art is naturalistic and the imaginative art ludicrous. Since he wants very much to be grown up and to fit into the adult world, he tries to follow what he judges adult patterns to be.

A child works seriously on his art, and, since he does not want it to appear ridiculous or amusing, he may avoid the imaginative. The child's growing awareness of his world brings these comparisons sharply to his mind, and he is deeply influenced by them. Older children need teachers who understand why they become so anxious about creating art that looks "real" and who know how to help them realize what is happening to their thinking. Children of this age also need teachers who are able to help them solve their art problems and who can give them the verbal guidance and the help they seek in depicting their ideas naturalistically, but who can *at the same time* keep alive and stimulate their imaginations, emotions, and awareness of design qualities.

The way in which a teacher helps children to keep in mind the qualities and values that make art exciting and interesting is shown in this example of a teacher working with his fourth-grade group as the children were either painting or working with chalk.

Following a field trip, which resulted from a science lesson, the children took a trip into the nearby woods to study, more closely, the coloration of the leaves in autumn. They were so impressed by the beauty of the trees and countryside that they suggested using this trip for a topic in their art class. Some wanted to work in colored chalk, feeling that this medium would give them the brilliance they wanted; others wanted to paint. Some children had a great deal of feeling for the subject and worked in an expressive, direct way. Others felt apprehensive about their inability to create a

49

When a child is impressed by something he has learned in another school subject, he may choose it for his art to express the emotion he felt.

naturalistic or realistic picture of what they had seen. They were confused by the contradiction between their feeling for what they had experienced and by what they thought were more adult ways of expressing an idea. As the teacher worked among the children in his guidance role, he tried to help some of them with this particular problem.

HARVEY: "Mr. Patterson, I want to make in my picture the path that went down the hill. Every time I try to draw it, it comes out different from the way it was in the woods. I want to try to get it just like it looked and I can't."

TEACHER: "Did it go straight down the hill?"

HARVEY: "No, it curved around. It was very pretty. I thought it was the best part of our trip. The path went along the hillside, and then it slanted down. Sometimes it went uphill and downhill as it went along. That part I can't draw at all."

Children need help with specific problems that they want to work out in a certain way. This child felt the beauty of the gracefully curving lines of the path and their relationship to the hill, but he needed help from his teacher in expressing his idea and feeling. Learning is effective when it takes place at the time of need.

TEACHER: "Think back about the way the path looked as it went uphill and downhill. Did you ever lose sight of any part of it?"

HARVEY: "Looking ahead sometimes I couldn't see down to the bottom of some of the dips."

TEACHER: "Did the path always look as if it came up out of the dip exactly opposite the place where it went down, or did it seem to come up a little to one side or another?"

HARVEY: "Almost always a little to one side."

TEACHER: "Imagine that you are feeling with your pencil along the edge of the very section of path you want to draw. Concentrate hard. When the path goes into a dip and you can't see it, stop drawing and move your pencil to the place where the path begins again. Feel along the path, keeping in mind that it goes downhill, so your pencil should move downward on your paper. Think more about how it feels and moves than how it looks. Remember, when your drawing is completed, it will have more of the quality of what you felt about the movement of the path than actually how it looked to the eye. A camera can, in just a second, record a picture of what it looked like. When *you* make the picture, it needs to show something of *you*; do not expect it to look mechanical or entirely visual. Don't try to think like a camera. There is more of you than just your eyes to react to the beauty of the path and the trees. I'll come back after a while to see how you are progressing."

The teacher did not point out the errors in Harvey's previous attempts; neither did he show the child how to draw or show him pictures of curving paths. He wanted to bring the child's feelings and awarenesses of his own particular path and idea about it more clearly into his active thinking.

ROSEMARY: "I am trying to make the farmhouse and the barn we passed at the foot of the hill and get some of the trees and the stream in it just as it was. I put them in just as they were, but it doesn't look right. I can't get it. I've tried and tried and I can't make it look as it looked to me out there. I guess I just can't draw so well any more, Mr. Patterson. I used to be good at it, but not in fourth grade."

TEACHER: "Don't be discouraged, Rosemary. Everyone has trouble with what he is doing some time or another. You are still good in art. I remember many lovely things you have done this year."

Children can become discouraged in art when they are distracted from their own purposes. Encouraging as it was, the teacher realized that simply reminding the child of past successes was no help in solving her current problem.

TEACHER: "You are trying to draw the house and barn you saw because you were impressed with their beauty against the hillside of trees and brightly colored leaves. I was impressed by them, too. But when we come to art class we try to remember that the house, barn, stream, and trees, which you have chosen to draw, were only a small part of the broad, wide landscape that could be seen. In your line of vision there were other houses, many mountains, thousands of trees, and a tremendous amount of sky. You chose one part to draw, and in doing so, you have already omitted a great deal. Therefore, it isn't exactly as it really was."

ROSEMARY: "But it was so beautiful right there."

TEACHER: "Yes, it was, but a part of the beauty came from your feeling about it. Not every child chose the house to draw. In fact, no one else did, so none felt as deeply about it as you did. You felt this great beauty and you are disappointed because the drawing you have made doesn't communicate this feeling to others—not even to you. Isn't that it?"

ROSEMARY: "Yes."

TEACHER: "In art we do not always draw a scene exactly as it appears to the eye. We choose a subject and use it as an inspiration in creating. We change its shape or size, rearrange parts, and exaggerate what we want others strongly to feel. We do this in telling a story, too. We tell it dramatically, emphasizing some words, repeating, and exaggerating a little so that people will not only hear what we say but feel the same emotion we felt. We have to do this because the listener was not there when it happened. The people who look at our art in school are not experiencing beauty by walking in the woods, either. In looking at your painting they will not feel the same beauty you felt unless you *make* them feel it through emphasis on how you felt, by exaggerating color and size and by rearranging objects to accomplish it. How could you rearrange the objects in your painting? What could you emphasize or exaggerate?"

ROSEMARY: "It wouldn't be the way it was."

TEACHER: "It might not look exactly as it was, but it would represent what you saw and express your feelings about it much more emphatically. Remember you weren't satisfied with your drawing based on how it looks."

JOHN: "I'm listening too, Mr. Patterson, because I felt the same. All pictures show things as they really look, but I see now what you mean about drawings being different."

TEACHER: "I'm glad you do. Most pictures in the magazines we look at, though, are photographs, not paintings or chalk pictures made by an artist. Some of the children had cameras on our trip that recorded the scene exactly as it was. Exactly reproducing a scene is the job for the camera and is done fast. This frees the artist to create."

MICHAEL: "I took the idea of some rocks and trees from our trip to the woods. I started out with that, then I just made it up as I went."

All the children in the group were hearing this discussion and learning something from it by having the emphasis on the imaginative and emotional in art repeated to them.

TEACHER: "That's the idea."

ROSEMARY: "I am going to start over again."

Rosemary had been disturbed by the conflict between her urge to express her emotions about the scene and the impact the bulk of photographic illustrations in periodicals had had on her thinking. The teacher knew it would take more than one explanation before the child could once again create freely and confidently, because education takes place slowly.

This example is representative of the problems children encounter in trying to overcome the forceful influence on their art of the mass of naturalistic and photographic illustrations they see daily.

Influence of Adult Values of Naturalism

Commercial illustrations are not the only source of naturalistic influence on children's art. Adults, who base their comments of children's art on naturalism, are a determining force in this direction. A great many adults understand no other art than the naturalistic and tend to feel that the more true to life a piece of art appears to be, the better it is. From the time most children begin to express emotion and feeling with art materials, the remarks they hear about their art expression are related to subjects they are expected to name. As a child becomes more skilled, his parents and relatives often encourage him to "make it look more like a house," or say "Don't you know a tree has branches?" When children come to school, all too many teachers ask them to tell about their pictures or ask them what they have drawn, thus making naturalism a valuable, if not the only, asset to art expression. Children are deeply impressed by the values teachers and parents have and transmit to them. When children are exposed to such influences until they reach the intermediate grades, they find them difficult to overcome.

The intermediate grades are crucial for children. Because they are becoming more sharply aware of the world around them and especially of adult ways and values, children tend to reject for themselves things that they feel are "babyish." They tend to discard, as immature, their former art expression. If these children are not cautiously guided by a teacher who understands children of this age and who understands art, they cast aside art qualities that they should retain, build on, and improve. Of course, there should be evidence of growth in art from the primary to intermediate grades, but imagination, design, exaggeration, and emotion in the children's art should not be sacrificed. The social pressures in the direction of naturalism in art are persuasive, and these influences should be pointed out to children so that they better understand how to deal with them. Teachers need constantly to emphasize the *art* values in art activities.

Knowledge Background

Children in the middle grades not only have a longer attention span than younger children, which helps them go further and do more with each idea, but they also have a deeper foundation of knowledge from which to draw ideas for art. This background of knowledge, experience, and skills gives them a remarkable insight into imaginative uses for art materials and increasing depth of perception in creative problem-solving in art. When an intermediate-grade child chooses the subject of airplanes for his art, for example, he knows a great deal more about the details of various types of planes than his third-grade brother knows. It takes more time and effort for him to put into form the many facts he knows about and wants to put into his art.

A teacher needs to feed this knowledge resource so that children can be helped to learn how to create naturalistic as well as emotion-centered or abstract art, and not resort to these latter forms because he does not know enough about objects to shape them in visually presentable ways. In the middle grades a child may paint an imaginary tree, but he still wants to know he can paint trees as they appear to the eye. Interest in art is often lost because children are not taught concepts and helped to develop skills that improve their fluency and competence in both design and naturalism in art.

Growing Importance of the Art Product

As children progress through the middle grades, the art products become increasingly more important to them. They want to produce something they can be proud of and are willing to spend much time and effort to achieve. The educational value and excitement of creativity is still inherent in the art process, but concern is extended to the product as well.

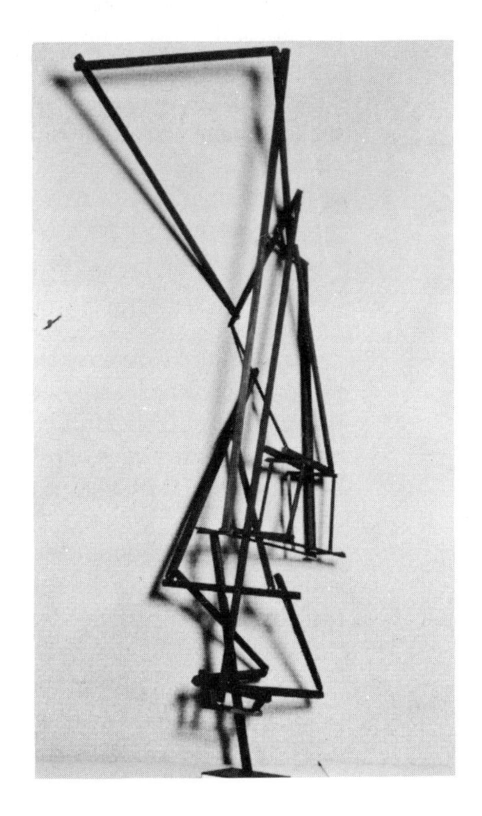

50

Sculpture of a construction type requiring the use of tools and giving the opportunity of freedom to shape it according to their own judgments quickens and holds children's interest as they work and make decisions about their art.

The utilitarian value of art appeals to children in the intermediate grades, and they are fascinated with complex and involved undertakings. Children of this age like to create art that "works," can be given as a gift, or can be put to some other practical use. They will spend a great deal of time working out intricate locks or openings for a valentine, for example. They want to create art products that they can operate, manipulate, bend, or change in some way. They are apt to spend a great deal of time making wheels that will turn for a wagon that will stand still in a specific place in a construction project. In spite of the fact that movable wheels are of no importance to the wagon for this project, they may spend as much time on this feature as they do on the rest of the wagon. They want to know that it works and that they can make it go; they are fascinated by this kind of challenge.

Older children enjoy art problems that include somewhat intricate steps in the process of working. Linoleum printing is an example of an activity characteristically enjoyed by children of this age. If they decide to print their own greeting cards, for examples, the children's motivation is heightened. Printing on textiles, because it can be used and seems permanent, is more interesting to them than printing the same design on paper, unless the printed paper has a specific use. They are often so impatient to begin cutting the block and printing, however, that they disregard design quality. A teacher, recognizing this impatience, needs to make children aware of the fact that art work *always* needs to have quality and be expressive and that eagerness to proceed with cutting is no justification for a poorly designed block. Teachers have a responsibility not to underrate the ability of children but to expect each to work up to *his own* best standards.

An intricate art problem, such as linoleum printing or the making of creative string marionettes, gives intermediate-grade children an opportunity to learn new processes and skills and to put into use the skills they have already learned. When children know the art products will be enjoyed by others, their more strongly developing need to function with and for others provides an incentive for work of high quality.

Self-imposed Standards

As children mature, they set higher standards for themselves. They are no longer satisfied with the art work they did when they were younger, although it represented their best efforts and had met their standards and expectations at the time. Sometimes these self-imposed standards are far beyond the child's abilities, and in failing to meet them he becomes discouraged.

Encourage children to learn more, to note general arrangements, shapes, and to study details in things they see: to look more completely and appreciatively. Help them. Have an art lesson occasionally in which you lead children in such a descriptive analysis based upon observations of an object.

An older child may occasionally discard or abandon his art work because his art product does not meet his self-imposed standards set by his inner drive for perfection; or he may not complete his art in the allotted class time because he wants to develop his maturity in art, as he does in other things, by carrying each project a little further than the last one, or because he now has enough insight to become involved in the challenges and problems in one aspect of his art. This testing and refining of his powers (a skill, form, or color relationship) may not only slow his progress at points but may also interfere with his simultaneous desire to get on with it and complete his art.

Because there is a wide range in the maturity of children in any group, many of the characteristics and qualities of the art of younger children will still be evident in the art of children in the upper elementary grades. There is no abrupt transition from the primary to the intermediate grades. Although children at any one age and grade level are more alike than they are different, mental, physical, emotional, and aesthetic growth takes place at rates that are different for each. A child may grow rapidly mentally and have little opportunity to grow aesthetically. Therefore, the range of maturity and ability will be greater for a group of children in the fourth grade than it was for the same group of children in the first grade. Some of the children will still be choosing ideas and expressing and organizing them in ways less mature than those of other children in their group.

In a learning situation in which individual differences are provided for, as they are in creative art expression, it is normal to find such an ever-widening range. As the teacher works with children in art, she needs to keep this fact in mind to avoid the temptation, which some adults feel, of trying to bring the work of the children in a group to a certain level or standard. It is the standard of *each child* that is important. This emphasis on individuality and on each child's standards as right for him is a continuous thread that runs through the art education of all children in every grade. Children beginning the fourth grade are very little different than they were when leaving the primary grades.

As children become older, more experienced, and better educated, and have greater motor control, certain differences in their art work and in their working habits become evident. This increase in ability to perform that enables them to work through time-consuming projects and to encompass a broader scope of art activities also stimulates children at times to undertake more than one art project. For example, an older child might be working on a lengthy project such as stitchery or papier-mâché and temporarily set it aside to work on fast-moving art such as painting or drawing.

Organization of Ideas and Feelings

The accompanying examples of the art expression of three intermediate-grade children are evidence of the well-organized expression of emotions of which children of this age are capable.

Marie's crayon composition of a haunted house shows how well she has organized the floating ghosts around the unhinged door (Plate XXIII). Their white color stands out sharply against the dark, cobwebbed interior of the house. She was skillful in expressing the unnatural transparent character of the ghosts by drawing the ghosts and the objects behind them as though one could look right through the shadowy figures. Other objects in the room add to the seasonal suggestion of Halloween.

Stanley's crayon composition, an unusual subject of a mother whale with her baby, is an example of good organization and successfully expressed emotions (51). There is a tender feeling between the mother and her baby. The small one looks frightened and huddles beside his mother, and she looks pleased and confident as she watches him. The baby whale is blowing a small spout; his mother blows a large one. Stanley must have experienced the strong, gentle emotion to have chosen this subject and to have expressed it so tenderly.

51

A tender feeling for relationships inspired Stanley's drawing of a mother whale and her baby.

Kenny calls his tempera painting (52) "Trouble." He said: "I am in trouble with my mother. She wouldn't let me go out and play in the ball game. I came downstairs dressed in my uniform to go and had to sit and watch out the window while the other boys went." The entire feeling of Kenny's picture communicates a feeling of dejection the child must have felt at being disappointed. The elongated forms in the picture help convey

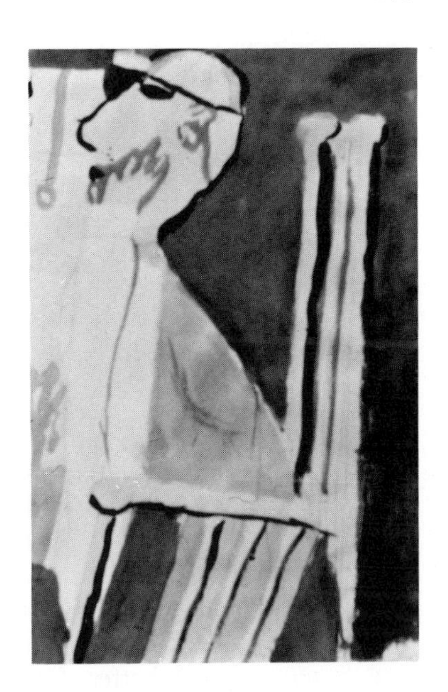

52

The art knowledge children gain plus a strong emotional feeling about the experience they are trying to express help them achieve results such as this example. The light colors are unified and show contrast against the dark background.

this emotion. Feeling an emotion deeply and concentrating on it as he worked has helped him express it so successfully. The design of the back of the chair against the deeply colored wall is beautiful and is emphasized and repeated in the design of the arm rest.

Proportion and Space

As they grow more critically aware, children in the intermediate grades want to be able to achieve proportion through a more visually accurate ratio of sizes between forms or among the parts of a form. They also want to know how to represent distance and the spaces between objects as they recede. This additional kind of knowledge is important to children, and they often ask questions about it or show frustrations because their attempts do not achieve what they hoped for.

Some awareness of proportion and space can be indirectly taught through the building of visual awareness in the primary grades, but older children need a direct focus of teaching on these and other topics. However, imaginative and design-centered expression needs to be kept alive and competences built in this, too.

Building concepts of how to express space is done through (a) helping children understand what happens as they learn to see more clearly, and (b) helping them conceive ways that space can be shown on a two-dimensional surface. (See Chapter 8 for a discussion of proportion in the human figure.) One example from the same art curriculum and a later grade:

> Distance and depth can also be shown by converging lines—lines that seem to come together as they move away from you. These two artists have used converging lines, as many artists do. Others do not.
>
> Knowledge of this kind is meant to help you express your ideas. If it

> gets in your way, forget it. High quality art does not depend on special ways of doing things.[2]

Let it be emphasized that knowledge is vital to art education, but at the same time the free choice of ideas and ways of expressing them is even more vital. Therefore, a teacher avoids requiring children to put any particular knowledge into effect in their creative art expression; but they have it to use or to disregard at their own discretion, for art must remain free and the artist without shackles.

SKILLS

Skills in art are important to older children, but are not important art activities for their own sake. Children need to feel a growing ability to control materials which develops as they become more experienced in art. Skills can be learned through the trial and error method, but education progresses faster if the teacher points out a few basic approaches and introduces children to some skills. If this teaching is done at a time when children feel a need for it, it is remembered better. If the skills are explained as the materials are presented or as the problem arises during the working process, interest is high, and the atmosphere for learning enhanced.

Teaching skills as separate art lessons places an undue emphasis upon one special way of working, and this can then become a block instead of a help. There is a great variety of materials, each requiring different skills or adaptations of them. When the learning of a skill is presented out of context, the application of it can become stilted and contrived. Skills are a means, not an end in art education, and they serve best when they remain subordinate to children's own inventive approaches.

Skills and techniques are not to be praised at the expense of creative, original art. Looseness in art, so evident earlier, is regained as children mature and gain greater mastery of skills which are developed only in limited ways in the middle grades. Intellectual freedom in art must be protected and provided for. Skills are only a means toward a broader scope of art processes.

The Teacher's Role

During these formative years in the middle grades, gradual improvement and change in children's art take place as the children delve deeper into the creative problem-solving situations in working out their art. The teacher learns not to expect the same growth patterns from each child but to recognize that each is working out these changes. She needs to communicate this recognition to the children and to build upon it through adding further concepts and incentives. Children need a teacher's help over difficult climbs onto the next plateau of education and expression.

---

[2] Page 11 from *My World of Art*, Book 6, by Blanche Jefferson and Clyde McGeary. © Copyright 1964 by Allyn and Bacon, Inc. Reprinted by permission of the publisher.

Although there is content in art to be taught and skills to be developed, the teacher must be constantly on the guard against restrictive requirements in creative art. Intellectual freedom of choice of ideas and ways of working must remain steady. This means the right to reject as well as to select. A teacher need not feel she has failed because a recently taught concept does not appear in every child's art. They learned it but may have decided not to use it at that time.

However, every child does at times need help with mechanical problems such as difficult fastenings or joinings. It is possible that both children may benefit if another child helps him. Under no circumstances should a teacher or any other person take a child's art work into his hands and work on it, because in doing this, the child is deprived of a precious feeling of accomplishment and loses the feeling of the work being his.

> The [teaching] crisis lies precisely at the point at which a child attempts to cope with external reality in a superficial way, and fails to penetrate it. . . . It is precisely an artist's view of art that is required if the child is to survive the crisis.[3]

SUGGESTED ACTIVITIES

Study a few pieces of art created by children in the middle grades (there are many examples in this text). Then:

(a) Note one art concept that you think they need more clearly to understand.

(b) Plan how you would present it.

(c) Indicate how you would provide for intellectual freedom in the art work period following this presentation.

---

[3] Arthur W. Foshay, "Art and Its Relationship to the Other Disciplines," *Eastern Arts Quarterly*, II, No. 4 (1964), 15.

8

Helping Children Improve Their Art

CHILDREN CREATE original art before they come to school: without art classes or teachers. Most children have already made drawings, designs, and used some art materials. Many pre-school children have also created sculptural forms using mud, sand, blocks, and other materials.

This tendency to create visual forms is a natural urge. People of all cultures, at all times in history and at all stages of civilization, have created works of art. Children, feeling this same universal urge, do so, too. They have a desire to create and construct, a natural curiosity to explore things, and an impulse to test their powers and abilities; and their art often has remarkable aesthetic quality.

It is not, then, the primary role of the art teacher to introduce children to art, for they have this informal beginning before their first art experiences in school. The teacher builds upon this background in a cooperative working partnership with children that helps them broaden their art experiences, strengthen their art interest, deepen their art knowledge, intensify their responses to art, and sharpen their discrimination of quality in art work.

To help children hold interest in art over the years and to build children's pride in their own accomplishments, both the teacher and the children need to see some gradual change and improvement in the children's art work. From one month to another, from one grade level to another, or from one level of education to another (primary to intermediate, for example) there should be some evidence of a developing mastery of each child's ability to express his ideas and feelings in a way satisfactory to him. Improvement does not necessarily mean that each piece of art work needs to be more qualitative than its immediate predecessor, for children need to explore new materials, ways, and skills. The results of explorations are at times anything but successful works of art. This is a part of learning and especially so in art where every piece of art work is expected to be something of an innovation, where each art material or process has skills and procedures that need to be brought under control, and where each idea requires forms and colors to express it.

There is a time for teaching art. There is a time for expressing it. Much attention has been given so far in this text to the role of the teacher in helping children express their ideas in art, because this is the area of art education least clearly understood and most frequently violated.

However, teaching about art does need to take place in the elementary school. Most teachers understand the need for continual feeding of new ideas to children, of review, reemphasis, of relating what has been learned to what is being taught, of seeing familiar knowledge in new settings, and of seeing new knowledge in familiar settings, of developing children's skills, confidence, and abilities.

Art needs to become art education as well as art expression. This means that some learning and progress needs to take place every year, every month, every day. Art expression and learning about art are not separate and contradictory. Both are a vital part of every good art program, for they nourish and develop each other.

Some teachers are afraid to teach anything at all to children about design or color, for example, lest they interfere with the child's right to self-determination in art, and this can happen when the teacher fails to recognize the kind of teaching practices that do cause a breakdown in the free flow of creative art expression. Teaching should never interfere with the confidence and freedom of each child originally and independently to deal with his art. It should enhance it.

Stagnation and discouragement result when knowledge about art is withheld from children either because of the teacher's fear of exerting too strong an influence upon the children's art, or because she may not know how to put this knowledge into terms simplified enough for children in the elementary school to understand. When this happens, children have the choice of repeating familiar ways of expressing forms and ideas or going ahead with the discouragements of trial and error without help from an educated adult. Children need help in the way of insight, *not* dictation. Let it be understood here that we all use familiar ways of expression as a base for more extensive ways of expression. To advance we need to feel the progress that comes from new ways and new knowledge. The trial and error method is essential to art, too, but it cannot remain the only road to learning. Trial and error are especially important in art, for art is open and inventive and rewards new ways and processes.

THE SPECIAL NATURE OF ART

Although education in general has common goals that run through all of the curriculum, each subject does have its own particular contributions to make, as discussed in the first pages of this text. When this concept of the

53

Nola's art shows the soaking quality of the rainstorm, and expresses a feeling of loneliness.

54 (*right*)

A child develops his sense of confidence as he undertakes more complex and demanding tasks. Children feel a natural urge to excel and to develop their own resources. An art class provides many such opportunities.

values of each individual subject is lost, much of the educational perspective to be gained from each different subject disappears.

The goals of art education are not necessarily parallel with those in other subjects. Art is different from other areas of the curriculum in its nature and in the meaning it holds for children. It has special values not found, or found to a lesser degree, in other subjects. It must follow, then, that art is taught somewhat differently from the other subjects.

Art itself is different from other areas of endeavor in its highly individualistic, creative, ever-changing, and often ambiguous nature. The self-directed, self-motivated, and self-judged ways in which artists work in their studios determine the rich and interesting world of art. Teaching practices in art education need to be related to the nature of art itself. To accomplish this objective, the teaching of art varies from the general methods of education to provide for these intangibles, in the highly subjective nature of art.

TEACHING TOWARD OPEN LEARNING

The need for well-planned, clearly presented lessons pointed toward the teaching of one new concept at a time is essential to education regardless of the subject. It is essential in art, too. However similar this need for well-presented teaching in all subjects is, there are major and vital differences in the *way* the art teacher provides for individual differences in learning and in the *freedom children must have to use, apply, or reject* new knowledge.

The teaching of art to children must be undertaken with an understanding of and a feeling for the special nature of art. It is *art* we are teaching to children. The nature of the art experience for each child is, then, basically the same as the nature of the art experience for the artist in his studio.

The artist learns, but he learns what *he* wants to learn and applies it when he wants to apply it and modifies it to suit his own purposes. He rejects knowledge that other artists accept. Selecting, learning, and using knowledge is highly individualized in art.

Learning must be kept on an *open* basis in art. The teacher protects each child's right to disregard any or all parts of whatever is taught. For a teacher accustomed to the techniques of teaching necessary for the mastery of skills in other subjects, this is difficult to understand or be able to do. It is not always easy to provide for this right of the individual to reject or modify knowledge that is presented, but excellence in teaching is never easy.

To keep art experiences on an open creative basis, the teacher cannot demand compliance from the learner. Teaching most subjects requires some expectation of learning what the teacher is teaching and some evidence that it has been learned and can be applied. In reading, for example, when a new word is introduced, the teacher tries to reach every child and have him learn the word and respond with it when he sees it that day and thereafter. The teacher follows through and reinforces the children's learning of this word until they know it and can read it. However, in *art* the teacher establishes a much *looser attitude* not toward teaching but *toward learning*. Learning and applying what is taught must remain on a *take-it-or-leave-it* basis. Otherwise, it is too influential.

Stress is sometimes put upon children to conform, even when children are given the opportunity to select their own ideas for their art—when the art experience has met the surface requirements of creative expression.

For one reason or another, a teacher who gives children some self-determination over their own art may still teach so insistently that children conform in ways which suit her adult purposes. Children can be reminded or cajoled into certain conforming patterns of art expression: for example, to shape large forms in their art, not to draw with pencils, to make big strong legs on sculptural forms, or color uniformly heavy with crayons. These are only a few. A teacher frees herself of such possible authoritarian ways by occasional thoughtful examination of her statements to children, or by studying their completed art work to search for similarities that might have resulted from over-insistence on her part.

THE CHILD'S OWN CREATIVE EFFORT

There are many experiences that provide opportunities for growth in art expression. One of these, which is of inestimable importance in improving the child's art work, is the actual working through of the creative process in art. Through facing the challenges of and solving the problems involved in this type of art work, the child learns by means of his own efforts many important things that help him better express his own ideas with materials. Coming face to face with a new situation, which the child feels must be overcome, presents challenges and makes demands on him. Overcoming the problems involved gives the child a sense of power and achievement. It is, however, difficult to motivate the child to accept another person's choice of such undertakings.

In order to understand more fully the tremendous incentive in self-determined activities and the growth resulting from them, watch a child's behavior in undirected activities with playground equipment. A child will make a free choice of a piece of equipment and then proceed to master the skills involved in using it. He finds his own ways of building these skills and of developing his own needed strengths to function with the parallel bars, slide, jungle gym, or rope for climbing.

Each time the child approaches the piece of playground equipment, he not only enjoys what he has already learned to do, but he also enjoys proceeding to a new and challenging achievement. He tries to turn himself over in a different way on the parallel bars, or to climb a little higher on the rope, or to balance himself on the top of the jungle gym. The new task he has set for himself will probably not be easy, but if the desire to do it is strong enough, he will keep working at it until he succeeds. The difficulty of mastery may in itself be a motivating challenge. The rewards are greater and the sense of power more profound when, through his own efforts, the obstacles have been overcome. In working through the physical processes involved in the use of playground equipment the child learns much on his own. Because his efforts are stimulated by his own desire, he becomes more capable and self-confident. The same thing is true of his art work. The child makes the decisions of what he can and wants to do, evaluates the results, sees his own growth, and proceeds at his own rate.

Children have a powerful desire to learn. A child cannot be prevented from learning if he is learning what *he* wants to learn. *No one, not even his teachers or parents, wants the child to learn as much as the child himself wants to learn.* Children have a strong desire to gain new powers and to grow up to do the things adults can do. The desire to grow and to learn physically, emotionally, and mentally helps a child gain more mastery, learn new skills, and better express himself through his own efforts. The child develops through his own efforts in working through the creative process in art. Through creative expression in art the child learns many new and valuable things and at the same time develops skills and judgments.

INSTRUCTION AND SUGGESTED TOPICS

Creative art activities should be the core and backbone of every art program. The nature of other art lessons should be derived from the children's needs as diagnosed from their creative art products. This can be the outcome of an evaluation discussion between the children and their teacher about their art work, or it can be the result of a teacher's analysis of their work.

After the area of weakness or need has been determined, the teacher should plan an art lesson for the near future, preferably the next art class, during which she will *teach* the children some general principles to help them understand and overcome their problem and to help them better express their ideas. The teaching will take the form of talking and explaining to achieve *understanding*. Understanding is achieved best by broadening and adding to the children's concepts and information, letting each child form his own mental pictures as the teaching proceeds. When teaching is done mainly by showing the children how to draw an object or through the use of illustration, the mental concepts of other people are impressed on the child. Therefore, if illustrations, which do have value, are used at this point, there should be a number of them covering a variety of approaches without too much emphasis placed upon any one other person's way of solving the problem.

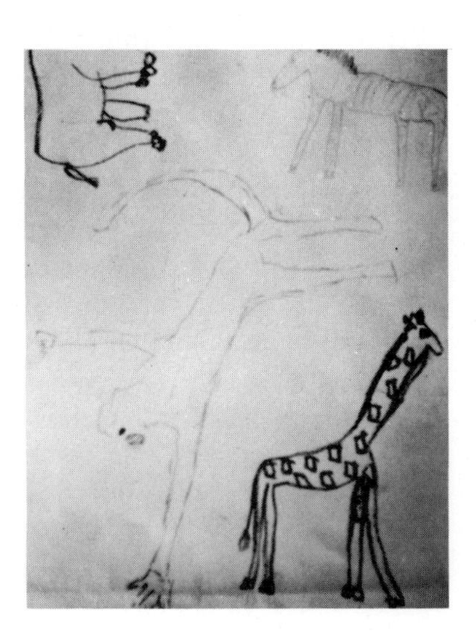

55

One way to help children improve their art is to give them practice in basic skills such as drawing. Interesting subjects stimulate progress. This is a page from one child's sketchbook following a trip to the zoo.

The overstressing of illustrations can influence the children's work. If only one or two illustrations are used, the children will tend to build a concept of a fixed form, which will limit their mental scope regarding the directions that can be taken to solve the problem. Not only is it important to teach the child about a particular phase of art, but it is also important that *at the same time* he be building a concept of creativeness about it. This can be done through illustrations that show many different approaches to the problem. Both naturalistic or representational and design-centered or abstract approaches should be included.

In most cases, showing selected examples of artists' work that illustrate the concept the children need to study, and pointing out the specific area of the art that involves this concept, will be enough to clarify it to children without further emphasis. However, there are times when most of the children would profit from a follow-up art problem in which the concept is involved. When this is done, it is necessary to emphasize that it *could* be a topic but not required. Neither should the inclusion of the concept just taught be required even though the topic be open choice. The fact that a topic is only suggested provides for those who may want to pursue it, and the others may elect to do whatever they choose. Many children need time as a buffer against the impact of their concentration upon the new idea. It can then at a later date take its place as a part of their idea for art and not dominate it.

The fact that the need for instruction toward growth in one particular area of art can be determined from children's creative art products does not mean that the results of every creative art lesson should be analyzed, weaknesses determined, and remedial instruction and remedial work undertaken. To do so might very easily cause children to regard creative art work with apprehension and to wonder what would be found wrong with their work. Frequently, creative art work should be undertaken for its own values and growth potential. Then, too, at times the teacher herself makes the examination of the work and plans certain art experiences according to her opinion of the children's needs. She draws her conclusions from watching the children work, studying their completed art work, and listening to their comments. Such diagnoses are made only when there seems to be a general need for improvement within the group. Children's art work is always to be considered from a viewpoint consistent with the age of the children. Their work will not meet adult standards; in no respect should it be expected to do so. It should be appreciated and enjoyed for its own qualities and accomplishments. Children build upon their successes in a very positive and encouraging way.

To illustrate how such an educational process takes place, an example of the way one teacher dealt with her fifth-grade group to improve their drawing of people will be described. This is a very common problem with children of this age.

After a creative expression experience with crayons, all the children's art was exhibited and the class conducted a discussion of it, indicating the achievements and strong points of each piece. When the discussion ended, this conversation took place:

TEACHER: "These are very interesting crayon drawings. You, as a group, have done an especially good job of using light and dark colors to emphasize certain parts of your work. Your coloring is emphatic. It shows up well from any part of the room. You have a wide variety of interesting subjects, but I notice only one of you drew any people in his composition. Gerald drew one boy in his picture. Why have none of the rest of you drawn people?"

JEAN: "It is hard to draw people."

PETER: "I can't draw them to look like anything."

TEACHER: "Why don't you draw people, Andy?"

ANDY: "I can't."

TEACHER: "Bill, why don't you?"

BILL: "I can't make them look right."

TEACHER: "How many have difficulty drawing people?"

Practically all the children raised their hands. The children had not, of their own accord, mentioned a need that they knew existed. They were aware of it but tried to conceal it, which is a natural thing we all do. The teacher helped them face their problem. She did it gently and without criticism, showing the problem simply as something to accept.

TEACHER: "Most of you have difficulty drawing people, or figures as we sometimes call them. Tomorrow in art class we will study some things about how people look that may help you draw them better. Probably proportion is one thing that troubles you."

Proportion seemed to be one of the figure problems they accepted as troubling them. Their general response to the suggestion had indicated that to the teacher.

TEACHER: "Between now and tomorrow, look into a mirror to see if you can find any relationships between parts of your body—arms and legs, for instance—that might help you."

The creative art work had been studied, the diagnosis of need made, and plans made for a teaching-learning situation. The children were encouraged to do a little exploratory work before the next art class. In doing this the teacher indicated to the children that there was much they could learn by studying their own figures. In fact, that is the way she planned to attack the problem on the next day.

The teacher began the discussion on the next day by referring to the suggested activity of studying their figures in the mirror.

TEACHER: "What did you discover about the relationships among parts of your body by looking into a mirror?"

GEORGE: "I couldn't tell anything except that my body is straighter and not so round as I draw it."

GRETCHEN: "I could see that my body was larger than I usually draw it and that my head is smaller. I have been drawing dancing girls, and I think I make their heads too large."

MARK: "I don't know what you mean by relationships to look for."

TEACHER: "What are relationships, or what are relations?"

SUSAN: "We are all the same family. We have the same father and mother, my sister and I."

TEACHER: "Yes, it is having something in common, something the same or similar, that makes a relationship between two parts of a thing. In studying about figures we need to look for things that are the same or nearly the same between parts."

56

When the teacher calls attention to points of success in a child's art, she is helping him to recognize design and other aspects of art. This fourth-grade boy's art is strong in design quality.

It was necessary to build an understanding of terms and art vocabulary before the teaching began, since the same word can have different meanings in different situations. *Figure,* for instance, means one thing in arithmetic and another in art.

TEACHER: "Stand on the floor far enough apart so that your arms do not touch each other when raised. Drop your hands to your sides. Your hand falls halfway between your hip and knee. A good many of you have been drawing arms too short. No matter in what position the arms are placed in a drawing they should be long enough to reach that far. When you draw an arm raised, judge with your eyes whether or not the arm is long enough to reach halfway to the knee if it is dropped."

The teacher talked about that point because it was a new experience for the children, and they needed to learn how to look for and to see relationships of sizes. The teacher takes the lead and then gradually draws the children into the discussion.

TEACHER: "Where does your elbow come in relationship to the whole arm?"

EDITH: "In the middle."

SHIRLEY: "And it only bends toward the front. But I knew this before."

TEACHER: "Yes, we already know many things about our body and how it moves and bends. Press your elbows in toward your sides. Where does the elbow come?"

GORDON: "Right on my belt."

AILEEN: "By my waistline."

TEACHER: "When you draw arms you have another relationship of sizes to think about. From the shoulder to the elbow is the same as the distance from the shoulder to the waistline. Notice how the body curves in at the waist. Now put the part of your hand that joins the wrist onto your chin. Put your hand over your face."

At this the children laughed and looked at each other in surprise. Many of them tried it again.

TEACHER: "You are surprised that your hand is that large. Now you can see how much too small you have been making them. Hands are much larger than you think. When you are trying to draw figures as they look, compare the length of the hands with the length of the face.

"Now locate on both sides of your body the place that indicates halfway from the top of your head to the soles of your feet. [Most children placed their hands on their waistline.] You think your waistline is the center of your body. Many of you placed your hands on your belt. While your hands are still there look around at your friends. Does it seem right or too low or high?"

ALEX: "It is too high, I think. It seems that the middle is lower."

TEACHER: "Move one leg a little and feel the place on the side of your hip where the leg joins onto the body. There is a ball-and-socket joint there, and that spot is about the middle of the body. Do you think it is exactly the middle for everyone?"

NORMAN: "Whee-u! Look at Morris! His legs are *long*."

TEACHER: "Yes, they are. Morris is tall."

During this time the children are looking around to see their classmates' proportions and to look for differences.

TEACHER: "That proves that not all people are alike and that what we have been saying about the relationships of sizes are only *general* guides. Almost every person varies a little from these general guides. Length of legs varies more than anything else. If you want to draw a tall man, how would you vary the legs from the guide we discussed?"

MABEL: "Make the legs longer. Is this the same for children?"

TEACHER: "Would it be?"

INEZ: "No, because children are just smaller than adults. So I think the middle would still be where the legs join onto the body."

TEACHER: "Yes, and there is something else about legs that I would like to call to your attention. While you are standing you notice that at the tops near the body, the legs touch. Then place your hands on your sides at the place where the legs join the body. You notice that both legs together are just as wide as your body at the place where they join the body. The legs get gradually smaller as they go down. Most of you know this, but you forget that the legs are as wide as they really are at the top. There is no sudden change from the body to the legs. You can see that it is a smooth line curving in as the legs go down."

All this time the children were exploring both by touching their own bodies and by looking at their classmates. The children were learning through three senses at the same time—by *hearing* the teacher's explanation, by *touching and feeling* the parts of their own bodies, and by *seeing* the relationships of sizes in their classmates' bodies.

TEACHER: "You were surprised to discover the actual size of your hands. Put the back of your hand beside the back of the heel of your foot. You had better sit to do it."

As the children made this comparison, they laughed a little and looked around to see if other children's feet were so much larger than their hands.

VALERIA: "Feet are much larger."

JASON: "They would look funny drawn that big."

TEACHER: "Most children draw feet much too small. To look at your drawings I sometimes wonder how the people would balance on such small feet. Feet have to be strong enough and large enough to carry us around and to support the weight of the entire body. Think about that sometime, too.

"There are many more size relationships that we can learn about people's bodies. We also need to know how people bend when they move. But we will leave that for another time."

MARK: "If I can remember this much for a while, I should be able to improve my drawing of people a lot. Are we going to draw people now?"

TEACHER: "I think it would be a good idea. You might want to try out some of the things you learned. The relationships of figure parts we discussed will help you if you want to draw people just as they look. Sometimes we don't want to do that, of course. Sometimes we purposely change these actual relationships to show a feeling of emotion. Let me show you briefly the works of some artists who have not drawn people as they actually appear to the eye. Artists are free to shape forms in any way they choose in order to suit their purposes."

The teacher had prepared six or eight illustrations to show different ways that artists formed people, and she commented briefly on each. The emphasis of the explanation had been so pointedly on naturalism that it seemed imperative for the teacher to remind the children that there were other approaches to art and to the way of forming the shapes of people.

TEACHER: "Mark suggested a little while ago that we might want to try some of the things we have just learned. There are other ways of doing this in addition to drawing. The illustrations I showed you were not all drawings."

MABEL: "No, some were like statues, like our clay modeling. We could make a person out of clay."

GORDON: "I think that would be good, because then we could see it and do it in three dimensions. It would be more real."

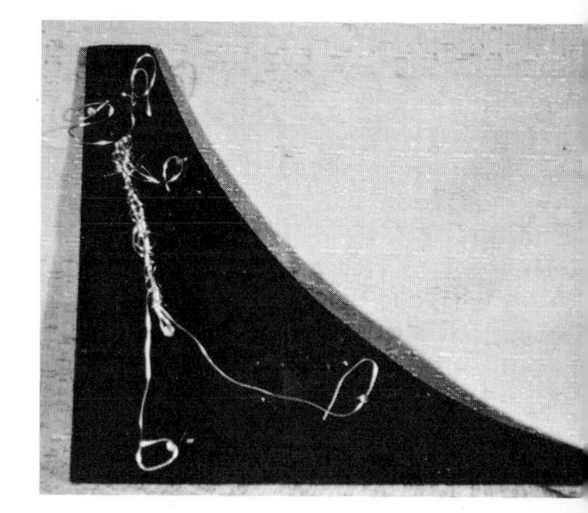

57

Bonnie started her work with this piece of scrap wood and then bent the wire to shape the figure according to the form of the wood.

EARL: "We could see better how big certain parts are."

TEACHER: "Suppose we plan to model people in clay tomorrow. You can be thinking about what you can make your clay figure be doing."

The teacher motivated the clay lesson as she would any assigned topic. (One way of motivating assigned topics was suggested in Chapter 5.)

After such a concentration of attention on improving the child's knowledge of and expression of the figure, it would be a good idea for the teacher to plan an art experience of a very different nature with materials of a different type, so that the children would not be so directly influenced by the emphasis shown by the examples or by any comments. Children enjoy and profit by change. They learn to be more flexible, and are stimulated and excited by a change of materials.

Research on Perception

This study indicated that perceptual training relevant to representational drawing can increase the amount of visual stimuli. . . . Perhaps students in the intermediate and upper grades would learn more from some areas of the art program if carefully structured content and direction were offered.

It appears that improved visual perception may not be a naturally occurring by-product of art activities, but a specific objective for which one must teach.[1]

Improvement Through Analysis

An analysis of children's art products provides insights that can lead to improvement of their future art work. As stated on pages 69–72 in Chapter 3, the positive comments made about their work gives recognition and sharpens awareness of the *art* qualities, thus building further bases for improvement.

The teacher's analysis of the completed art work also contributes to the general upgrading of children's art, when she, as a responsible professional, silently appraises their art and decides upon its shortcomings as a springboard toward further teaching, as discussed earlier in this chapter. Teachers, especially in the middle grades, need to do this.

Children, too, make silent appraisals of the exhibited art. It is necessary occasionally to provide both levels of appraisals, because a child perceives his world, of which art is a part, differently from the way an adult sees it.

SUGGESTED ACTIVITIES

From a set of finished art work of any medium done by children in any one of the elementary grades, study:

(*a*) *The strong points of the group as a whole.*

(*b*) *Any general weakness of the group's work.*

(*c*) *The procedures you would use for helping the children to improve their future art work.*

---

[1] R. A. Salome, "The Effects of Perceptual Training Upon Two-Dimensional Drawings of Children," *Studies in Art Education*, National Art Education Association, Washington, D.C., VII, No. 1 (1965), 32–33.

9

Curriculum in Art

One of the reasons for the lack of general support for art education and for its present minor place in school programs is the absence of planned and organized teaching curriculum materials that make the art education program visible. In other fields of study in the elementary school there are sets of sequentially planned textbooks and rich amounts of related materials used, but this is most often not the case in art education. These carefully planned, graded, and tested materials not only give stability to art education, but they also make the art curriculum and its purposes discernible to children and adults.

Education is a serious and expensive involvement, and people tend to lack confidence in whatever part of it appears to be unorganized, piecemeal, or structured only on a local level without the support and backing that a basic program, developed and tested on a broad scale and refined over a period of time, offers.

A PLANNED BASIC PROGRAM

Sensitivity to the fact that art is open, free, and highly individual in nature has caused some educators to avoid using programmed educational materials lest they influence children toward one specific way of working. This, of course, needs to be of concern to art educators. Evaluations need to be made of all kinds of art teaching aids, and only those put into use that widen the opportunities for imaginative thinking and freedom of intellectual response as well as fulfill the purposes of conceptual learning in art education as was discussed in Chapter 2.

The use of such a teaching tool as a sequentially planned series of art curriculums in the elementary grades would insure that many important concepts about art, skills, and appreciation materials were provided for the children somewhere in the course of their art education in the first six grades. This series would, hopefully, provide only a basic program that would become a floor under art education supporting many additional teacher- or student-initiated art experiences.

A basic program would be flexible enough to encourage a teacher to present any concept, skill, or medium when it is needed regardless of the placement of it in the basic art curriculum, for any art concept is strengthened by repetition in another context at another time and skills are perfected only by repetition.

58

The irregular shape of the outer edges adds distinction to the head Janet carved. Consider how it might look with a regular round edge.

Art education cannot content itself only with providing for the child's immediate interests. Art education must do this first and continue it as a thread running through all art education. Since art is creative in nature, each must have full opportunity to use his ideas and his own ways. Yet, this alone is not enough. The child must also be educated for the future.

Teaching art to children implies that some art be taught: that some educational purpose lie behind and through every art experience. Although the earlier chapters in this text stressed the identification of quality art experiences for children and described helpful methods of teaching to implement them, something needs to be said about *what* is taught and *when* to teach it as well as *how* it is taught. All three are important and related.

A great deal has been said in this text about the methods or processes of creative art education. The content of an art curriculum and the grade level in which experiences are most effectively presented are also of concern in the teaching of art to children. Every art program needs to be based upon an organized, tested, and appropriate basic curriculum open-ended enough to provide for exciting new ideas, materials, and processes as they emerge, and also to provide for units of art education within the teacher's particular area of strength and interest in art. If, for example, a teacher has a strength in ceramics, a curriculum should provide time and opportunity for children to take advantage of this teacher's depth of study and skill in ceramics. Another year, their teacher may have a depth interest in art history, for example, or printmaking and would be able to provide rich learnings from this area of specialization. If a curriculum is not too tight, children gain from depth study with each teacher as they also build common sequential concepts and skills through a basic curriculum.

> The content of the subject matter of art has for too long been given second place in importance in our American public schools. We have been over-concerned with methodologies (namely, how we teach) at the neglect and expense of the subject matter (namely, what we teach).[1]

Throughout any curriculum in art it is necessary to keep the experience close to the nature of art itself and to the open ways of creativity. For example, a lesson in design can be taught in a way that helps children understand some ways of improving the organization of their work and at the time inspires them toward imaginative original work. On the other hand, the same topic "design" could be taught in an imposed and restricted way that would leave little opportunity for children to escape from the domination of the teacher or the application of certain "rules." Under such circumstances it is the individuality of the children's art work that suffers. There is a danger that a teacher can become restrictive during or following an explanation of a new art process or concept. At every step of the way the teacher needs to keep in mind that she is broadening opportunities and needs to avoid making any restrictive demand that the process or idea she was explaining be immediately applied in each child's art. This is too much direction and too close to dictation.

The teacher walks a tight rope which requires a balance between teaching and liberating, between putting new ideas and knowledge into children's minds, and yet giving them the full right to make up their own minds and use their own ideas and ways.

Isolating one thing, focusing upon it, explaining it, and helping children understand it is what constitutes teaching, and this is a necessary and vital part of every art education program. All new knowledge is added to whatever other knowledge a child already has and becomes a part of his total resource. Every child receives the material that is taught differently and reacts to it differently, depending upon his readiness for it at the time it is presented and upon his emotional state at that time. In one mood, a child may warmly receive any thought; in another he may reject almost any. This is all part of the vital internalizing and individualizing of experiences that is necessary to art. The knowledge, insights, and improved skills that children gain from this focus provide a resource of background materials which children can draw upon to help them improve the expression of their ideas and feelings in art. Unless this educational provision is made, children lose the stimulation that comes from increased competence. Increasing competence can

---

[1] Leon Frankston, "The Case for Depth in Art," *Art Education*, National Art Education Association, Washington, D.C., XX, No. 7 (1967), 5.

most effectively and efficiently be done through long-range planning for the inclusion of basic concepts about art in the curriculum.

Some teachers, afraid that teaching will too heavily influence children, avoid it, preferring instead to let children improve by independently working through their own problems. Changes and improvements do take place in this way, of course, but only those the child is able to see from his own limited experience. He needs and deserves the enrichment and enlightenment that come from an educated teacher knowledgeable in art.

Other teachers, realizing that the educative process includes instruction, revert to teacher-controlled art education methods to support their concept of their function as a teacher.

Neither position is a sound one, and this dilemma need not exist if teachers understand how and when to teach and clearly comprehend the nature of the art experience and their role in it.

ART AS A DISCIPLINE

A discipline is a subject that is taught, a branch of learning, a field of study. From this simple definition, art, too, as well as other subjects in the elementary school, is a discipline, for learning takes place in many ways and under various conditions in art. It is a subject in which there is a great deal to be taught, learned, and explored in many ways. The achievements of art through the ages and in the present; the many directions, branches, and facets that art takes; the highly creative nature and changes within every artist's work, all make a tremendous body of subject matter for art. Although art offers this gigantic body of content that can be approached and studied systematically, this does not mean that every part of the educational process in art is like that in every other of the disciplines. As was previously said, even though the content is presented in organizational form that makes the study of art more efficient and effective, the learning of it must not be dictated but must remain free and open, providing for a different well of resource material for each person, so that art expression can remain varied and individualistic. This awareness of the particular quality of art education also makes it difficult and perhaps inadvisable to readily compare works of art.

The nature of art and of the art process is hard to grasp and to describe, for the two are greatly concerned with the subconscious and with feeling: with the heart as well as the mind. Just how much of feeling, intuition, and sensing go into the creating of art and how much of a role that reason and the conscious play would be difficult, if at all possible, to determine; and it is questionable if such a general determination, once made, would contribute to either the creation of art or to the response to it, for it varies greatly with the person and his purposes. The whole process of either is so complex and distinctive for each person that generalizations might do more to mislead than to instruct. Art is a kind of educational experience that molds, strengthens, and perfects the mental facilities and the capacity for emotional expression.

Knowledge about art can be learned, and a child's competence in art work strengthened, by the study of the main areas in the discipline of art. Knowing something about design, for example, means that it is understood by and can be applied according to the will of each person.

Methods of teaching are important, especially so in the teaching of art, but a study only of the process of teaching art is not enough for a teacher. It cannot be a substitute for a study of art itself. The same applies to children. It is important for them to study and perfect the methods of working with materials in art to create original works, as well as to study the discipline: structure, content, and history of art.

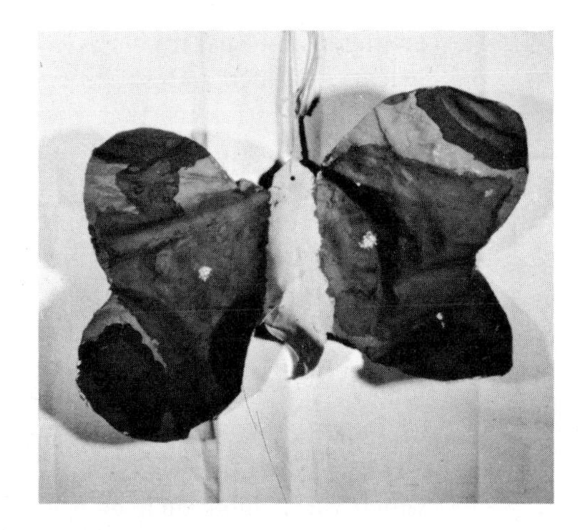

59

Sculptural forms are often created from wire and papier-mâché. The ideas and feelings the child puts into his art are what help give it art quality.

It is not necessary for a teacher to instruct children in ways of grasping inspiration for art and expressing ideas and feelings from its drive, for this is intuitive. Children begin to create art, at their own level of skill and performance, before they meet teachers in a formal school situation, as was indicated in Chapter 8. It is, however, necessary for a teacher to follow a curriculum in art that provides intellectual learning activities for children as well as providing art work to do. Children do not need to be busy every minute creating something with their hands to be studying art.

FEEDING THE RESOURCES FOR ART

Children learn from everything that happens to them both in and out of school. These experiences feed children's knowledge and sensitivity, and become additional stock in their resources for art. When a teacher helps children become more acutely aware of their activities, environment, and of nature, she is encouraging them to build richer resources by profiting more deeply from everything they see, do, feel, and imagine.

However, there is much knowledge about art that children would not be at all likely to grasp for themselves. They need to have these things pointed out, explained, and illustrated to them. This kind of information supplies still further richness to their resources for art, and can be used as intellectual tools to help facilitate the organization and expression of their experiences that children need for all kinds of art work.

Teachers need to make available to children a continuous stream of new knowledge, which is consumed to an extent determined by their personality demands at the time. Children need this wealth of personally selected resources so that they have abundance from which they can pick and choose for their art.

It is the individual character of each child's distinctive internal well of resources that provides for his originality in art, and makes art such a fascinating realm in which to work or observe. To maintain this important personal quality in art it is necessary that each child be permitted to include among his internal resources only those that seem important to him. When a teacher's influence is so strong that each child feels required to feed back through his art ideas that the teacher fed to him, the individualization of art breaks down.

The instructional process must be strong, clear, and interesting, so that all of the children will comprehend the goals toward which they are being taught. But at the same time, the presentation and follow-up needs to be undemanding, giving each child the privilege of deciding how and when he will use it, to reject it altogether, or to modify it to suit himself. In this way the individual character of children's resources for art is strengthened and built.

New knowledge, when dynamically presented and clearly taught, blends and strengthens children's store of intellectual reserves and becomes material which they, upon their own choices, *may elect* to use for their subsequent art work.

Although some exercises in the application of the new knowledge may be a part of the teacher's presentation, when the children approach creative art work, the choice of using this or any knowledge or skill is up to each child individually. New knowledge as a vital basis for intellectual growth and for art achievement is essential to art education, and practically every child profits from all well-planned explanations in some way even though identifiable evidence of it may not appear in his art. Teachers need to be prepared in art for this flexibility of acceptance and use of new concepts, for this is consistent with the nature of art and is reflected in the works of mature artists.

A teacher who really understands the nature and importance of individual differences, of providing for them in education and who does not simply pay lip service to this important area, considers it no rejection of herself as a teacher when a child does not use in his art some knowledge she has worked hard to teach. What is sometimes difficult for a teacher to understand is that some children will internalize the knowledge slowly, postponing or never using it in the form in which it was given, but letting it affect their other resources and flow in this way into their art without conscious effort. To insure the ever-changing original aspect of art, art education must remain on this open take-it-or-leave-it basis.

What the planned curriculum in art needs to supply is not so much the experiences that children can derive elsewhere, but rather the art concepts that help them express these experiences.

> If the stereotyping of responses and the suppression of novelty in the use of materials are to be avoided, information should be taught with only that level of motivation needed to maintain relevant activity.[2]

A SEQUENTIALLY PLANNED CURRICULUM

Concepts in art that require some previous background knowledge with which to relate are more difficult to understand than others. Since learning involves identification and understanding, it is wise to organize the materials to be learned so that the most basic and simple concepts related to a phase of art are presented first, and ample opportunity is given to children to identify them in a variety of situations, understand their meaning, and apply them when, how, and if they wish. Then a length of time should elapse before presenting the next related step, to allow for assimilation, familiarity, and a feeling that children are "at home" with the first basic concepts before introducing the next. In art it is especially important to provide this margin of time for a child to transform and incorporate new concepts into a blend with his own distinctive substance, for fluency in art requires smooth and easy access to all of a person's resources without labored concern in dealing with a concept still very much on the immediate conscious level.

In considering sequential planning of concepts through a curriculum in art for the elementary school, it is advantageous to children to space the concepts at intervals through the six grades, beginning with the simplest and advancing to the most difficult. For example, there are concepts and facts about color that are a vital part of art education and which can and should be taught in the elementary school, for children use colors, select them, and observe them in their environments before they come to school and throughout their entire lives.

The conscious study of basic knowledge about color adds another dimension to children's natural feeling for color. The learned concepts need not replace a child's natural feeling for color and its uses, but rather extend and refine it and enhance a color resource that is exclusive with each individual.

One basic curriculum in art for elementary schools presents color sequentially in this way:

FIRST GRADE: Naming and identifying basic colors.

SECOND GRADE: Use of a wide range of colors; identifying light and dark colors; mixing colors to make them light and dark.

THIRD GRADE: How color is used to unify a painting; changing colors by texturing them; effect of various backgrounds on color; pri-

[2] Sheridan Dauster Speeth, "The Rational Design for Toys," *Journal of Creative Behavior*, Creative Education Foundation, Buffalo, N.Y., I, No. 4 (1967), 398.

mary colors (identification), concept of them, and mixing them; identifying colors that are mixed with other colors.

FOURTH GRADE: Identifying and understanding shade; mixing various shades of one color; identifying warm and cool colors.

FIFTH GRADE: Related colors; warm and cool colors; colors considered warm and cool by comparison; receding and emerging quality of colors.

SIXTH GRADE: Shading; contrast; individual use of color; closely related colors.

Throughout this curriculum knowledge about and use of color is presented in almost every art experience.[3]

When a total study of color is presented in any one grade, it often becomes technical, tedious, and confusing. When presented sequentially and reinforced throughout later grades, time is provided for the assimilation of various aspects of this complex topic and color and becomes related to every other aspect of art in the total on-going art activities. By thoughtful sequential planning many topics such as design, drawing, sculpture, architecture, line, texture can be presented at the level most appropriate for them and their study broadened and deepened in subsequent grades.

DIRECT AND INDIRECT ART EDUCATION

A curriculum in art provides for direct teaching through structured sequences of concepts, skills, and creative art work; but it also needs to provide amply for indirect education through art as well, for there are some qualities about art that can better be taught indirectly: aesthetic judgment is one, sensitivity to personalized expression in art is another.

THE CHILD AS LEARNER

An example of direct and indirect art education can be studied by referring to color Plate XXVIII which is a teaching page from a current new curriculum in art. The direct purpose of this page is to teach first-grade children to recognize and name the basic colors. Yet, at the same time, they also see and *indirectly* absorb, in individually varying degrees, the fact that all reds are not identical—that there are varying shades and tones of every color. Many will also notice that each color block is a design. Some noticing the designs will also become aware of the simplicity of them and aware of the varying designs on the page, thus absorbing some measure of concept about design.

Both direct and indirect learning again take place as children study with their teacher the works of professional artists, deepening the children's awareness of and feeling for art as the teacher calls their attention to certain

[3] From *My World of Art* Series by Blanche Jefferson, Barbara McGeary, Barbara W. Fredette, and Clyde McGeary. © Copyright 1963 and 1964 by Allyn and Bacon, Inc. Reprinted by permission of the publisher.

qualities of the art and discusses these with them. While this is taking place, the children may perceive certain additional and unmentioned aspects of the art. For example, if the teacher were to use the painting by Corneille (Plate L) as a means of helping children deepen their response to art, they would be consciously aware of the qualities of the painting that she emphasized. As the teacher points out and describes the ways the artist organized the parts of his art, "direct" learning takes place. But "indirect" learning is quite possibly also taking place, and different children may be absorbing different aspects of the art. Some may notice the shapes of the forms, others the patterns of dark and light, still others the textures or the enriched colors. Without the benefit of words or direct pupil-teacher communication this important and personalized learning takes place.

The Pre-service Teacher as Learner

This text is written basically for the college student who will teach art to children. Throughout the text and in the illustrations with their captions much "direct" teaching is evident. The prospective teacher learns, hopefully, from it. But there are other facets of his educational experience also being "indirectly" fed. For example, both direct and indirect learning can be found in Illustration 20 in Chapter 3. The caption calls attention to the fact that the teacher is giving individual guidance to each child as he works on his original piece of crafts. But the observant pre-service teacher will *indirectly* learn more. She will notice that in a painting project the children's clothing is covered with aprons and the table protected by newspapers. She will also notice that the children work in small groups, sharing colors as they are supervised by their teacher. There is an atmosphere of orderly informality in this working group of children. The concentration of each child as he is involved with his original art work can also be observed. All of this, while presented "indirectly," is important information for a teacher to have.

Another example of direct and indirect learning is shown through Plate XXI. Direct teaching is inherent in the caption that calls attention to torn paper as an art medium for first-grade children. One who studies the plate closely can also learn that newspaper gives an exciting textural area to the composition; that torn and cut edges contrast and enhance each other; that children care little about the naturalistic appearance of objects as shown in the chimney on the house or the witch's eyes; and that the whole art work has a feeling for Halloween.

"Art is more 'caught' than taught" is a well-known adage, and the inclusion of materials to be presented indirectly adds richness to the curriculum and remains an effective tool in art education.

BASIC AREAS IN A CURRICULUM

At every level of study an art education curriculum needs to cover three basic areas:

(a) Concepts about art to understand.

(b) Creative art work to do.
(c) Works of art to study.

They are not listed here in preferential order, for one is just as important as another. These three fundamental approaches to the study of art feed each other in building a comprehensive art education.

Structuring these areas within a curriculum offers strength to both comprehension and competence. As these three approaches to art education are brought to bear upon the study of texture, for example, the statements explaining the concept of texture bring one kind of enlightenment. Examples of works of art that show the use of texture clarify ways that texture is used and how it helps add meaning to a work of art. The actual involvement in finding ways of expressing textural surfaces and applying texture to works of art adds personal interpretation to the study of texture and gives the learner an additional tool for broadening the resources from which he can more acutely individualize the character of his own creative art expression.

Concepts

A concept in art is the understanding of a general art term or idea that includes a grasp of its essential meaning. It is more than just an explanation of a term; it includes a knowledge of, an appreciation for, and a feeling about the main idea running through an aspect of art.

A concept in art can be introduced in an elementary way in one of the primary grades, broadened, and built upon as children advance. The introduction of the visual concept of color as described earlier in this chapter was enlarged at various intervals through the elementary grades, broadening the concept of color.

The concept of design can be built in the same way. In the first grade, children can become visually aware of design in their environment and be able in this way to recognize it and have some feeling for its use and diversity. Design as a plan, as a pattern, and as decoration are extensions of the concept that can be presented sequentially in an art curriculum.

To effectively help children come to terms with some of the complex qualities of art, it is necessary to simplify statements about them. This is not as easy as it sounds, for much knowledge about art is gained from a feeling for it and from working through the problems involved in it. People whose concepts are built upon this foundation may never have verbalized them or needed to, but teachers do need to use words to explain concepts to children; and when these words and phrases are simplified, understanding of them is easier. It takes time and effort for a teacher to do this. If programmed art education materials include tersely worded basic and sequentially expanding concepts, the teacher's time can be devoted to illustrating them and helping individual children see them in art and put them into practice.

However, it is out of place to unduly emphasize the teaching of concepts to children, because overconcern with them can destroy the spontaneity and freedom that give to child art much of its charm and vigor. Children work best when they have no restrictions on their thinking, no "set rules" by which they feel they should be guided.

Art knowledge influences children to bring order and control into the expression of their ideas. It should be introduced, explained, but not overstressed. Concepts need to be taught in the spirit of increasing visual awareness and building art judgments and *not* as inflexible rules.

> In our zeal to leave children free to express themselves we have lost track of the importance of knowledge to freedom. We have seemed to assume that to try to increase children's knowledge would impair their freedom. But, as a matter of fact, freedom is usually dependent upon knowledge.[4]

Creative Art Work to Do

Researchers and others in art education along with those in general education have been centering a great deal of attention upon aspects of creativity to the point where it concentrates almost a disproportionate amount of attention upon this one phase of art, overshadowing others. Important and basic as it is, there are other aspects of art education that also deserve stress. Design is one of them, for design is actually the supporting structure of any work of art.

60

A small line or spot can become a point of departure for creativity in art. Illustrations 61–65 are examples of art work created around this given line.

A balanced curriculum in art, built upon the philosophy of creative expression, bases every art experience upon creativity as it deals also with other essentials. Chapters 1 and 4, particularly, describe and emphasize creative art work for children to do, and Chapter 2 deals with reasons for it. Since it has been the thread through this whole text, further detailed emphasis of it seems unnecessary here. However, many kinds of art work with various media do need careful consideration within every curriculum.

The five compositions done by second-grade children in Illustrations 61–65 from the given line in Illustration 60 show another approach to the development of originality in art. The use of a line, shadow, bit of texture, or color variation on a piece of paper is a departure from having to confront a blank sheet of paper, and can occasionally be used by children as a springboard for creative art.

The challenge of meeting a fragment of something and utilizing it as a part of a new art composition not only gives variety to the way creativity can be developed, but this fragment found by the child on his paper pro-

---

[4] Merritt, *op. cit.*, p. 38.

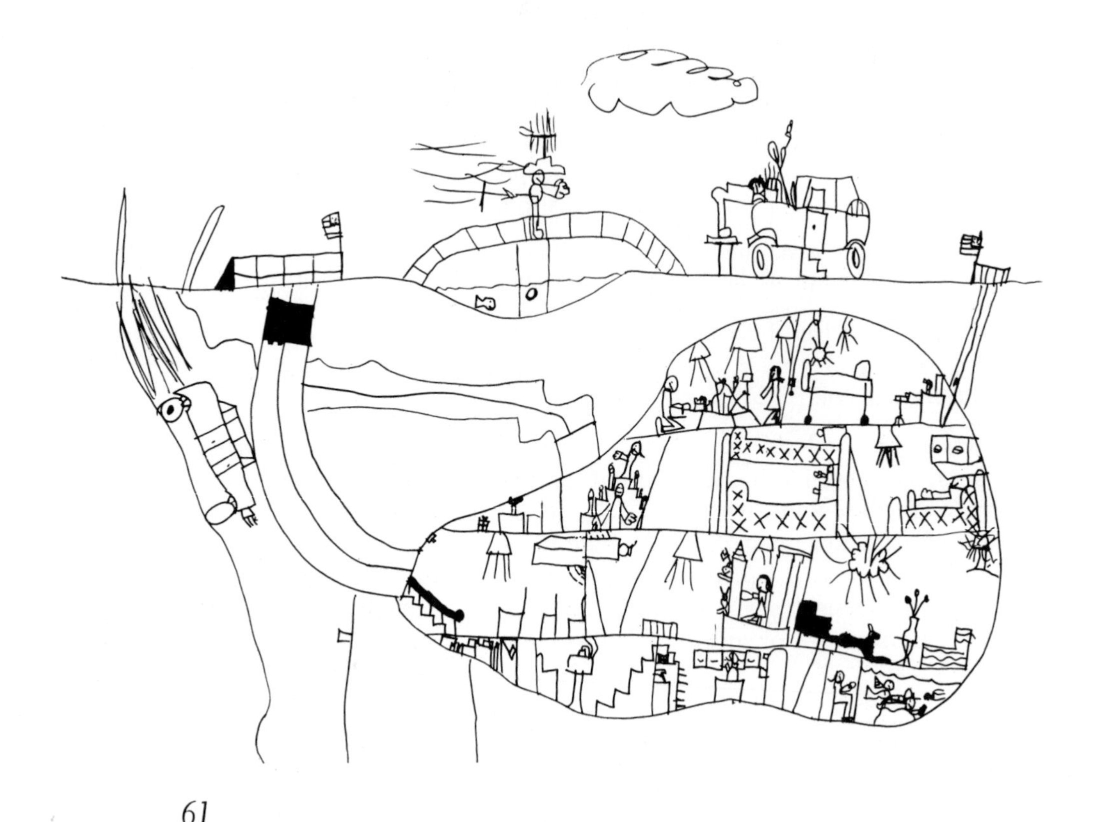

61

Larry's drawing is complex and imaginative with well-conceived space divisions and interesting details of how people might live underground.

vides its own motivation. The imagination goes immediately to work, suggesting numerous ideas that can be developed from this simple and flexible beginning. As children turn their paper vertically (62) other possible ideas occur to them. Turning it upside down as Illustration 64 shows stimulates thinking in other directions.

Educationally, children need increasingly more types of situations in which they can use their imaginations and resources to solve problems creatively, for ways of working, communicating, and dealing with situations change fast; so do the vast number of products we use and need to adjust to. Then, too, the very nature of art itself demands a constant search for new uses of materials and new ways of expressing ideas and emotions.

The use of a visual motivation instead of a verbal one also brings the nature of motivation closer to the essential quality and essence of art than verbalization does. This is not to imply that the use of such a "found" object in either drawing or sculpture might replace plain paper and unformed materials. It is simply to suggest it as an occasional variation of the approach to art.

When using a "found" visual motivation, it is sometimes (but not always) helpful to children if the teacher conducts a pre-work discussion of possible forms and ideas that can develop from the cue, much as creative expression in art is motivated, as discussed in Chapter 4.

Not every visual motivation can be placed at any grade level. Some are successful with one age group and not another. They need to be carefully studied, tested in use with children, and placed at the grade level in which they stimulate the highest quality art.

Works of Art to Study

Blended with and fortifying the creating of art and understanding concepts about it is the encountering of works of art to study. Examples of art from various periods in history need constantly to be in children's line of

62

Lucinda's drawing is strong and direct. The slanting arm and purse overlapping the tree unify these objects. The line helps form the body.

63

Eugene brought his lunch to school, and in art class, from the given line in Illustration 60, he drew himself eating. The large desk organizes the small shapes on it, and the bent drinking straws carry the eye back to the child.

vision, and displayed pieces frequently changed lest children become indifferent to them. Representations from various types of art such as architecture, furniture, fabrics, painting, collage, pottery, sculpture, printmaking, and drawing are desirable. They should also represent a broad cross section of styles of expression, and not just what is in popular taste or representative of any one person's preference.

At times attention may be called to the displayed examples and possibly a discussion begun; at other times the art is simply there for children to see, to react to, and to adjust to. Response to art may actually suffer from verbalization. To talk about art is to deny a basic aspect of its nature: that it is a silent visual language. Not to discuss art at all with children may, on the other hand, deny them the educational asset of involvement with art on another level: to sound it out, to share it, and perhaps in this way to see something in a new light.

Because art is a visual area, children need to learn to see it, to look at it, to have it where it can easily be seen. Children can, then, focus upon it and

64

In drawing both the above- and below-ground growth of flowers, Jimmie correlated art with nature.

65

Alex's crayon composition shows a car going over a bump in the road (the given line) near a farm. The verticals balance the horizontals and help organize the many elements in the picture.

return to it. Unconsciously and indirectly art becomes more a part of each child. Response to art will be studied in more depth in Chapter 12.

The vast number of works of art available for study continually increases as the art changes, so the necessity for including quantities of examples of them in the art curriculum becomes more demanding.

66

An art curriculum needs to include some drawing for the sake of improving skills. Jan's drawing not only shows competence but also the lonely feeling of the girl at the window.

The world of art can seem and perhaps be ambiguous and often contradictory. Expression in art moves from one point of view to another. No sooner does a person studying art begin to grasp current expressions than he is faced with vigorous new works that challenge him toward a broader acceptance of kinds of art expression, new forms possibly running counter to existing ones and to each other. It is vital, then, that every work of art be approached as a new world free of preconceived ideas of skill, taste, and content. A free mind, closed only to prejudice, can be refreshed and enriched by art. Their teacher's example may be all that children need to help them respond openly to works of art.

BUILDING AWARENESS

A constant that runs through a well-planned curriculum in art education is the building of awareness, particularly visual and artistic awareness. The more things that children know about, the more ideas they have available for art; the more they know, sense, and feel about anything, the more expressively they can create from it in art. A background of knowledge and reactions is necessary to feed a child's constant need for creativity. Because children learn all the time, because they are exposed to a wealth of materials and to emotional stimuli, it may not seem necessary for a teacher to add much; but a child can see and learn only to the extent that his maturity and experience make it possible. Children need the help of adults to extend their capacities and to open new vistas, and they often feel helpless without this teaching.

The art teacher can help children increase awareness of nature, art, and their environment and at the same time point out art elements in what they see. For example: in art, when discussing their completed work or the work of a mature artist, call attention to the uneven spaces between the objects within a group, or help children see the various shapes of objects and forms; in nature, help children note the different shapes of trees or the diversity of coloring of birds; in their environment help children become cognizant of the differences in the shapes of buildings and the characteristic shapes of some of them, as well as the many textures in objects they encounter and how that texture enhances the form.

The ever-present effort to increase the breadth and depth of children's awareness should become a steady stream of conscious alertness to all kinds of visual, emotional, auditory, and other stimulating influences to which children and teacher together can help each other build greater sensitivity. Children can be helped to give attention to the ways their own individual personalities answer each contact, not only as factual feedback, but especially to the physical and emotional reactions they have. The avenue into the area of the personality that contributes greatly to expressiveness in art has predominantly to do with physical senses and especially with the emotions.

Meanwhile the intellect is also being soundly strengthened through these same procedures. People learn faster and remember better those things to which they have responded through more than one facet of their total being.

Art requires the total involvement of the emotions, the bodily senses, and the mind. Thus, the building of awareness is one of the essentials in art education that needs to be a daily experience. Since in many other areas of the elementary school curriculum children concentrate upon objective facts, it is important that emphasis also be given to the subjective responses and to awareness to objects and experiences in art, nature, and the environment that may not be found in the study of other school subjects.

> One of the most important things that a teacher or parent can help children to retain as they mature is their awareness of experiences through the use of their senses and emotions. The creative person keeps his openness to experiences and in this respect he is childlike. The child does not feel that a new experience will be a risk to him. He perceives the world without feeling he has to make judgments about it. During early childhood he collects much raw material without deciding "what" or "how" he will use it. How much information is collected and what is done with it will determine his creative potential not only as a child but as an adult.[5]

> Art is a matter of perception as well as expression, and children cannot reasonably be expected to express their interpretations of their environment unless they have keenly observed that environment.[6]

TEACHING-LEARNING AIDS

There has been a tremendous growth in the amount, variety, and excellence of teaching-learning aids in art; yet these tools are not used in the elementary school art program as much as they might be.

Teachers' study of and investigations with new kinds of consumable art materials have kept many so busy that they have not given time to explorations of the possibilities of teaching-learning aids in art except, perhaps, in the use of motion pictures and slides. Others hesitate because they fear a mechanical device or a programmed educational tool might influence or channel children's thinking in prescribed ways; and, of course, teachers should evaluate every device they consider using to insure that it will not only instruct, but also do it in such a way that it inspires original ideas. There are such educationally sound aids available now among the films, slides, serialized textbooks, reproductions, educational television programs, and other teaching-learning tools which are becoming less expensive and at the same time contain a greater amount and higher quality of color.

Some of these tools present materials that will help a teacher make her point by adding well-organized, highly selective content that would be difficult for individual teachers to procure and time consuming to arrange and unify. Others can be used more independently by a child to help him in referring to sequences within a complex art process, such as printmaking. In this way he learns to use resource materials in managing complicated processes and doing it at his own pace. Having this help available to him as he needs it gives him more confidence since it frees him from the teacher as a reference for this kind of information. Meanwhile, the children's individual use of these teaching-learning aids allows the teacher to work with the children on a different level: in guiding their designs, stimulating them to further their ideas, opening up new doors to them, and helping them achieve to their own highest standards.

The wealth of knowledge existing about art and the extensive facets of art in which artists work make it imperative to extend every educational op-

---

[5] Linderman and Heberholz, *op. cit.*, p. 11.

[6] Merritt, *op. cit.*, p. 39.

67 68

The making of puppets can be as creative as any other form of art if the teacher places the activity within a creative context, as these two illustrations show.

portunity as much as possible to give children some knowledge about art along with many experiences in creating it. Since time is a factor in every school schedule, the educational value of each art work period can be amplified through the use of highly selective teaching-learning aids.

SUGGESTED ACTIVITIES

1. *Plan the kind of an art awareness notebook that a child might keep and use. Think of possible titles for it. What would children put into it? How could these notebooks be shared with other children?*
2. *Study and discuss in a group published curriculums in art for the elementary grades, evaluating each from:*
   (*a*) *The three basic areas necessary to a balanced curriculum (pages 183–184 of this text).*
   (*b*) *The creative viewpoint toward art education.*

10

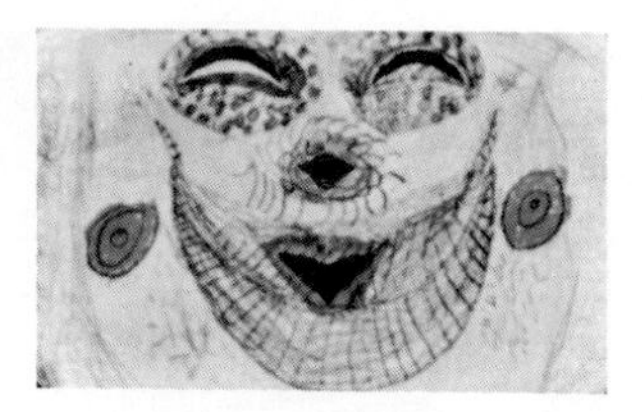

Relation of Art to Other Subject Areas

ART IS RELATED to every human experience and emotion. There is an existing connection between the activities and feelings of the artist and the art work that he creates whether the artist is an elementary school child or a mature professional.

Art is inspired by life situations and by the imagination that finds its basis in an experience. A very important part of the experiences and activities of children in the elementary school is their curriculum of studies. Art is a part of this curriculum. Relationships exist between art and the other areas of the curriculum. Some of these areas show direct influences and associations; others are less direct in their relationships.

It is important for teachers to understand that such relationships exist and that learnings from the one reenforce, intensify, and magnify the learnings and understandings from the other areas. It is just as important, however, for a teacher to realize that every area of the curriculum has its own merits and qualities and that the teacher has a responsibility not to let one subject become subordinated to or to encroach on the other.

The particular values derived from art and art education were discussed in Chapter 2, and the nature of art is covered in Chapters 1, 8, 9, and 11. With these distinguishing qualities and contributions of art and art education in mind, consider throughout this chapter your evaluation of the effects of "correlation" upon art and the act of creating art.

CORRELATION

Relationships between one subject and another or among several subjects mean that there are particular ways in which these areas extend into each other. In teaching art it is wise to be aware of the close connection between it and other areas of the curriculum and between art and life experiences out of school. Art depends for much of its subject-matter content on these activities. Art has no subject matter of its own, so every art expression is a *correlation* with something. Learnings from other areas of the curriculum are frequently transferred to art. In poster-making, for example, it might be interesting to list the skills and knowledges involved that were acquired in the study of other things—such as spelling, for one. All learning depends on integration of the new experience with past learnings; art education does, too. The more extensive the integration, the more easily the new knowledge is learned and remembered.

Teacher-Structured Correlation

For some years educators especially in elementary education, interested in more effective education, have resorted to correlating art with other school subjects as a way of reenforcing and extending learnings in another school subject. They believed that the need for children to put what they had learned from the other area of the curriculum into visual form through art would cause them to review and reenforce what they knew about the subject and find the additional knowledge about it needed for their art work. Since art allowed freedom of choice of a topic for an art experience, they thought (erroneously) that the choice of a subject did not, then, make any difference and that here was another opportunity to advance and strengthen the other area of the curriculum.

This freedom of individual choice of a topic—so basic for the artist and in art education—can, in this and possibly other ways, be misconstrued unless the necessity for intellectual freedom in art is understood as a part of the art process itself.

The imposition upon children's right to determine their own topic for art and the invalidating of intellectual freedom in art was, they believed, justified if it served their adult purposes which were unrelated to art. In these cases, the teacher often guided the on-going art work as a history lesson, for example, and in a different way than would have been done in an open creative art experience (as described in Chapter 8, pages 164–165), expecting children to disregard their preferences for her purposes.

These educators, and they were (and still are) many, failed to understand the nature and purposes of art, and supported the practice of infringing upon the art experience in the belief that this was one of art's contributions to education.

Recently, however, educators studying new subjects for the elementary school and more effective methods of teaching all subjects developed new and personally meaningful ways of conducting the teaching-learning situations. The New Mathematics and Science for the Elementary School are examples of what has resulted.

As educators reexamined ways of individualizing instruction and freeing children to learn by setting the tasks and paces for themselves, some found that the contributions art makes to the entire field of education is in the *methods* or *processes* inherent in the creative teaching and working in art

69 (*top*)

What is learned in other subjects motivates a child in art. The intense red background dramatizes the impending danger of the Indian following the Pilgrim through the woods.

70

A lesson about butterflies motivated a second-grade child to paint a boy holding a butterfly. Note the functional proportion.

as presented in earlier chapters of this text. Instead of art "serving" education on such a shallow basis as concern only with the subject matter of art, these educators have recognized art's contribution to other school subjects is, rather, in the self-determined open approaches of working and teaching.

> When a capable coordinator isn't available, how does one begin teaching science as a way of investigating one's total environment? If a teacher conducts an art class as recommended by Dr. Blanche Jefferson of the University of Pittsburgh in her elementary series, *My World of Art*, the teacher is also capable of guiding students in the field of science.

71 (*top*)

The first-grade girl who drew this picture was so impressed by her role in a dramatization of a reading lesson that she not only used it as a topic for art but also exaggerated the size of herself in comparsion to the boy and the audience.

72

"Robby the Thinking Robot" is a title in keeping with our present technology.

> Art can help a child to see and understand his environment. In art, the child usually gets an idea and often comes up with some type of conclusion or solution. A good science teacher, then, works somewhat like a good art teacher.[1]

> . . . in 1952 an International Society for Education Through Art was founded, sponsored by UNESCO, and held its first General Assembly in Paris in 1954. INSEA, as it is called, now has branches throughout the

[1] Emil Abramovic, "New Approaches to Elementary Science Teaching," *American Teacher*, American Federation of Teachers, XLIX, No. 1 (1964), 20.

world, but this does not mean that its claim—that art should be made the basis of education—has been widely recognized. It conflicts too directly with the technologically motivated education of advanced industrial societies. But the progress of this simple idea in twenty years has been amazing, and I believe that it may yet conquer the world.[2]

Sometimes two areas of the curriculum are tortured into a correlation such as attempting to model or paint what the music says or to express the mood of the music. Music is an auditory area and art a visual one. There is no reason why children should try to shape into a visual form the music they hear, for this implies that music arouses in the listener some visual images. This is not necesarily so. Music has its own qualities, and each person enjoys it in his own way. Modeling or painting what the music says is just about as absurd as taking a painting to a piano and playing it.

The development of creativeness, inventiveness, and originality is a vital purpose of art education. When this is discouraged or forbidden, the child loses the type of experiences that were meant for him when art was included in his school life.

There is, basically, one factor that determines whether the child is provided with opportunities for his *art* growth or whether the time allotted to art is being used to teach and to emphasize other learnings. This factor is the *basis on which judgments are made* throughout the working process. The basis for judgments in art should be *art qualities*. To be an art experience the activity must be centered in *art* purposes, *art* judgments, and *art* education.

Child-Selected Correlation

Without any particular intent to frame a juncture between two areas of the curriculum, children often choose such relationships because of their interest in them. The example explained in the discussion between Janice and her teacher in Chapter 5 shows that the child's interest in reading a story became the subject matter for her art. In the early part of Chapter 8 the children and teacher discuss the ratio of sizes existing among the various parts of their own bodies. A direct dependence on the knowledge gained in this way was used by the children to improve their art expression. Such relationships between art and other areas of study occur every day. They are so common that, frequently, we take little notice of them.

At its best, the correlation of art with another area of the curriculum can add a new dimension to learning when it is truly an art experience. Since art relies heavily upon the imagination and the emotions, it can add the emotional dimension to factual education, making the educational experience more personal to the learner and more true to life. Every human action has its accompanying reaction. Since we have some feeling about everything we do, art, with its expression and reflection of emotion, adds this depth to learning. If a child chooses the early settlers as a topic for his art, the teacher

---

[2] Herbert Read, "Whatever Happened to the Great Simplicities?" *Saturday Review*, February 18, 1967, p. 48.

might help him more closely relate the topic to the nature of art and, at the same time, add another dimension to his appreciation of these pioneers through questions that would personalize it to him and bring his imagination into it by helping him focus upon the emotional aspects of their experiences and not simply the recording of factual information. For example: If you were a ten-year-old pioneer boy, how would it feel to come face-to-face for the first time with a group of Indian children playing in the woods? How could you show this feeling in your art?

Correlation that comes easily, that seems to flow naturally into children's minds, usually results in the richest art work. Some exciting school experiences are sources for individual art activities. However, much of the factual representation is lost in correlation with art as both the teacher and children concentrate upon the transference from chronological sequences or the dominance and subordination of characters and events in the factual subject to the kind of dominance and subordination required in an art composition. In art, color affects size, and the need of the composition determines size and placement. The feeling to be expressed affects colors and causes exaggeration of some things that may not have been important to the factual material. For the sake of the art expression, items may be omitted altogether that were important to the other area of the curriculum. Art has its own

73

Children apply their art knowledge to solve problems that arise in a variety of situations. These first-grade children are painting a church window to use in their Christmas play.

values and makes its own demands which require the person doing the art sometimes to sacrifice the factual, to change it, adapt it, or omit it.

GROUP PROJECTS

Group projects are a common way of correlating art with another school subject. A small or large group of children works on one piece of art and attempts to develop a unified composition. Usually one person's idea is chosen as the main theme, and the group works it out as it is or may reorganize it first. What usually results is that one person's idea is executed on a large scale by several persons whose own ideas are subordinated to his. Although it is true that a large display piece results, it is questionable if more than one child in the group had an art experience.

74

Knowledge from science inspired this crab; but because it is art, it need not adhere to the realism of science.

Whatever social or other values group projects may have for children, they have limited art value. Art is and always has been a highly individual way of working. What great works of art were ever created through the group process? It is *art* we are teaching to children, and the qualities and practices of art education should be closely related to those in fine art.

WORKBOOKS

In the elementary grades, workbooks are frequently used as one of several aids to promote learning in some of the school subjects. Realizing the advantages to be gained by relating art experiences to another area of the curriculum, many of these workbooks contain pictures that may illustrate the work of another subject, by providing opportunities for children to color inside outlines or even to copy pictures. In fact, many of the workbooks contain specific instructions for children to copy a certain figure and to color it with a particular hue. This is particularly true of many workbooks used in the primary grades. The intent and purpose of preparing such workbooks is to relate the textual material to the drawing and coloring activity in order to promote learning through more than one type of experience. In doing this, emphasis has been placed on the desired effect on the subject-matter learning, and little regard has been given to the effect such workbook copy experiences may have on the children's art.

Art educators have long been aware of the possible effects on children's art of these copy activities as well as those requiring the children to color within prescribed lines. As explained in Chapter 1, such activities have very little or no value for children. In fact, they may often have detrimental effects on the child's confidence in his own ideas and on his creative art concepts. Interfering with the child's ideas and displacing his own concepts of form with prepared shapes can cause mental and emotional confusion and affect his creative work.

The effect of workbook copy experiences on the creative concepts of children was measured in an experiment with 28 first-grade children.[3] Early in the term, before the children had been exposed to workbooks, they were each asked to make several individual drawings of objects that were later presented to them on reading and arithmetic workbook sheets. The workbook sheets each involved a copy experience. Following this, they were again asked to make individual drawings of the same forms on 9 by 12 inch drawing paper.

Comparing the second drawings against the first showed that few children were able to withstand the influence of the workbook forms given them to copy; their second drawings showed various degrees of resemblance to the workbook forms. The quality of the art work in their second drawings had deteriorated, and many were noticeably smaller in size after the copy exposure. Many of the second drawings were more difficult to recognize because of the conflict between the child's idea and that imposed upon him by the workbook.

The accompanying examples of two children's work show how workbook copy experiences affected their art (75, 76). Three drawings are shown with each example. The first shows the child's creative concept of the form before the workbook experience. The second is a line drawing enlarged many times from the very small one used in the workbook, and the third is the same child's drawing of the same subject following the workbook copy experience.

The first example of Curtis' work shows a well-developed concept of a house. It has a robust, solid look of strength. Details such as roof shingles, the attic window, and the boy in the foreground help to enrich Curtis' art.

---

[3] Irene Russell and Blanche Waugaman, "The Effect of Workbook Copy Experiences on the Creative Concepts of Children," *Research Bulletin*, Eastern Arts Association, Kutztown, Pa., Vol. III, No. 1 (1952).

75

Curtis drew the picture to the left before he colored the workbook form (center). The drawing to the right, made afterward, shows the barren effect of the workbook experience.

76

Lucille's art expression shows marked deterioration as a result of her workbook copy experience.

The center line drawing is the enlarged workbook form. The last drawing of a house is one made by Curtis following the workbook experience of copying the form of the house. The second drawing greatly resembles the workbook form; many of the meaningful details are lost, and it lacks the interesting art qualities of the first.

Lucille's work is another example of the deterioration that took place following a workbook copy experience. In the first example, done before the workbook experience, the girl in the picture looks happy and is holding her doll, an activity common to little girls and one they all seem to enjoy. Her arms are bent to hold the doll (not an easy thing for a six-year-old to attempt to draw). The body, arms, and legs of the girl have solidity. The girl is drawn in a front view, which most small children use in their drawings. Lucille has included a doll carriage to complete her picture.

The enlarged workbook image in the center is a grotesque drawing of a girl. Children, themselves, know better. Study details of this figure, compare it with Lucille's first drawing, and you will see how much more interesting and well developed her drawing is.

In looking at Lucille's second drawing, you can see the deterioration in aesthetic quality and in the concept of the figure that has taken place. Lucille still wanted the girl to hold her doll, but she found it difficult with a side view. The girl is holding the doll by the hair with one hand, which is not only an unnatural position but also causes the picture to lose much of its warm, human, emotional appeal. The only item in both Lucille's drawings that did not appear in the workbook copy experience was the doll carriage. Nothing interfered with her concept of the carriage, so it remained the same.

Since areas of the curriculum are related, and since transfers of learning take place from one to the other, teachers need constantly to appraise the experiences they provide for children. Teachers who believe in creative art and who would not consider using copy work or prepared outlines in art often are proud of the numerous workbooks they use with children. Often teachers use the workbooks without having regarded the possible consequences of the copy experiences many of them contain. Coloring inside a form is actually a copy activity because it forces the child to follow the form.

Just looking at the very small size of the spaces provided for children to color should be evidence to teachers of the inappropriateness of such work for small children, who have not yet developed enough manual dexterity to control their work in such small areas.

A few teachers may try to justify workbook experiences on the basis of the importance of such work to reading or any subject. It seems questionable whether the emphases of activity in some workbooks are those connected with the subject the exercises are intended to develop. Sometimes the matching of a word is the only subject-matter activity—the emphasis of the child's time being given to the drawing or coloring activity.

Teachers need to be discriminating in their selection and use of materials in every area of the curriculum because subjects are related, and learnings from one affect learnings and expression in another.

SUGGESTED ACTIVITIES

1. *Study the examples of children's art in this volume, then list those in which the topic for the art was influenced by content from another area of the curriculum.*
2. *Study a modern up-to-date workbook from a subject in another area of the elementary school curriculum to determine whether or not there are any experiences in it that would be in opposition to the art education philosophy of this text.*

11

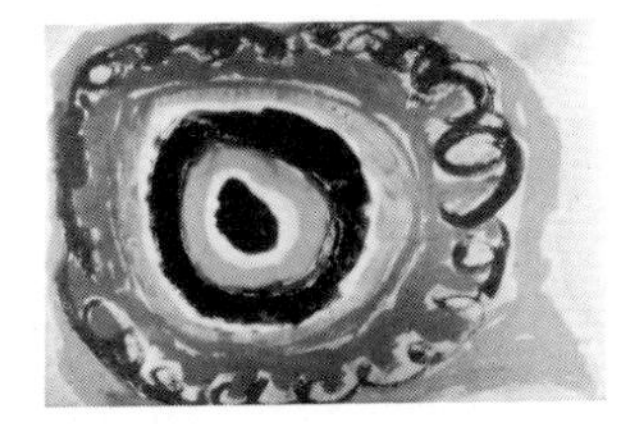

Influence of Individuality and Experiences on Art

THE INDIVIDUAL DIFFERENCES among children, developed from heredity, environment, and experiences, influence and determine the child's art products. The individuality of the child is shown in his personality as qualities that distinguish him from others. His experiences encompass everything that has happened to him: the things he has done, seen, read, heard, imagined, felt, or dreamed. His personality and his experiences interact in a way to influence each other. Because each child is different, widely varying reactions to activities occur. Because experiences affect each child differently, each develops in a way that makes him unique. This uniqueness determines the child's art work. Since the child himself decides upon the subject matter for his art, he draws upon his personal resources for ideas, thus learning a self-reliance that strengthens him.

Even though several children are exposed to the same activity at the same time, each is impressed differently by it. Each is attracted to that aspect of it that personally impresses him the most. Therefore, he does not actually have quite the same experience as the others.

It is the purpose of this chapter to show how some of the factors that make up the personality and background of a child determine his art. Some of the areas to be included will be the way in which the child's reactions to an experience affect his art product, and also the way his background, as well as cultural differences, determines what he selects for his art and how he expresses it. These two factors are not separate. They are both present in every piece of art work. The examples chosen to illustrate this point contain influences from both the child's personality and experiences. Emotional blocks, too, influence the child's art. This chapter is not an extensive inventory of factors that determine the child's art, but a selection of samples to represent broad and complex areas that are influential factors in the child's art expression.

REACTION TO AN EXPERIENCE

Involvement in an activity brings to the person physical participation, mental stimulation, and emotional reaction. The child's emotional response to the event depends on his individual personality and on the effect that similar or related previous experiences have had on him. The way he feels influences the way he expresses his ideas. Differences in the ways children react to the same experience are shown in the examples of the art work of two boys (Plates XXXVIII and XXXIX).

77

Children often fear what they do not understand. Emily said, "I was afraid of my grandmother after she died." She expressed her deep concern in this art.

One day the second grade went outdoors to have its art class. No instructions were given to the children about what they were to draw or how they were to do it. Before the children left their classroom, the teacher motivated the work as she would have for any creative art work. Some of the children drew buildings and trees; others developed abstracts. Excavation for a new building caught the attention of some of the boys, and they drew it. As Andrew gave his picture (Plate XXXVIII) to his teacher after it was finished, he said: "I like to do that. Let's do it again tomorrow." Although he chose the excavation as the topic for his art, his picture has a pleasant look. Birds are flying overhead. The picture is brightly and smoothly colored. It communicates the feeling he had about his experience.

Christopher drew the steam shovel and the excavation—a subject almost identical to Andrew's. His art (Plate XXXIX) shows that the same experience had a different effect on him. When he gave his picture to his teacher he said, "Boy, they're sure tearin' it up out there."

The rough way his composition was colored and the absence of gay objects show that he was much more sensitive to the destruction of the lawn and trees that was taking place than Andrew was. The different personalities of the two boys influenced their reactions, and each plainly showed in his art work the effect the experience had on him.

BACKGROUND OF EXPERIENCES

Through examples of their work and through voluntary statements they make about some of their experiences, insight is given into the ways in which background determines children's art. Background is considered to mean the broad experiences that make up the children's home, school, community life, and relationships with others, particularly family relationships. These experiences help to build the knowledge and reactions that provide sources of ideas for art.

Plates XL and XLI are the work of one child and dramatically show the way in which her family relationships, home life, and school life have affected her art products.

In second grade Florence painted the picture of herself by her house (Plate XL). Most of her drawings and paintings showed the same subject repeated over and over again, and this one, like the others, is depressing. She has painted the girl with brown and black, looking unkempt and dejected. The sun, which is usually bright and important in children's paintings, is dim, with little color. There seems to be a lack of orderliness even in the arrangement of the windows. Florence always depicted herself alone.

Florence was withdrawn in school. She repeated the first and second grades, and this painting was done in her second year in second grade. In class or on the playground she very rarely communicated with anyone. None of the children wanted to play with her. At recess she always stood against the side of the school or in some obscure spot. None of her teachers could remember her approaching them to tell about little incidents that had happened, as children so often do. Being two years older, she was, of course, larger than the other children in her group. She sat slouched down in her seat most of the time. Even when called on in class, she just sat still.

Florence seldom wore a dress that was ironed, and none of her clothes looked as though they originally had been bought for her. Her hair was seldom combed. It is not difficult to imagine the effect these things had on her. Children are sensitive and find it difficult to understand why they cannot have what others have or are not as well cared for as their classmates.

Florence was, no doubt, feeling the effect that frequent illnesses of both her parents had upon their family life and upon their economic status. Her father was unable to work regularly, thus reducing the family income and the advantages Florence might have had, and her mother's limited strength was used for only the most essential jobs in caring for her family of four children, of which Florence was the youngest.

Florence made the second picture (Plate XLI), of two children picking flowers, several weeks after the first one was painted. The effect of this picture is quite different from her other one. It looks gay and pleasant. For the first time she has shown another person with her. Every leaf on the trees and every flower is meticulously placed and colored. The arm of one child is long enough to reach down to the flowers, showing functional proportion, which is a normal way for children to solve such a problem. Florence's art work showed a sudden and dramatic change. A certain change in her life at home had brought about a change in her emotional outlook.

An older sister, Mary, had gotten a job and from her first pay had bought Florence a new pink coat with gold buttons. The first time Florence wore it to school, she went right up to her teacher and showed it to her, telling her about Mary's taking her to the store and getting the coat; this was the first time she had sought out a teacher to talk to her. After recess she told the teacher she had lost a button from the new coat that meant so much to her, and naturally she was upset. The teacher, who had encouraged the child on every possible occasion, took advantage of the opportunity she saw to call the attention of the group to Florence in a personal and happy way. She showed the coat and its remaining buttons to the class and asked all the children to help find the lost button. The teacher was wise enough to know that the few minutes required to find it was time well spent in building a relationship between Florence and the rest of the group. This was an unusual experience for the child, one in which she felt that people were working for her and with her.

The next illustration shows how the particular relationships a boy had with his father affected his art (78).

Vincent was a happy, well-adjusted child, pleasant to work with. He had a great many friends in school. He was proud of his father and talked about him to his third-grade teacher and to his friends. The father was a coal miner who spent a great deal of time with his son, talking to him about many things, including his work in the mines. About this picture, Vincent said: "Last night my daddy was telling me about the mines. That's where he works. The coal is all around. See, I made it like that. It's dark in there. The men have to wear lights on their caps. He eats in there. My mother packs him a bucket. They dig the coal, then put it on the cars like this, and the mules pull it out to the motors. My dad often tells me about the mines." Vincent's interest in the information about his father's work is evident in this piece of his art. Children's art shows the influence of their experiences

78

Vincent's close relationship with his father made him feel pride and interest in his father's work as a coal miner.

and their relationships with others, the most important of which is their relationship with their parents.

CULTURAL DIFFERENCES

Differences in cultural background cause differences in the art of children. Eileen, a Hopi Indian girl, drew this picture of her mother and her house (79). The way of life determines the kind of house, and Eileen's many experiences with her house have taught her how it looks and how it functions. The approach to her house, above the ground floor, is also typical of her culture. She has drawn her mother walking up the ladder in an upright position, as Hopis do. Food is hanging to dry on the outside wall. The row of candles on the edge of the roof is lighted and placed there in celebration of Christmas.

The other illustration (80) shows Eagle Katchinas dancing to the music of two Hopi drummers; many Indians sit or stand on top of the pueblos to watch the dance. The white sand and the violent red mountain help convey the feelings of the heat of the day and the excitement of the dance. The traditional style of painting, as done by the people of this fourth-grade child, has become a part of her experiences and shows in the way she expresses her art. The cultural background of the Hopis and the influence of their en-

79

Eileen's art shows the influence of her home environment and her way of life in a Hopi village.

80

The activity of the dance, the heat of the day, and the traditional style of Indian painting determined this Hopi child's art.

81

The major industry in Sammy's home town was the production of steel, which is reflected in this composition.

82

Hawaiian children are familiar with trees typical to their environment and the cool relief of shade they give against the hot sun.

vironment have made their creative art distinctly different in content from that of another culture.

Children from other cultural backgrounds create art that reflects their own particular life. In a town in which steel production is the major industry much of the life is influenced by the mill. Most of the children's fathers work there (81). They have learned many things about the mill from their close contact with it. A child who lives near a mill gets acquainted with it through all his senses. He smells the smoke and hears the noise night and day. He feels soot on his skin. He sees many workmen on the streets at specific times as they change shifts. He sees raw materials go in and finished products taken out, and he must watch out for the big trucks transporting steel. It is necessary for a child to have such first-hand acquaintance with something in order to use it so freely in his creative art.

The culture of the people of Hawaii is not as different from that in the continental United States as the American Southwest Indian culture is, but some of the existing differences are evident in the art of children. A fifth-grade Hawaiian child painted the row of bamboo trees shown in Illustration 82. This type of tree is not found in the other illustrations of this group because a bamboo tree is not found in the environment of the other children. The intense Hawaiian sunlight is shown by the warm colors in the sand. In a warm land the shadows seem cool and inviting and make a sharp contrast to the sunny areas, as this child has shown. The child is also familiar with the structure of the trees and with their quickly moving, long, thin leaves. Cultural differences give the child different ideas and experiences that help to determine his creative concepts as well as other factors in his art.

EMOTIONAL INFLUENCES

Emotional problems affect a child's art, and the art products change as the emotional problems are solved. Change sometimes comes about slowly, however, as it did in the case of Winifred whose mother died when she was born. Her maternal grandparents reared her, giving her many material advantages. In trying to prevent Winifred from being injured, the grandparents overprotected her and restricted her play. To protect her from the cold, she was required to wear clothing unlike that worn by other girls of her age. She was the only girl in her group who wore long stockings and long-sleeved dresses. Winifred's father thought the grandparents were overstrict, and when he visited them, there was often quarreling. On one such occasion, without forewarning, he picked up his daughter and took her to the new home he had established since his remarriage.

At this time Winifred entered the third grade. She had always been shy and somewhat withdrawn in school and seldom smiled. After any new experience, she merely dabbled in the art medium. She usually had clay or finger paint all over her or she painted mixed-up puddles. Sometimes she used so much paint that it ran off her paper onto the table, and the teacher would have to gather up her paper and pour her painting into the sink. It was not possible to save any samples of this stage of her work.

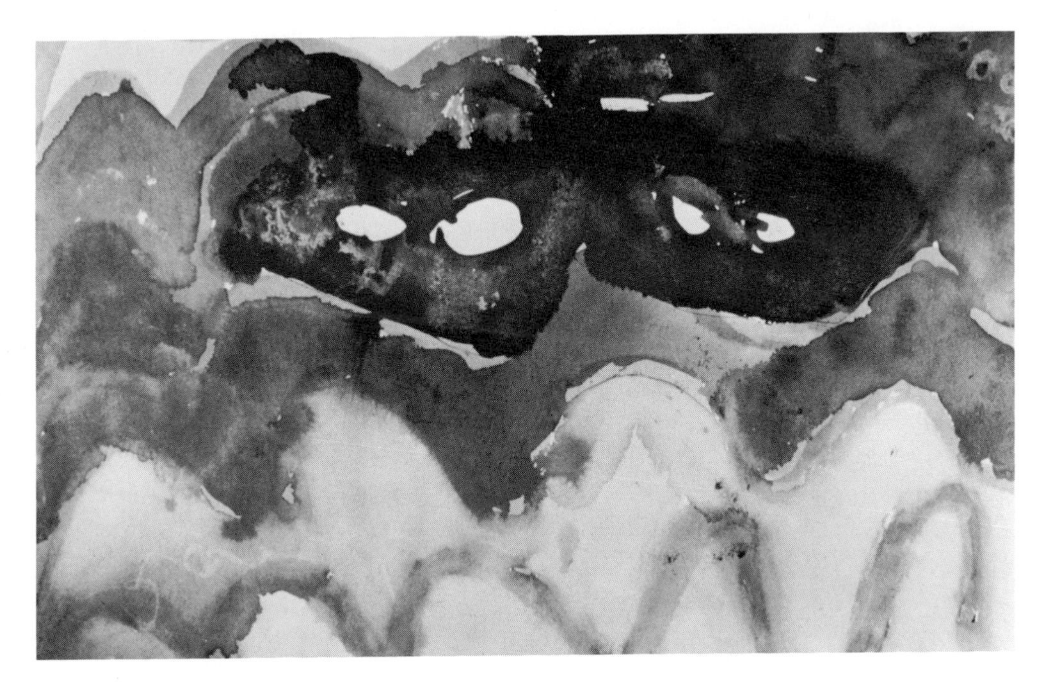

83
Personal problems, too, help to determine a child's art. When Winifred's emotional problem was most acute, her art was indefinite in form and morbid in feeling.

84
Forms in Winifred's art became more distinct as she began to work out her emotional problem.

In the first illustration of her work (83) Winifred has made a design. She offered no explanation for the forms that look like two pairs of eyes. In Illustration 84 the colors are dark, and the whole feeling is morbid; the dark eyes, alert and watching, add to this effect. In a cut-paper composition Winifred made the figure of herself in her house (85). She is as large as the house, and again the piercing effect of the large eyes is felt. The strip of red paper below the center of the girl is her skirt.

85

Frequently Winifred's art showed preoccupation with herself and little control of the art medium.

The swimming picture was made by Winifred in the last part of her third-grade year (86). About this time she began to choose gay colors and subjects. Her work has lost most of its morbid quality, although some confusion is still evident. This picture is better organized than her earlier ones. The body of water fits around the interesting variety of shapes at the bottom of the page, and the children are having fun together. By this time much of Winifred's art incorporated many interesting things that probably reflected her own broader scope of interest. She seldom painted puddles any more but continued to be slow to complete her art and hesitant about beginning another problem. All three of her primary-grade teachers helped her by accepting and encouraging whatever art work she did. The healing, uplifting, stimulating effects of art and the warm friendliness of her teachers were supporting Winifred and freeing her to express her ideas.

These typical examples of Winifred's work were selected to show how home and school experiences affect a child's art. The experiences make up a long series of incidents and relationships with her family. The illustrations show the changes that occurred in her art as her home life and her relationships with her family changed.

In working with children it is wise for a teacher to disregard an occasional deviation in a child's art. For instance, if a child is usually interested in and does interesting art of a variety of types, a teacher is wise to ignore the time he does not do well, the day he paints all over his work, or the moment of discouragement that prompts him to destroy his work. We all have days and moments when we are emotionally upset. It is only when such deviational behavior becomes a pattern of action that the teacher should feel the child needs help. As she sees such a pattern developing, the teacher, of course, should encourage the child and build his confidence in himself. When she sees him repeating an idea or form one time after another, she should encourage (but not pressure) him to try other ideas or variations of the favored idea. When this fails, she should seek help from someone whose speciality is work with problem children, such as the school psychiatrist or psychologist.

Teachers do not have the knowledge to diagnose and prescribe for children's emotional problems. There are many things a teacher can do, however, to help such children. She can be gentle, understanding, and sympathetic, accepting the child and his art and refraining from harsh criticism or using a sharp, cutting tone of voice. It is helpful if the teacher encourages the children whenever she can, without making the encouragement appear false or artificial. Although a teacher can do helpful things, she

86

As her emotional problem became resolved, Winifred's art showed the inclusion of other people, more complex organization, brighter colors, and better control of the medium.

is limited by the pressure of the needs of many other children who deserve as much of her attention as the problem child. *Every* child is important, deserving, and needs some special personal attention from the teacher every day.

The more the teacher knows about the child, the better she can appreciate his art. The more the teacher knows about art, the better she can appreciate the child who creates art.

OTHER INFLUENCES

The methods used in the teaching of art are also among the school experiences that determine a child's art. They can directly determine the art produced by teacher-dictated processes, copy work, prepared outlines, and patterns. Methods used by teachers can have a long-range effect on the art of children, as shown by John's work in Chapter 1.

Experiences from other areas of the curriculum affect and determine children's art. Workbooks are frequently used in the elementary school, and many contain pictures that children copy or color. Such experiences are the same as copy work or prepared outlines that are sometimes used in the time scheduled for art by teachers who do not understand the values of creative art.

Emphasis on naturalistic representation without regard for the intent of the child or without concern for the other bases for expression are other school experiences that influence art.

SUGGESTED ACTIVITIES

Study Plates XV, XX, *and* XXXVI *in the color insert. Try to decide which ideas, forms, colors, groupings, proportions, and sizes were determined by the child's personality influences, which from his experiences, and which from a combination of both.*

Discuss your findings with at least one classmate, and compare your decisions.

12

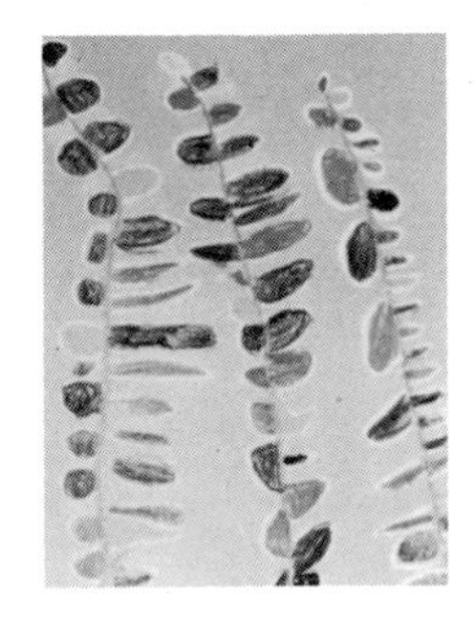

Response to Art

EVERYONE MAKES personal responses to art. Works of art are seen daily: on the walls and in other places in homes and buildings, the building forms themselves, in publications, in clothing styles, and in decorations of many kinds. Colors, forms, and arrangements are so constantly present that many times they are disregarded. Art is a part of life, and the involvement that art holds for people ranges from indifference and insensibility to absorption and exhilaration; reactions spread from pleasure to aversion. The depth of personal absorption with art can lead to greater breadth and depth of our pleasure in seeing. It adds richness and beauty to life and occupies a part of conscious thinking with an uplifting attitude toward the anticipation and experiencing of beauty and visual pleasure. It has an uplifting effect upon thinking and behavior. Art has always had a cultural and refining influence. It is vital, then, that awareness to art becomes an integral part of every child's education, that children learn to be sensitive to visual aesthetics, and learn how to make discriminating judgments about art. Exposure to art is the avenue through which this capacity is achieved. Hearing comments about art increases appreciation.

Insight into the qualities of art can be greatly sharpened. Responsiveness to art can be educated, guided, elevated, and enriched. This ability not only applies to works of art, but can be transferred and applied to the discovery of pleasing groupings, color harmonies, and shapes seen in nature and in the environment. A deeper appreciation of art through art education can also lead to closer personal identification with a greater variety of types of art expression. The rewards in seeing can be greatly enhanced.

People have never been satisfied with the bare necessities and materials of existence. They have always tried to bring beauty and harmony into their

87

Children need exposure to a variety of art of different types and from different historical periods. Occasionally the teacher points out certain elements in a work of art; at other times children simply look at and study it for themselves.

lives and into their homes and artifacts through art. The earliest cave dwellings had wall paintings to beautify them. Since the earliest traces of mankind on this earth, art has been a powerful influence, and people have created it and have responded to it in ways which were influenced by the spirit of the times in which they lived, by their needs, and by their own personalities.

Art transcends time and space. People of this age who study the paintings on the cave walls of Lascaux or Altamira are able to comprehend them. The ageless values of art provide a bridge that has helped us understand cultures of the past long buried and forgotten. It is largely through the study of recovered art objects and architecture that knowledge of these ancient peoples is gained. Although art does provide this powerful means of communication, expression is even more basic to art, for an idea must be expressed before it can be communicated. However, when art is reduced to communication, it becomes mere correspondence; and art is much more than that. Art crystallizes an experience as it expresses underlying feelings experienced by other people as well as by the artist. There is a spirit about a work of art that contains an intangible expressive quality.

> True art must remain an emotional contact with the inner man, with deep seated human emotions. But there is a kind of mystical universality which results from the human drives and aspirations common to all people and it

is this personal universal quality on which art depends. This has been called the collective unconscious. Herein lies an explanation of the fact that art is a common language and as such we must search for the secret of the creative impulse in some common factor. If, as often happens, the work of one period in time or particular culture is unappreciated by another it is because the mind has been overlaid with prejudice or is unequipped to grasp the subtlety of an accomplished expression. The potential to be moved aesthetically is always present.[1]

THE MEDIUM

Art is creative activity with materials for the purpose of bringing into existence original forms expressing feeling and thought. Art is also the finished products resulting from creative activity. Both the activity and the product are referred to as art, and study of both is needed in a well-rounded art education program. Ability to create is often enhanced through a study of works of art, and, conversely, appreciation for works of art is often enhanced through creative participation with art materials. Value and education in art comes from both study and execution of original art works. The combination of the two leads to a fuller understanding of and feeling for art than either could accomplish alone. This chapter deals especially with building appreciation for art through the study of works of art and the resources and methods the teacher uses to promote it.

Art products take many forms, for art represents continual change and innovation. Art may be flat or three-dimensional. In fact it is often difficult to tell where painting ends and sculpture begins. Sculpture sometimes has color added, giving it qualities of a painting, and it can be used as either a floor or wall piece. Some framed paintings have three-dimensional effects, giving them sculptural qualities. Architecture often has sculpture, mosaics, or paintings planned as a part of the whole visual effect.

At one time the concept of art was limited to three clearly defined categories of expression: painting, sculpture, and architecture. Today these divisions are vanishing. The materials used were also limited in scope. Today art includes many materials and many areas of visual form such as ceramics, metalwork, and fabrics. These areas were, at one time, considered as crafts and not thought of as fine art. This distinction has also disappeared. Art now includes a broad and full meaning of creative visual forms, and an equivalent change has come about in our concept of what art is.

The materials associated with art are not as easy to classify, either, as they once were, for everything available to the artist becomes media for his creative expression. Resourcefulness in the use of the many materials that modern technology has developed is itself a part of art. Art now involves a search for new aesthetic forms utilizing an amazing variety of materials and ingenious uses of them, which in turn requires constant adjustments to new bases for art appreciation.

[1] Walter Read Hovey, "The Creative Spark," from Topic 5, *Creativity and the Arts*, Washington and Jefferson College, Washington, Pa., III, No. 1 (1963), 41.

The form of art has also changed radically and continues to depart from previous forms. Throughout history recognizable subject matter dominated most art. Although abstract or conventionalized design was also an art form, it had a place of secondary importance, being used mostly as decoration for objects and not as art form in itself. But the dominating force and form in present-day art is abstract or nonobjective. The twentieth century aesthetic is an attitude toward beauty based upon these new forms of expression; an appreciation of them is determined by wholly different concepts of what art is, how relationships within it are made, and how it expresses feelings and drives.

88

Raoul Ubac's "Cut Slate" is concerned with shapes, including outside shapes, and the relationship of shapes and spaces. (Courtesy of Museum of Art, Carnegie Institute, Pa., Patrons Fund.)

The changing forms in art have come about because artists have found another much more personal source of inspiration for their art forms. Traditionally, artists used what they saw as inspiration and form for their art. Now most artists have turned to the deeper forces and drives within themselves for their inspiration.

This expansion in the materials used in art, in the forms used to express ideas and feelings, and in the types of art products has greatly amplified the whole field of art, requiring proportionately increased efforts toward art appreciation.

People can no longer approach art with preconceived ideas of what it should be or what it should look like. To make contact with this open, free world of art expression requires an open, free attitude and a flexible, adaptable mind. Every work of art needs to be considered as an individualized expression different from all others. People can no longer set one standard for art or expect all art to be "pretty." Art expresses feelings and emotions common to people; not all art can possibly be "pretty," because not all emotions are "pretty." Some are disturbing. The drawing (89) by Michael, age nine, effectively expresses his strong and disturbing feeling of grief, and so communicates it to those who study his drawing.

However, in the final concept of art, it is not the range of materials, their uses, or the directions art is taking that are vital to a work of art. It is, rather, the integrity and sincerity of the artist, his vision and expression that give life to art.

Art has the capacity for freeing us from the mechanical ways of cognition that can dominate our awareness and from these same ways of comprehending the world around us. Art is different in nature from these ways of knowing, and accordingly operates on different elements, principles, and purposes. Therefore, ways of studying, conceiving, and responding to art need to be related to its basic nature and purposes.

> . . . [thinking] of a few works of art widely separated in time which indicate an awareness of the source that gave them being we find that although the terms may differ there is always the consciousness of an unknown factor. The Greeks called this factor inspiration and it was imparted to the artist by the Muses. The Middle Ages referred to it as revelation and this, like a shaft of light, came from God. The "Moderns" refer to it as intuition and the source for that is psychic phenomena. This intangible something which gives rise to creativity clearly partakes of incommensurate qualities.[2]

> Perceiving himself to be an inseparable part of the natural world, the contemporary artist offers himself as an organic medium through which its mysterious forces (though not subject to his command) can reveal themselves. Being part of his own field of perception, he willingly submits himself to the only role that becomes him from this human position. He rejects the vain and willful ego as a false master of the human situation turning instead to revelations of that deeper and more elusive self that has been called the "human spirit."[3]

THE RESPONSE

Every person who approaches a work of art makes contact with it and draws from it to the extent of his knowledge about art in general and to the extent of his contacts with and study of art of many kinds. This knowledge

---

[2] Hovey, *op. cit.*, p. 42.

[3] Gordon Bailey Washburn, Introduction to *The 1961 Pittsburgh International Exhibition of Contemporary Painting and Sculpture,* Department of Fine Arts, Carnegie Institute, Pittsburgh, Pa.

89

Michael's drawing, made in the home of a friend, is a strong expression of his deep feeling of sorrow at the loss of his pet dog.

about art and experience in looking at it help people respond more deeply to it.

Response to art is an art activity, an ability that can be developed through art education as other art skills can. Response does not depend upon ability and skill in creating art, but creating art does bring people close to its meaning. It helps the artist understand what goes into the accomplishment of a work of art, and it helps him know how much of the heart and spirit must go along with ideas, imagination, concentration, and hard work. However, there are a great many people who find pleasure in looking at art, even though they do not engage in producing it. They are appreciatively responsive to beauty or to some particular quality in works of art.

Many things affect responses to art: knowledge about art, attitude toward art, prejudices, the mood or spirit in which art is approached, as well as expectations at the time of viewing.

To respond to and to more deeply appreciate art, each person must actively enter into it by giving it his special attention. The act of response is a two-way process. To find some value, pleasure, support, peace, stimulation, or feeling in art, a person allows himself to be outgoing and projects himself into the art; at the same time he is receptive, letting qualities of the art project into his mind and feelings. The viewer lets it go beyond his conscious awareness and into the deeper resources of his being.

To learn to probe the depth of art, it is necessary to free the mind and allow the image to enter and to make its own impressions. Each piece of art needs to be appreciated for what it is. Expecting it to be consistent with other art leads to disappointment, for there is a tremendous variety of styles of art, countless different purposes in creating it, and innumerable personal expressions made in it. Response, like art, is a personal thing. Not all people respond to the same object in the same way, but all can be helped to respond to more art and to deeper enjoyment of it.

Response to art and the appreciation of it is both an intellectual and an emotional action. When satisfaction can be gained from both these approaches, the viewer is doubly enriched. The intellectual access implies enough understanding to enjoy and admire its excellence. Art also contains emotional expression to which a person responds to the extent that the emotion or feeling expressed has personal significance for him. If the viewer has experienced a feeling in the same context as it is shown in the art, he will be in deeper and more immediate involvement with the art. Meaningful contacts with art most certainly include personal interpretation. But personal likes and dislikes are not bases enough for discovery and translation of art.

Some people may say that they know little about art, that they know what they like or do not like. What they like depends very often upon the personal association they can make with art. They tend to like the art that has some familiar note about it. To like it means that they find it personally agreeable. They may be, therefore, rejecting or ignoring quantities of art, for art reflects life, and not all of life is pleasant or agreeable; neither, then, is all of art. Subject matter alone is a shallow criterion by which to evaluate art. True, viewers do react to the subject, but they also need to study the way it has been expressed and note the consistent relationship of this to the content. The quality of the art should not be disregarded because the artist has chosen subject matter, such as social distress, that is not considered "pleasant" by some people. The viewer must apply vigorous interpretation, looking for sincerity of expression, for the daring and the original. Likes and dislikes alone are a thin and shallow base for art appreciation. As children learn what to look for, as they are exposed to more and more art, they reject the words "like" and "dislike," replacing them with more descriptive words and phrases. They learn an art vocabulary which can act as another bridge to art, and at the same time they broaden the range of their art appreciation.

The primary purpose in presenting children with a variety of art work and in discussing it with them is to deepen their pleasure in seeing, to increase the number and types of art forms they can enjoy, to deepen their intellectual and emotional satisfactions, and to strengthen their awareness of the importance of art.

Response to art takes place within the child often without any outward sign that it has occurred. Teachers need to be aware that this is a quiet internal art experience and should not expect children to be verbal or demonstrative about it. Because this response is different from most other learning situations, it should not bewilder or discourage her. To help children gain value from a work of art, it needs to be approached with the expectation of finding something interesting in it as well something new and different. This attitude and effort alone can help the viewer discover at least something of its worth.

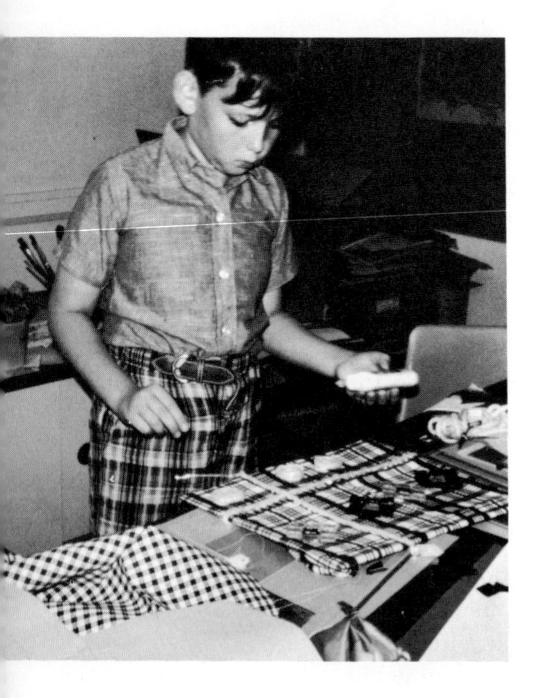

90

Through their own creative efforts children learn many things about art that cannot be put into words.

The essential and pivotal point in response comes through the reaction to art that results from sensitivity to it, and the focal point of sensitivity is most generally the feeling of the art. Understanding this, children can let their feelings move toward the art and thus open the way for this intimate reaction. Other, more tangible areas of sensitivity can also be developed which can lead to a warmer, more total involvement with art. Sensitivity to textures, shapes, colors, and relationships wherever they are found can lead to awareness of these same elements in art, helping to bring art more readily into consciousness and toward greater appreciation of it.

To deepen response to art it is necessary to go beyond study into empathy with the works of art. To understand knowledge of art structure, its symbolic meaning, and be able to intellectualize about works of art are all important; but to fully experience the impact of art, to feel its meaning and to respond to its vigor, it is necessary to add to this intellectualizing still another dimension: the immersion in creative activity itself. Otherwise, an important element in the response to art is missing. A person may coldly analyze a work of art, but when he participates in creative original works of art, he becomes personally and emotionally involved with art in another way. He then feels a kinship with the creator which opens another avenue into his response.

Efforts to help children become aware of, to want to become acquainted with, and to admire art help them realize that art has been a constant and important influence in the lives of people even before the first written records were made by man. It is important to know, for example, that the first recorded communications were through pictures. Writing grew out of art, and a few cultures used picture-writing until very recently.

> The aesthetic or undergoing phase of experience is receptive. It involves surrender. But adequate yielding of the self is possible only through a controlled activity that may well be intense. For to perceive, a beholder must first create his own experience. Without an act of re-creation the object is not perceived as a work of art.[4]

> The inner force of the rhythm is conveyed to the observer who is moved by it according to his nature, but it is rare for even the suspicion of a psychological or cosmic significance to rise to the surface of his consciousness, although he may perceive its dynamic essence.[5]

BUILDING RESPONSES TO ART

The philosophy of modern art education and of this book is one of appreciation. As the teacher helps the children see the art quality in their own and other children's work, she is establishing an attitude for favorable responses to it. Even before the art work begins, the teacher's acceptance of each child's verbally expressed ideas shows appreciation. Her effort to help each child release his own responses to the art materials shows her confidence in and appreciation of the unique abilities of each child, which helps them respond appreciatively to other people's art expressions. As the art work of each child is exhibited and as each child makes his own private responses to it, appreciation takes place. In fact, this philosophy of appreciative acceptance of each child's achievement is so vital in art education that it not only affects the extent of responsiveness to art, but any reversal of it can stop the free flow of creativity altogether.

One of the most direct influences upon building a positive, receptive, zealous feeling toward art is the teacher's own enthusiasm for it. "Appreciation is more 'caught' than taught," to vary the adage mentioned earlier. The teacher herself must be interested in art, alert to reproductions of it that she can bring to children, and on the watch for newspaper and magazine articles about it that she can call to their attention or tell them about. Children quickly catch and reflect their teacher's intensity for art. Her own voice and manner reflect this intensity. If she encourages children to attend art exhibitions, she is shaping the kind of attitude that leads to art appreciation. If a teacher wants to become a dynamic influence in art as, of course, she

---

[4] John Dewey, "Having An Experience," in *The Problems of Aesthetics*, Eliseo Vivas and Murray Krieger, eds. (New York: Holt, Rinehart and Winston, 1953), p. 340.

[5] J. E. Cirlot, *A Dictionary of Symbols* (New York: Philosophical Library, 1962), p. xliii.

91

Children indirectly absorb the values of art when art work is displayed in the classroom. Art is a visual language, and communicates most effectively through silent study.

expects to be in all of her teaching, she must have and continue to build a knowledge about art through contacts with actual works of art.

The most personalized approach toward response to and appreciation for art, and the most convenient materials to use, are those in which children have the most interest—their own art. There is an abundance of child art in every school program resulting from the open opportunities for choices in creative art expression. Their art is approachable for children because it is on their own level. The very fact that it is their own, has come from their own efforts or from someone they know, gives them a receptive feeling for it. During the art work period they were intimately involved with it. Actually creative art expression. Their art is approachable for children because it is already sensitized to it when it is exhibited and when the discussion begins. Therefore, since it is not strange to them, they are helped, through positive comments about its merits, toward more comprehensive awareness of its qualities. They are helped toward more quickened responses to it and toward appreciation of the *art* qualities in it. Study and discussion of the strengths of each lead toward an expectance of variety in works of art, toward an intellectualizing of many ways aesthetic qualities can be achieved, and toward a broadening of the kinds of art for which each child can develop a feeling.

The description in Chapter 2 of Jane's painting (12) is an example of some of the comments made about a child's art that lead to deeper awareness of and response to it. In Chapter 1 the positive statements pointing out achievements made in the examples of children's art give further insight into the method of helping children appreciate art through becoming aware of their own accomplishments. It is better not to dwell overlong on any one child's work for three reasons:

(a) Children's attention spans are short.
(b) They prefer to spend more time doing art than talking about it.
(c) More emphasis upon one child's work than upon that of another can influence children in the direction of the work receiving the emphasis, thus indirectly stimulating a child to copy the work receiving the most attention.

Other examples of comments about child art that lead to fuller appreciation of it might be some of the following. In Illustration 53 there is a feeling for the soaking quality of the rain, that the rain is heavy and that the little girl will be very wet. Another kind of feeling is shown in the painting of a baseball player in Illustration 52 in Chapter 7. His facial expression, his hand holding his chin, and his bent-over sitting position as he looks out of the window all help to convey the feeling of disappointment the child had in not being permitted to join the other boys who were playing baseball. In this same painting, attention could be drawn to the pleasing pattern made by the light colored chair back against the dark wall, and to the slanted pattern of the chair arm against the dark baseball uniform. Structurally, the verticals of the chair back and the boy's arm give strength and support to the composition and help to form somewhat of a rectangle with the arm of the chair and the baseball cap. This rectangle is interestingly divided by the curved line made by the boy's back, neck, and head. The light and dark are balanced within this painting, and each is well organized. The light areas are connected, flowing one into another, and seem to create interesting shapes themselves.

Although all of these comments and more could be made to children about Kenny's art, they are pointed out here to try to help teachers understand an approach to art study through children's own art. The teacher might well be able to make a great many more favorable comments about this or any one piece of art, but she might also choose to make only a few to the children. She selects and guides what is said according to the age and background of the children and to the educational purposes she has in mind at the time.

If the teacher herself participates in art and occasionally brings pieces of her work to class, children may be able to make somewhat immediate responses to it because of their relationship with their teacher and because she may be better able to interpret her own work. But it is not at all necessary for a teacher actually to participate as an artist to stimulate intellectual and emotional responses to art. Her interest and knowledge about art, her ability to be conversant about it, the excitement in her voice as she discusses it are all vital factors in guiding the way.

The teacher's leadership in helping children more thoroughly see a piece of art will help them respond more thoroughly to it. Although it is difficult to verbalize about art, some discussion does help understanding. When the teacher points out what she sees, the children, focusing upon it, may be helped to see those same things more completely. When children try to put into words what they see or how they feel, others trying to find the words or attempting to define a feeling are helped toward crystallization of it. Some of the particular points to watch for in art might be the relationships within the colors and the forms; the movements and counter-movements; the overlappings and transparencies; the uniqueness of parts or of the whole; the variety and unity within it; and the effects it has upon viewers.

The new awareness to art that results from learning how to recognize, to become involved with, and to be drawn in by the finer qualities of one art form can transfer to other art forms. For example, a person who studies form, balance, surface treatment, organization, and expression in sculpture can usually make more discerning decisions about other three-dimensional forms in fine art. He is aware that these qualities are important; he has learned how to look for and to see them; he has built a basis for judgments; and he has acquired a feeling for quality. This is often what is referred to as good taste.

It is important for children to learn how to assess and to become absorbingly occupied with qualities in art, because it is not only enrichment and personal pleasure, but it also opens the way to more extensive responses to art. Learning how to make discriminating judgments of one type of art can lead to insights into the qualities of other art works. It is exciting to feel a personal contact with a work of art, for it brings a rewarding glow to the deeper mental and spiritual areas of life. A desire to broaden and extend these indescribable satisfactions leads to a search for them in other pieces of art. Interest in sculpture, for example, can lead to a study of the sculptural qualities in furniture—the shape, organization of its parts, and the overall visual effect it has. Although art knowledge gained from a study of one area of art can be transferred, more is gained by direct study of each area.

It is necessary to help children build an art vocabulary, for without it they are less able to intellectualize about art, to communicate about it, and at times less able to identify their own working problems. An art vocabulary helps children be more verbally eloquent as well as more expressive with art materials.

Some knowledge about the structure of art helps children respond to one kind of its values. Knowledge of design, color, line, and form is one facet through which pleasure in seeing can be enhanced. Some works of art might first be approached through a study of their structure, others through an emotional approach.

There are multitudes of sources from which to draw the materials for helping children respond to works of art. In addition to the painting, sculpture, and other forms generally associated with art, there are many different kinds of consumer goods; in a sense, everything is shaped and designed by an artist and can, therefore, have artistic values. Comparisons, appraisals, and judgments can be made of such items as wallpaper, drapery fabrics and designs, floor coverings, dishes, utensils, clothing, and automobile designs.

Reproductions of many works of art are also more available than they have ever been before. There are quantities of reproductions of paintings, collages, sculpture, and ceramics which are often inexpensive, making it possible for individuals and schools to own them.

Some educational television programs help children learn about art and help them project themselves into art more deeply. Books and some periodicals are further sources of materials for art appreciation.

Field trips stress the importance of art: that art is significant enough to make a trip to see, that people cherish it. In addition to art museums and galleries, visits to art rental galleries help children learn to enjoy and to become acquainted with art. For a small sum the group may pick out a piece of art to rent for their classroom for a period of time. Visits to artists' studios can put art study on a person-to-person basis. Meeting the artist and hearing him talk about his work as he shows it can be a most impressive experience. Seeing the equipment and materials as well as the partially finished and completed work inspires both art activity and depth of feeling for art. Hearing the artist's comments helps to make his art clearer and more intelligible. If such a field trip is too difficult to arrange, inviting the artist to bring his works to school can be an alternative.

Other field trips may include walking tours of the architecture in a city: churches, important buildings, homes, and factories. Just calling attention to the architecture is, of course, meaningful, but when the teacher has made some study of the buildings and is able to point out their distinguishing features, it helps children not only to see more, but also to learn how to look at architecture.

Nature offers a great many materials for increasing perceptiveness of beauty: the shapes and textures of stones, running water, mountains, tree shapes and groupings, flowers, grasses, plants, sunsets, clouds, birds, fish, and people; the lights and darks, the shades of green, the colors in the earth, and the way weather affects colors and our reactions to them. Our man-made environment also has an infinite assortment of forms, colors, and structures: churches, homes, industrial buildings, street surfaces and intersections, bridges, railway tracks, poles and wires, television antennas, smoke; the patterns we see in window arrangements, in paving and building materials, in the rhythms and flows of traffic; and the arrangement and beauty of lawns and gardens. Contact with both their natural and man-made environment enriches children's sensitivity to beauty.

Possibly the most familiar way of building knowledge that can lead to greater responses to art is through a study and an exchange of comments about works of art. When children are accustomed to the content, the subject matter, the form, or style of the art, they can move more readily into a discussion of it. But it takes time to adjust to a new and strange art expression. When the whole work seems overwhelming, it helps to pick out one small part and study it. Choose one spot, one form, or one color combination; then add to it by studying the part next to it or going to a similar spot in the art. Sometimes a movement through the work can be studied in isolation, then the counter-movement, and then other features of it. This study procedure is recommended only for individuals or groups having problems making contact with a work of art.

PROBLEMS IN GUIDING ART STUDY

Teachers often feel insecure in the unseen and immeasurable processess of children's responses to works of art. In art work with materials, there are definite resulting products than can be seen, touched, and hung for all to see and study; but the results of efforts at guiding art study are intangible. A child may be deeply touched by seeing a whole work of art, yet make no outward indication of it in any way. The same work may have little or no effect upon another child. Their outward behavior may be similar. There is no way of knowing or judging how children have responded to an art exposure. Verbal statements are not always an indication, for the silent thoughtful child may be the most impressed. Because it shows little tangible results of their teaching, many teachers avoid their leadership role in this important area of art education. It is important for them to realize that this very vagueness is part of the process and that they should not withdraw or retreat because that area of art education cannot be stated or measured in general terms as so many other areas can be. When every teacher seriously attacks this important responsibility with enthusiasm, children caught in the excitement of it enter a study of art with a feeling of warmth, opening the way for further knowledge about and feeling for art.

The naming of objects in a work of art can be a pitfall. It is not critical to either the art qualities of the work or to an individual's reaction to it that he be able to identify the forms in the art work he sees. This is especially true today, since much of our contemporary art has little recognizable subject matter. The same can be said for factual information about the life of the artist. It is the *qualities inherent in the art* that are important in the personal reaction to it: a feeling for the subject, the consistencies within it, the uniqueness of it, and possibly some of the structural elements.

Because art encompasses such a broad variety of styles, purposes, and materials, some teachers may feel inadequate to guide art study. This should not deter them from presenting art forms that are new to them and to their children. No comment about the art may be needed. Teacher and children can look at the art and gain whatever they can from it.

It is inadvisable for a teacher to impose value judgments on certain styles, periods, or kinds of art. A teacher's prejudices about art can limit the scope of children's art experiences. Emphasis upon current styles in art can deprive children of contact with important works of the past, and a teacher's opinions may be outdated by the time children become adults. Styles in art change with the times. It is better to keep open the contact lines with a great variety of art so that the teacher and children can openly evaluate these works.

Too much talk and too much analysis can detract from the feeling of deepened visual enjoyment a teacher is trying to build. Asking a child why he likes a work of art can be overwhelming, for that is, indeed, a difficult question for even the professional artist or the art critic to answer. Sometimes an answer is given, but it often seems lame and appears to miss the mark. Words are inadequate for a rich visual experience. Art must be seen to be felt and appreciated. To accomplish this, the concentration is placed upon these inward intangibles and not upon hearing and verbalizing.

Attempts have been made to isolate children's preferences for works of art. Children have been shown a variety of types of art and asked to list them in order of preference. Lists of these choices are available, but choices made from these lists would not provide a sound basis for selections of study of works of art, for they represent only the familiar and accepted. Education is broadened and deepened to the extent that children stretch to encompass new ideas and deepen their absorption with them. Children need to have opportunities to see again and again examples of art to which they can make contacts of their own.

Studies have also been made to try to discover what happens when children are confronted by a work of art. This is a difficult thing to isolate, measure, and compare, because so much of what happens as we look at art is felt and sensed. It would be difficult if at all possible to put this into verbal form. This particular area of education may not lend itself well to research or studies, because just as art is an individual expression of its creator, the response to it is an individual impression of its viewer. To make a statistical study, certain factors would have to be brought to a common denominator, and this denies the personal, individually different responses. Individual differences are the very source of art and are the agent of art appreciation. There may be some measurable factors, but they would reveal only a part of the process and perhaps not the most important one.

Watch children's responses as you show them either original works of art or reproductions. Try to present art in an atmosphere charged with anticipation. This showing of art should be a regular part of classroom activities. Children should feel that art is not remote.

Art appreciation does not respond to pressure. It takes leisure, time, and a feeling of ease and freedom. One of the most important things to keep in mind is that children in the elementary school respond to art as children, in "childish" ways, and with a viewpoint often different from that of adults.

SUGGESTED ACTIVITIES

Begin to collect and organize reproductions of works of art to show to children or to hang for them to study.

Take a child to an art exhibition. Listen to his unsolicited comments. Watch his expressions and note the length of time he spends looking at different parts of the exhibition.

With a small group of your friends, try guiding the discussion of one or two pieces of art work.

During a visit to an art exhibition, make a particular point of identifying your own reaction to some of the works of art.

13

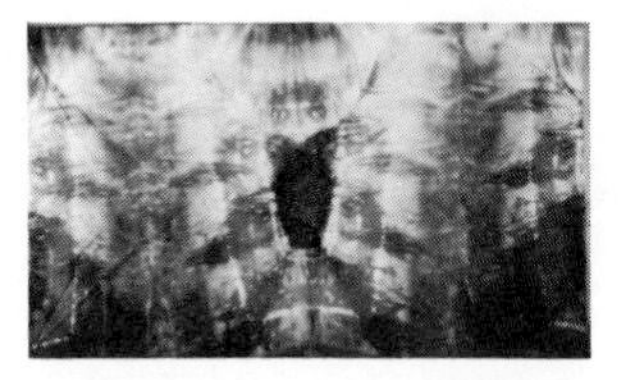

Competition, Contests, and Grading in Children's Art

THROUGHOUT THIS BOOK the emphasis has been on methods of teaching art to children in the classroom and in situations involving direct relationships between the teacher and the child. There are other practices associated with the teaching of art to children to which teachers need to give thoughtful attention, even though these practices may involve less direct relationships. Some, associated with the children's daily art experiences, can affect the processes in the art work, the art products, and the way the children feel about the art experiences. Others may come into play only occasionally but can have immediate as well as lasting effects upon the children's art and their attitudes toward it. By calling attention, in this chapter, to some of these practices—particularly competition, art contests, and grading—it is hoped that teachers will give thoughtful attention to some of their influences. Through evaluation and discussion of these practices, teachers may gain some criteria by which they can make critical judgments of other practices that have some relationship to art. It is important for teachers of art to understand and evaluate any practices or factors in classroom or community life that may have effects on the art experiences of children. Anything that affects the child's art also affects the child.

ART CONTESTS

A contest is a competition for some advantage over some other person or group. It involves a struggle to win over adversaries or a fight to gain superiority over other contestants. Each contender in a contest is deeply concerned with establishing his own excellence above that of all others. A contestant is not only trying to do the best he can but also to do better than anyone else. In order to accomplish this victory, a contestant must be, from the beginning, deeply concerned with an accomplishment that is closely related to the purposes of defeating others as well as to developing his own interests and purposes.

Conflict arises from the contestant's struggle between what he may feel is right and what he feels is necessary in order to gain the advantage over others. The contestant may feel an urge to express himself in a certain manner, or he may be drawn toward the selection of ideas that attract him, but neither of these factors can be the final basis of his choice. He must also consider the chances that his choices will have of winning and make a decision with this in mind. Conflict arises also in his feelings toward other contestants. He loses his feeling of cooperation in favor of a competitive one. If he helps another contestant, the other may win, and he may lose. He therefore cannot afford to be helpful in ways that might endanger his chance to gain the winning advantage.

Purposes and Problems of Art Contests

Because art products are tangible, have form, and can be seen and handled, those who propose contests seem to regard art as a field well suited to competition.

The purposes of contests vary. Sometimes a contest is associated with an exhibition of art. Each exhibitor selects his "best" work for the display. From among these pieces so selected, one "best" is chosen to receive a prize. In this way, an exhibition also becomes a contest for the superiority of one or a few pieces. This selected work then receives a great deal of attention and publicity. In many cases the amount of emphasis placed on the prize winner is out of ratio to the difference in quality between it and other pieces of art work in the exhibition.

Since rewards are given to a select few from among those entering a contest, some method of determining the winners must be decided. Usually, one person or a panel of a few persons is appointed to make the final decision. If there are many entries, some selection and elimination usually takes place before the judges face the task of making a final decision. Therefore, the works of some children have no chance of even being viewed by the judges.

Judges are usually selected from among those persons who have little or no involvement with the sponsors, the contestants, or the processes of preparing the entries. The aim is to find an "impartial" jury which cannot know the personal struggles, hopes, dreams, and emotions that have gone into the making of each entry. Yet, this personal involvement of the artist is the very essence of creating art. Every judge necessarily approaches the selection with his own prejudices, special interests, reactions, tastes, and experiences.

Since contest judges differ in personality, background, and value judgments, it is evident that they will not all make the same decisions. Sometimes each judge has selected, as his choice for a prize, a different piece.

When this happens, a compromise must be made. There have been instances of a prize being awarded to a piece of art that no judge had selected as his first choice; it was simply one on which they could all agree.

The most difficult problem of all, of course, is the selection of one piece of art work above all others. One composition appeals because of a certain quality; another, not having this quality, attracts because of a different reason. The difficulty is not so much in finding attractive and interesting art work to choose as it is in having to reject work of quality. A judge, sensitive to various distinguishing factors in art, regrets having to withhold prizes from excellent pieces. He is confronted with a job that is extremely difficult to do in a completely satisfactory way.

Some persons, faced with making a final choice of one among several excellent pieces of art work, feel that they cannot make a mistake because whichever work is selected will be a proper choice. They feel that someone will be pleased by having won. Yes, some *one* will be, but the others will find it difficult to understand why this certain piece was selected above their work or over that of some other person.

Effects of Contests

What happens to the *winner* of a contest? To be elevated above many others because of the quality of his work is most certainly an intoxicating success for a child and greatly builds his morale. He is strongly motivated by the reward and recognition, which can fortify his interest in art and in education. It is a triumph that he can remember and can point to with pride. It can encourage him to do more art work, but it can also impede his art progress. Some winners repeat the successful art form in later art experiences in order to continue to receive recognition. They become afraid to try new or different ideas and materials lest the result fail to be as successful as the prize-winning one. Winning an art contest can also cause the winner to have an exaggerated opinion of the quality of his work. Such a success may cause him to think he is more capable in art than the other contestants, whereas another judge possibly might have chosen another child's work. Whether a child's art was selected or not, the quality of it remains unchanged, but the child will be either elated or discouraged by the value judgment that some-one else places on it.

The winner is also sometimes affected by his parents, relatives, or friends, who are justifiably proud of the successful child and praise him and boast about him to other people. Praise is a rich incentive, but when carried too far, it creates a reputation for the child that he may not be able to maintain, thus causing him to become discouraged. He may lose interest in art or turn from it rather than reveal his inability to always produce art of such a high standard. He may not want the stress that such a reputation can put on him to do more art work.

The *loser* is deeply affected by defeat. Children in the elementary school are too young to understand why their work was not chosen. Each takes the promises of the contest personally and expects to win. Children react in this way and should not be expected to behave as adults. Even adults are disappointed by not winning a contest, but children are more sensitive, more tender, and more expectant and so are hurt more deeply. At such an impressionable age, these deep failures and frustrations can bring about lasting damage and cause the child to associate art with failure.

Children who lose an art contest tend to be influenced in subsequent attempts by the pieces of art that won the award. The awarding of prizes showed the children what the judges liked, and even if the children do not repeat the same idea that won the prize, they are often greatly influenced by it.

92

Competitions of every kind (for prizes, grades, or selective exhibition) are restrictive. Only through creative expression can the opportunities for imaginative art be widened, as this piece in which a "really big fish" is caught.

Although the sponsors maintain that one of the aims of the contest is to increase the children's interest in art, the opposite effect happens after the contest is over and the entries judged. Since most children are disappointed, they are reluctant to try such activities again. Contest sponsors find it difficult to understand why children's participation in an annual contest wanes and why prizes are no longer the inducement they once were.

The kind of structured competition that pits one child against many others in a struggle to gain victory for only one is inappropriate for children. Children have their own private challenges. They compete with themselves by successively trying to do better work. A child will secretly compete against another, as, for example, in trying to ride a bicycle faster. Children will often compete without a spoken word between them. These personal strivings for a better place or for achievement are normal. The child feels these for himself and can control them as he wants. In that respect they are very different from imposed contests the child did not initiate and cannot control.

Some persons think children should be exposed to the practices of competition in order to give them experiences that prepare them for adult life, and the earlier they begin the better. Some persons think children who compete in contests become adjusted to this practice and learn how to cope with it. Children profit by early experiences with many things, but not with all things. There are some things that are right and logical for adult life, but not for children. Many experiences are reserved for adults because they can best be dealt with by mature persons.

Although competition is a major factor in the private enterprise system upon which American economics is based, structured competitive art experiences for elementary school children do little to prepare them for life in our culture. Before an individual can compete, he must be prepared to do so by feeling confident in both the skills he has mastered and is able to use to his advantage, and in the broad knowledge he has acquired and can draw on and manipulate to serve him best. Children in the elementary school are still in the process of the development of skills. Some areas of education have not yet been presented to them in school. Children of this age lack sufficient background for structured competitive experiences in art.

Children are also emotionally unready for such activities because in elementary school they are more ego-centered than older persons. When a contest is presented, they regard it and the winning of the prize in reference to themselves.

Teachers and others who work with children should carefully consider the effect that losing has on the children. Since so very few win in proportion to the much greater number who do not, attention should be given to the greatest good for the greatest number—the many should not be exploited in favor of the few. Our democratic ideal is based on the dignity and worth of every human being. Activities in which children participate should help them put this objective into practice; contests for children are not among these activities.

Contests and Art Education

In reading this chapter, up to this point, it should have become obvious that art contests are contradictory to modern methods of teaching art. Some of the reasons for the contradictions follow:

(a) *Contests emphasize the importance of the finished art product.* The quality of the completed art work *is* important to both the child and his teacher. Both must feel a pride in the child's achievement as evidenced by his art work. *Educationally,* however, it is *what happens to the child during the creative process* that is significant. When such emphasis is placed on the clay piece, the painting, or the poster, children tend to do what they already know how to do and feel certain they can do reasonably well. They hesitate to experiment lest it not compare well with the work of their classmates. They are reluctant to try new ideas and new ways. Learning is affected. To ensure an acceptable result, a child may be tempted to copy a picture or shape instead of creating his own. The detrimental and injurious effects of copy experiences on a child's creative art are made clear from the research study discussed in the previous chapter.

Some teachers, too, are influenced by the stress placed on the completed art product. When prizes are given, teachers are anxious for their children to win. When a child wins, recognition comes to him and, indirectly, to his teacher. Teachers want to receive this focus of favorable attention on themselves and their students and to have their work honored. For these reasons, some teachers are tempted to pick out those few children most likely to win and spend most of their time with them. In other instances, teachers might actually pick up the materials and work on the children's art, changing it and making it conform more nearly to adult standards. If adults are tempted to cheat in order to gain indirect recognition for themselves, it must be obvious that children, who are directly involved, are much more likely to feel enticed to do so. It is unfair to elementary school children, who are still building character, to place before them such temptation. By placing value on the end result, the child may be made to feel that any means to achieve this end is desirable. "The end justifies the means" can be an attitude resulting from contest emphasis. The end does not justify the means; it is a product of the means.

(b) In a great many contests the *topic* is determined by someone other than the child. Other restrictions and limitations are also placed on the contestants.

(c) The strength of modern art education lies in the value and worth it places upon every child. By recognizing the successes of every child, each is dignified and encouraged to build upon his achievements. These important processes build into the child value standards and behavior patterns that will make him a more confident person and a more appreciative world citizen. One basic characteristic of a contest, on the other hand, is that recognition is *not* given to the successes of every child. Modern art education and competitions stand, therefore, in educational opposition to each other.

(d) Sponsors of contests are right, to a certain extent, when they say that contests strongly motivate children. They do; but when contests or competitions are advertised or presented, the opportunity for one or a few to win is stressed. No mention is made of what will happen to the majority of children. Children in the elementary school are too immature to foresee that most of them will not win. They are so dazzled by the prizes and by the power of the contest motivation that they concentrate on the awards, each believing that he will win.

(e) In a contest most children are defeated regardless of the fact that they have followed the prescribed rules and have done their best work. They often *lose confidence* in themselves and in their abilities in art. Children tend to lose confidence in their teacher, too (or whoever presents the contest to them), because she made promises to them of awards for winning, but because of the nature of contests was forced to withhold prizes from most of them.

(f) A child *cannot understand why he does not win.* The reasons for his not winning are very difficult for the contest judge or sponsor to explain and much more difficult for the child to accept. Since the child cannot understand why he lost, he becomes confused. He is not concerned with the fact that many other children besides himself also lost but thinks of it only in relation to himself.

(g) Contests are also inconsistent with the purposes of elementary education. Elementary school teachers are anxious to have every child learn all subjects and to make progress and to feel successful. Teachers realize that every child will not learn to the same extent, make the same progress, or experience the same measure of success. Neither teachers nor children expect uniformity, yet teachers strive to have *every child* feel the satisfaction of even a small amount of success, and they praise each child for his achievements. For example, Sam has difficulty with reading and cannot seem to remember words. Therefore, on the day that he reads with more fluency and comprehension than he previously has done, the teacher is pleased and praises him. She thus gives him recognition for his achievement even though he is still a slow reader. His classmates are pleased, too. Children are accustomed to this practice but are not equipped to deal with the mass failures brought about by contests.

GRADING OF CHILDREN'S ART

A grade, as it applies to art in school, is a symbol used in rating the attainment of a child in that particular art problem or to indicate the quality of his work over a certain period of time. A grade is usually a number or a letter indicating which one among several degrees of quality or achievement the child has attained.

Grading systems that indicate varying degrees or classifications of excellence separate the work of children into categories or divisions. This practice suggests that every piece of work within each of the different steps on the rating scale is of the same rank or standard of quality. This exact categorizing of art is extremely difficult to do. Since each child was motivated toward originality and individuality in his art, each resulting art product should be different in subject and feeling from the others. There is, then, no standard or uniformity by which the children's work can be measured.

In art, the work of the child is closely tied up with his feelings, emotions, reactions, ideas, and personal experiences. When children's art is graded, it almost suggests that the personal characteristics of each child are rated, too. When children begin to feel that their backgrounds, ideas, and feelings are going to be evaluated, compared, and graded, they tend to withdraw from exposing these intimate characteristics. Such individually distinguishing features are the essence of what makes art interesting, exciting, and expressive. Therefore, whatever discourages children from expressing feelings and emotions in art should be avoided.

Grading of children's art is inconsistent with creative expression as a way of working in art or as a method of teaching art. Since creative expression gives to every child the opportunity to choose the subject matter for his

93

These examples reflect the varying backgrounds and abilities which children bring with them to school. Since the teacher's preferences and a child's previous experiences in art are virtually the only bases for grading, it is unfair to attempt to grade children's art.

art, to organize, and to express it in his own way, it implies that the work of each child will be accepted. The art product that results from every child's serious attempt to solve his art problem should be received by his teacher with the same warm approval that is given to every other child's work. The acceptance of every piece of art work emphasizes the worth and value of *every* child, and if this emphasis is interfered with, the warm, mutual exchange of confidence between children and teacher is affected.

Influences of Grading

Elementary school children need to build their self-confidence, skills, and motor coordination before they are ready to be subjected to such competitive practices as grading. A feeling of success and confidence is necessary to the child in order to sustain him through the sensitive years when he is most actively learning. He does not yet have a resource of power, which comes from education and skills, to draw on. He needs to have the support of confidence in order to know his strengths and limitations and to understand why certain gradings or ratings are right for him, requiring much more maturity than children have. Since grading puts art on a competitive basis, its effects are similar to those of competitions and contests.

Children, being sensitive, are hurt by a practice that puts them in a position of being rated lower than others. Many things can happen to a child and to his art as a result of grading. The child may form a dislike for art when he receives grades lower than those of some of his classmates and friends. He may copy the approved art work, thus abandoning his own ideas in favor of someone else's. In doing so, he forfeits his chance for developing his inventiveness, creativity, and imagination, as well as for developing his ability to make decisions based on discriminating judgments. In their formative years children should be indoctrinated with ways and means of working and living together and of developing viewpoints and attitudes that contribute to the constructive level of their uniqueness and that help to maintain freedom of choice in art and in every facet of life.

In art, both the end product and the working process are interdependent and important, but grading emphasizes the end product, and when this happens, children are apt to become more concerned with the visual appearance of their art than with the experimenting, the learning of new skills, and the free approach to art.

Parents, too, are influenced by the grading of their children's art. Parents tend to regard the grade as the total statement of their child's ability in art, his interest in it, the quality of his work according to his ability, and the quality of his work in comparison to his classmates' work. Actually, what may also enter into the grading are the teacher's personal likes and dislikes in the children's art expression.

Some Bases for Grading

Failing to understand the nature of art, some school teachers and administrators require letter or numerical grades to be determined for each child in art. Creative art does not lend itself to being measured, categorized, or graded. Teachers, faced with this requirement, realize they will need to devise some standard that can be applied to all children's work. Such a basis is extremely difficult, if at all possible, to find because of the contradiction between creative art and grading.

One standard sometimes used is the amount of improvement shown within a stated period of time. If samples of a child's art show growth and improvement over a six-week period, he receives a higher grade than a child whose art showed less of an advance. One objection to this viewpoint is that children's art often does not show such a regular chronological pattern of growth. Because of intense interest in a topic, a high pitch of emotional involvement with it, or other reasons, a child may create a composition of a higher than usual quality of excellence. Even though he may consistently work hard in art class, his work will probably vary in complexity and art qualities. Over a long period a child's work should show general growth in a number of aspects, but this is difficult to measure.

Another difficulty with improvement as a standard of measurement is that very often only the flat work is kept for grading. Three-dimensional work is difficult to store and therefore is seldom kept for long periods. Memories being what they are, scarcely any teacher is able to accurately recall the work of each of her children over a period of time, so that if the three-dimensional work is omitted, the grade is then a partial one.

Children of greater mental capacity will usually make more progress than their less fortunately endowed classmates. Mental power, then, is being rated, and since children find it difficult to understand or to accept this basis for grading, they can become confused and emotionally upset by it.

Quality in children's art is such a difficult thing to measure that various persons arrive at different grades when attempting to measure it. Any measurement of quality is difficult for children to understand because of their level of maturity. Therefore, adult judgments are imposed on the products of children's thinking and feeling.

Effort is sometimes used as a basis for grading children's art. Teachers, realizing the difficulties in making quality judgments of children's art, rely on the apparent amount of work the child has put forth during the art class. One difficulty with this basis is that so much art work is mental. How can the amount of mental effort be measured or judged? When effort is determined by the child's degree of busyness, time spent in the making of decisions and in contemplation is ignored or negatively evaluated.

Art grades determined by effort alone are misleading. A child whose mental capacity is relatively low will work harder and achieve less than a child whose mental capacity is greater. This means that the slow child, working hard all period and achieving less, may actually receive a higher art grade than the child who achieves more with less effort. The less complex or lesser quality art may receive the higher grade. When the art grade is based on effort, it is quite possible that a child may receive a high grade in art and low grades in other subjects. The child and his parents may form the false impression that he has some specific art talent. People also get the false impression that children who cannot do the more academic work are successful in art or that artists have less general intelligence than persons in other fields. The opposite, however, is true; art ability is often related to general ability.

When grades are given in art, children, wanting to make a good impression, to be successful and to compare favorably with their classmates, will substitute for their own motives and purposes the basis on which the grades are determined.

Since grading of the art work of elementary school children is such a difficult thing to do, and since it is incompatible with creative expression as a method of teaching art, it seems evident that children would be freer to grow in art if no grades were given. When grades are given in art, children develop a fear of failure. This fear restricts their freedom.

One school system, in which discriminatory grading in art had prevailed for several years, changed the art grading to a nondiscriminatory reporting symbol that indicated that each child had made some achievements in art.

Several of the teachers affected by this change felt that when children were no longer motivated by grading, they would no longer put forth their maximum effort in art. The teachers regarded grades as motivation, feeling that children needed the threat of low grades to stimulate their work. The children were happy about the change and worked at least as diligently as and much more freely than before. The quality of their art work actually improved when the fear of failure was removed. Teacher time previously spent in grading art work could be spent on instruction and motivation, which were other reasons for the improvement of the children's work.

The words *satisfactory* and *unsatisfactory* are used to some extent in reporting children's progress in art. In this case, children whose art products appear to have some acceptable quality are rated as satisfactory, the others as unsatisfactory. The word *satisfactory* conveys the impression of work that is mediocre or merely acceptable. When a child receives the highest grades in his other work, the "satisfactory" rating that he receives in art seems not to measure to other grades. The word *successful* would have a better effect upon children. The use of the opposite of these words is closely connected with failure, which is of no encouragement or help to children, and therefore should not be used.

In order to show the difficulty in grading children's art, one college teacher showed his class several pieces of child art and asked them to assign a grade to each. This demonstration took place near the end of a course in art education, after the teacher felt the students had some background for it. Using the grading system of A, B, C, D, F they were asked to record grades for the paintings which had been numbered for identification.

Plates XLIV–XLIX show six paintings that are representative of the group. There were 24 students in the class, and the chart below shows how their judgment of the quality of these first-grade children's art varied.

Paintings Identified by Number	GRADES				
	A	B	C	D	F
1	14	10			
2	8	10	6		
3	6	9	8	1	
4	5	11	7	1	
5	4	9	9	2	
6	6	10	7	1	

Some things are evident from this chart. One is that the students were influenced by the fact that there were five different grades within the grading system. The power of suggestion to use the various grades was strong and was reenforced by their own school experiences with grading. Since the range was given, most felt impelled to use it. In spite of the fact that they had just completed a course in which acceptance and appreciation of each child's creative art was stressed, they failed to apply it when faced with a practical test of its application. During the course in art education, these pre-service teachers had discussed and studied the effects upon children of discriminatory choices and selections of their art work, yet they regressed to this very practice when dealing with child art. In spite of the special nature of creativity, most of them applied to art the same measurement used in the skill and content subjects.

Then, too, the personal reactions and the likes and dislikes of the one assigning the grades must, of course, have been a determining factor. Neither the quality of the child's art nor how hard he tried to express himself made much difference in the grading. What made the difference was the selection of the particular person he could get for a teacher. The teacher's own personality was a factor. How justifiable is this as a basis for grading? One teacher might give him an A grade, stimulating him and giving him pride and confidence in himself and in his work. Another teacher, dealing with the same child and the same piece of art, would from the evidence of this chart give him a D grade, indicating poor and unsuccessful work. The effect of this grade upon a child who found both pride and satisfaction in his painting would be discouraging and cause him to be confused by the discrepancy between the teacher's verbal motivation toward individual creative art and the grade she gave to this work. She had encouraged open individual originality, yet she selected some for encouraging grades and rejected other individually creative work.

This demonstration and its analysis shows how easy it is for teachers to disregard the child-centered educational methods they were taught in their professional preparation and to revert to methods less conducive to children's education and general development welfare.

It also indicates how inappropriate this or any similar system of grading is for art. Art by its special nature depends upon individual differences and seeks new and inventive approaches to them. Such a system of grading, even if used for other school subjects, should not be applied to art, for it can retard or destroy the natural incentive to create which every child has. If some grading symbol must be used for recording purposes, every child needs one that is both encouraging and positive.

Art offers a wonderfully open opportunity for the deep satisfactions and gratifications that come from the knowledge and feeling of creating, originating, inventing something new and pleasing. The highest quality art teacher opens the door wide for each child and holds it open so that he can work as he alone can do and achieve an art product close to his highest standard for that time and with those materials.

Selections of ability in art have little or no validity in the elementary school, first, because it is too early to make any kind of decision about who has "talent" or who should pursue an art profession. Then, too, children change and vacillate in their interests and apparent commitments. Also, they have yet to experience the new and fascinating fields of study in the high school. The best we can do at the elementary level is to keep all of the lines of opportunity open and available to every child.

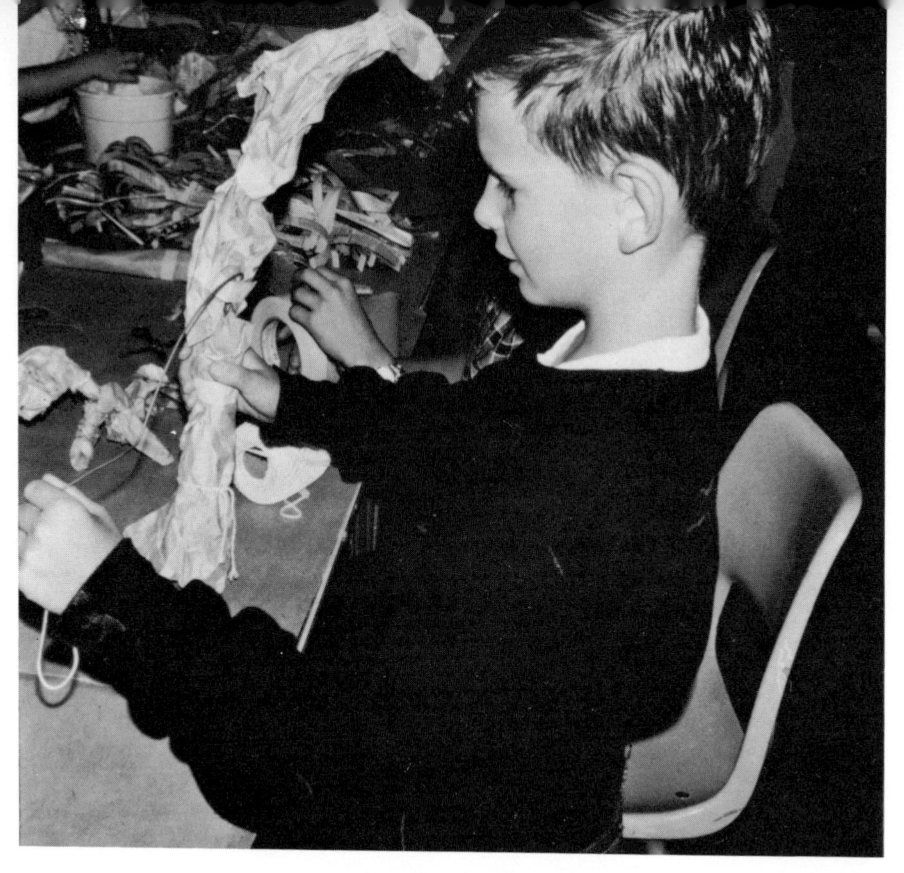

94

At the conclusion of this text one point to be reemphasized is that the *child* and his growing competence are the center of all art education. Every art activity, every guidance and evaluation procedure, and every contact the teacher has with a child should contribute toward developing the child's confidence in his ability to work out his art problems.

> The development of the power to think is a slow affair, and it is all but impossible to measure the character and the direction of that growth at any one moment of operation and take this as a sure statement of generally advanced capacity. Since we are, for the most part, committed to measurability, and thinking power seems to defy the available instruments, we find ourselves turning toward what is immediately measurable.[1]

> We (adults) destroy the disinterested (I do *not* mean *un*interested) love of learning in children, which is so strong when they are small, by encouraging and compelling them to work for petty and contemptible rewards —gold stars, or papers marked 100 and tacked on the wall, or A's on report cards, or honor rolls, or dean's lists, or Phi Beta Kappa keys—in short, for ignoble satisfaction of feeling that they are better than someone else.[2]

> Discussions of the teacher's evaluative practices and issues concerning external evaluation in general led us to formulate the hypothesis that in-

---

[1] From *Education as a Discipline* by Marc Belth. © Copyright 1965 by Allyn and Bacon, Inc. Reprinted by permission of the publisher.

[2] John Holt, *How Children Fail* (New York: Pitman Publishing Corp., © 1964), p. 168. Reprinted by permission of the publisher.

dividuals working under unevaluated practice and with encouragement to experiment freely would produce better creative work on subsequent occasions than individuals working under conditions of evaluated practice.

To test this hypothesis a classroom experiment was conducted in grades one through six in a public elementary school. . . . The results indicate that younger children (grades one through four) are apparently affected more strongly by adult evaluation than are the older children (grades five and six). For the former an unevaluated period free from the fear of making mistakes seems to be somewhat more conducive to creative work in general than for older children.[3]

SUGGESTED ACTIVITIES

To see for yourself how difficult it is to accurately categorize the art work of children and to see how inconsistent the judgments of different adults become when faced with the task of grading art, separate the creative art products made by a group of children into four levels of excellence. Record the results of your selections. Put this first listing out of sight. Mix the art work so that you leave it in no particular sequence. A week later reclassify the work and record your selections in each level of grading. Compare your two listings to see if you may have changed your decisions about any of the work.

Ask one or two other adults whose tastes or points of view may be different from yours to rate the art work. Compare their findings with your own to see if they made any decisions about the grading of any of the art work that are different from yours.

---

[3] Paul E. Torrance, *Rewarding Creative Behavior* (Englewood Cliffs, N.J.: Prentice-Hall, © 1965), p. 161. Reprinted by permission of the publisher.

Bibliography

ABRAMOVIC, EMIL, "New Approaches to Elementary Science Teaching," *American Teacher*, American Federation of Teachers, October 1964.

ALSCHULER, ROSE H., and LABERTA W. HATTWICK, *A Study of Painting and Personality of Young Children*, 2 vols. (Chicago: University of Chicago Press, 1947).

BANNON, LAURA, *Mind Your Child's Art* (New York: Pelligrini and Cudahy, 1952).

BELTH, MARC, *Education as a Discipline* (Boston: Allyn and Bacon, 1965).

BLAND, JANE COOPER, *Art of the Young Child* (New York: Museum of Modern Art, 1968).

BROWNE, SYBIL, "Beginning Art Teachers Appraise Themselves," *Art Education*, National Art Education Association, Washington, D.C., November 1954.

BRUNER, JEROME S., *On Knowing* (Cambridge, Mass.: The Belknap Press of Harvard University Press, 1962).

BRYCE, MAYO, *Fine Arts Education in the Soviet Union* (Washington, D. C.: U.S. Department of Health, Education and Welfare, 1963).

CARSON, RACHAEL, *The Sense of Wonder*, photographs by Charles Pratt (New York: Harper & Row, 1956).

CIRLOT, J. E., *A Dictionary of Symbols* (New York: Philosophical Library, 1962).

COLE, NATALIE ROBINSON, *The Arts in the Classroom* (New York: John Day Co., 1940).

CONANT, HOWARD, *Art Education* (New York: Center for Applied Research in Education, 1964).

COUSINS, NORMAN, "What Matters About Schweitzer," *Saturday Review*, September 25, 1965.

D'AMICO, VICTOR, *Creative Teaching in Art* (Scranton, Pa.: International Textbook Co., 1953).

DE FRANCESCO, ITALO, *Art Education—Its Means and Ends* (New York: Harper & Row, 1958).

DEWEY, JOHN, *Art as Experience* (New York: Monton, Balco and Co., 1934).

__________, "Having an Experience," in *The Problems of Aesthetics*, Eliseo Vivas and Murray Krieger, eds. (New York: Holt, Rinehart and Winston, 1953).

EASTERN ARTS ASSOCIATION, "Art: The Balance Wheel in Education," *1948 Yearbook*, State Teachers College, Kutztown, Pa.

__________, "Integrative Function of Art Education," *1950 Yearbook*, State Teachers College, Kutztown, Pa.

ERDT, MARGARET HAMILTON, *Teaching Art in the Elementary School*, rev. ed. (New York: Holt, Rinehart and Winston, 1962).

FAULKNER, RAY, EDWIN ZIEGFELD, and GERALD HILL, *Art Today*, 4th ed. (New York: Holt, Rinehart and Winston, 1963).

FOSHAY, ARTHUR W., "Art and Its Relationship to the Other Disciplines," *Eastern Arts Quarterly*, Eastern Arts Association, Kutztown, Pa., April-May 1964.

GAITSKELL, CHARLES, and MARGARET GAITSKELL, *Art Education in the Kindergarten* (Toronto: Ryerson Press, 1952).

———, *Children and Their Art*, Willard P. Spalding, general ed. (New York: Harcourt, Brace & World, 1958).

GARDNER, JOHN, *Self Renewal* (New York: Harper & Row, 1964).

GHISELIN, BREWSTER, *The Creative Process* (Berkeley, Calif.: University of California Press, 1952).

GREENBERG, PEARL, *Children's Art Experiences* (New York: Holt, Rinehart and Winston, 1966).

HARRISON, ELIZABETH, *Self-Expression Through Art* (Scarsborough, Ont.: W. J. Gage, Ltd., 1951).

HAYAKAWA, SAMUEL I., "The Revision of Vision," in *Language of Vision*, György Kepes, ed. (Chicago: Paul Theobald and Co., 1945).

HOFFER, ERIC, *The True Believer* (New York: Harper & Row, 1951).

HOLT, JOHN, *How Children Fail* (New York: Pitman Publishing Co., 1964).

HOOVER, FRANCIS L., *Art Activities for the Very Young* (Worcester, Mass.: Davis Publications, 1961).

HOVEY, WALTER READ, "The Creative Spark," from Topic 5, *Creativity and the Arts*, Washington and Jefferson College, Washington, Pa., spring 1963.

JEFFERSON, BLANCHE, "The Color Book Craze" (pamphlet), Association for Childhood Education International, Washington, D. C.

JEFFERSON, BLANCHE, BARBARA MCGEARY, BARBARA W. FREDETTE, and CLYDE MCGEARY, *My World of Art* Series, Books 1–6 with accompanying Teachers' Manuals (Boston: Allyn and Bacon, 1963–64).

KAGAN, PAULINE WRIGHT, *From Adventure to Experience Through Art* (San Francisco: Chandler Publishing Co., 1959).

KAINZ, LOUISE, and OLIVE RILEY, *Exploring Art* (New York: Harcourt, Brace & World, 1951).

KAUFMAN, IRVING, *Art and Education in Contemporary Culture* (New York: Macmillan, 1966).

KINCAID, CLARENCE E., "The Determination and Description of Various Creative Attributes of Children," in *Creativity and Art Education*, Lambert Brittain, ed. (Washington, D. C.: National Art Education Association, 1964).

KRAUSS, RUTH, *A Hole Is to Dig* (New York: Harper & Row, 1952).

KUH, KATHARINE, "An American Critic Reports on Art in the Soviet Union," *Saturday Review*, August 24, 1963.

LARK-HOROVITS, BETTY, HILDA LEWIS, and MARK LUCA, *Understanding Children's Art for Better Teaching* (Columbus, Ohio: Charles E. Merrill Books, 1967).

LINDERMAN, EARL W., and DONALD W. HEBERHOLZ, *Developing Artistic and Perceptual Awareness* (Dubuque, Ia.: William C. Brown Co., 1964).

LINDSTROM, MIRIAM, *Children's Art* (Berkeley, Calif.: University of California Press, 1957).

LITTLE, SIDNEY W., "No Grade," *Art Education*, National Art Educational Association, Washington, D. C., October 1949.

LOWENFELD, VIKTOR, *Your Child and His Art* (New York: Macmillan, 1954).

LOWENFELD, VIKTOR, and W. L. BRITTAIN, *Creative and Mental Growth,* 3rd ed. (New York: Macmillan, 1957).

LOUGHRAN, BERNICE, *Art Experience* (New York: Harcourt, Brace & World, 1963).

MATTILL, EDWARD L., *Meaning in Crafts,* 2nd ed. (Englewood Cliffs, N. J.: Prentice-Hall, 1965).

MC ILVAIN, DOROTHY, *Art for the Primary Grades* (New York: G. P. Putnam's Sons, 1961).

MC VITTEY, LAWRENCE, *An Experimental Study on Various Methods in Art Motivation at the Fifth Grade Level* (Doctoral dissertation, Pennsylvania State University, 1954).

MENDELOWITZ, DANIEL M., *Children Are Artists* (Stanford, Calif.: Stanford University Press, 1954).

MERRITT, HELEN, *Guiding Free Expression in Children's Art* (New York: Holt, Rinehart and Winston, 1964).

NATIONAL ART EDUCATION ASSOCIATION, *Report of the Commission on Art Education,* Washington, D. C., 1965.

NATIONAL EDUCATION ASSOCIATION, *Art and Music in Our Schools,* Washington, D. C., 1963.

NATIONAL SOCIETY FOR THE STUDY OF EDUCATION, "Art Education," *Sixty-fourth Yearbook,* W. Rein Hastie, ed. (Chicago: University of Chicago Press, 1965).

PARKHURST, HELEN, *Creating with One's Hands,* a recording (New London, Conn.: Alpark Records, distributed by Arthur C. Croft Publications).

PURCELL, VIRGINIA, "Art Is a Personal Matter," *Art Education,* National Art Education Association, Washington, D. C., 1957.

RANDALL, ARNE W., and RUTH ELSIE HALVORSEN, *Painting in the Classroom* (Worcester, Mass.: Davis Publications, 1962).

READ, HERBERT, *Education Through Art,* 2nd ed. (New York: Pantheon Books, 1945).

———, "Education Through Art—A Revolutionary Policy," *Art Education,* National Art Education Association, Washington, D. C., November 1955.

———, "Whatever Happened to the Great Simplicities?" *Saturday Review,* February 18, 1967.

ROGERS, CARL R., "Learning to Be Free," *Art Education,* National Art Education Association, Washington, D. C., March 1963.

RUSSELL, DAVID, *Children's Thinking* (Boston: Ginn and Co., 1956).

RUSSELL, IRENE, and BLANCHE WAUGAMAN, "A Study of the Effects of Workbook Copy Experiences on the Creative Concepts of Children," *Research Bulletin,* Eastern Arts Association, Kutztown, Pa., April 1952.

SALOME, R. A., "The Effects of Perceptual Training Upon Two-Dimensional Drawings of Children," *Studies in Art Education,* National Art Education Association, Washington, D. C., autumn 1965.

SCHAEFER, ROBERT J., "Anti-Intellectualism in the Pursuit of the Intellectual," *Teachers College Record,* Teachers College, Columbia University, New York, November 1963.

SCHAEFFER-SIMMERN, H., *The Unfolding of Artistic Activity* (Berkeley, Calif.: University of California Press, 1948).

SHULTZ, HAROLD, *Art in the Elementary School* (Urbana, Ill.: University of Illinois Press, 1948).

SMITH, JAMES A., *Setting Conditions for Creative Teaching* (Boston: Allyn and Bacon, 1966).

SPEETH, SHERIDAN DAUSTER, "The Rational Design for Toys," *Journal of Creative Behavior,* Creative Education Foundation, Buffalo, N. Y., fall 1967.

TAYLOR, HAROLD, *Art and the Intellect* (New York: Museum of Modern Art, 1960).

TOMLINSON, R. R., *Children Are Artists* (London and New York: Penguin Books, 1947).

TORRANCE, E. PAUL, *Guiding Creative Talent* (Englewood Cliffs, N. J.: Prentice-Hall, 1962).

———, *Rewarding Creative Behavior* (Englewood Cliffs, N. J.: Prentice-Hall, 1965).

WACHOWIAK, FRANK, and THEODORE RAMSEY, *Emphasis: Art* (Scranton, Pa.: International Textbook Co., 1966).

ZIEGFELD, EDWIN, ed., *Education and Art: A Symposium* (Paris: UNESCO, 1953).

Index